Representing China on the Historical London Stage

This book provides a critical study of how China was represented on the historical London stage in selected examples from the late seventeenth century to the early twentieth century—which corresponds with the Qing Dynasty (1644–1911), China's last monarchy. The examples show that during this historical period, the stage representations of the country were influenced in turn by Jesuit writings on China, Britain's expanding material interest in China, the presence of British imperial power in Asia, and the establishment of diasporic Chinese communities abroad. While finding that many of these works may be read as gendered and feminized, my study emphasizes that the Jesuits' depiction of China as a country of high culture and in perennial conflict with the Tartars gradually lost prominence in dramatic imaginations to depictions of China's material and visual attractions. Central to the book's argument is that the stage representations of China were inherently intercultural and open to new influences, manifested by the evolving combinations of Chinese and English (British) traits. Through the dramatization of the Chinese Other, the representations questions, satirize, and put in sharp relief the ontological and epistemological bases of the English (British) Self.

Dongshin Chang is Assistant Professor in the Department of Theatre at Hunter College of the City University of New York.

Routledge Advances in Theatre and Performance Studies

Representing China on the Historical London Stage

From Orientalism to Intercultural Performance

Dongshin Chang

 Routledge
Taylor & Francis Group

NEW YORK AND LONDON

First published 2015
by Routledge
711 Third Avenue, New York, NY 10017

and by Routledge
2 Park Square, Milton Park, Abingdon, Oxon OX14 4RN

Routledge is an imprint of the Taylor & Francis Group, an informa business

Library of Congress Cataloging in Publication Data

Chang, Dongshin.
Representing China on the historical London stage : from Orientalism to intercultural performance / by Dongshin Chang.
 pages cm — (Routledge advances in theatre and performance studies ; 38)
 Includes bibliographical references and index.
 1. English drama—History and criticism. 2. China—In literature.
 3. Chinese in literature. 4. Theater—England—London—History. I. Title.
 PR635.C53C63 2015
 822.009'35851—dc23   2014036221

ISBN: 978-0-415-85571-6(hbk)
ISBN: 978-0-203-73494-0(ebk)

Typeset in Sabon
by codeMantra

MIX
Paper from
responsible sources
FSC
www.fsc.org   FSC® C013056

Printed and bound in Great Britain by
TJ International Ltd, Padstow, Cornwall

To my parents

Contents

List of Figures

Acknowledgments

It is with great pleasure and heartfelt gratitude that I acknowledge the people and institutions that have been instrumental in bringing this project to fruition. My foremost thanks go to the faculty and staff in the Department of Theatre at Hunter College, City University of New York (CUNY), for offering care, support, and a nurturing environment to which I feel privileged to belong. Especially, Mira Felner, Jonathan Kalb, and Claudia Orenstein have offered invaluable comments on drafts of the manuscript as well as mentorship and guidance, while Barbara Bosch and Joel Bassin, in their capacity as chairs, have ensured the time release and administrative assistance I needed to complete the project. The tremendous backing the department has provided reflects the support I have received from the college and CUNY. I thank Hunter's President Jennifer J. Raab for the multiple rounds of faculty funds and travel awards, and I am very grateful to CUNY's Faculty Fellowship Publication Program (FFPP) and the PSC-CUNY Awards, which have enabled me to conduct research, obtain copyright permissions, sharpen my writing, and share my findings with my peers.

Besides my academic home base at Hunter and CUNY, my admission into the Frederick Lewis Allen Memorial Room at the Stephen A. Schwarzman Building, New York Public Library, has provided me a writing haven and access to the library's rich resources and dedicated staff support. I would like to thank Jay Barksdale, Study Rooms Liaison, and Andrea Felder, at the library's Permissions and Reproduction Services, for their onsite assistance and timely help.

Earlier drafts of this book, from its dissertation form to its various parts rewritten later as conference papers, journal articles, writing-workshop materials, and the book proposal submitted to Routledge, received constructive criticism and invaluable feedback from its receptive readers. Marvin Carlson, to whom I am indebted beyond measure, has nurtured the project with tender and staunch support since its inception. Ted Ziter, my adviser, who I will never be able to thank enough for his dedication to this project, has assisted me in articulating my critical position. My dissertation committee—Ziter, Carlson, Barbara Browning, Karen Shimakawa, and Jill Lane—recommended ways of deepening its theoretical engagement, which helped me reconceptualize the project for this book. My discussion on Restoration and eighteenth-century drama has been informed and inspired by the expertise and scholarly rigor of Judith Milhous, and my drafts on early nineteenth-century British popular entertainments were critically and insightfully remarked on by Jody Enders, Penny Farfan, David Mayer, Ric Knowles, Carlson, and my FFPP mentor Shelly Eversley and my cohorts: Gloria Fisk, Hyo Kim, Tara Pauliny, Richard Perez, Belinda Rincon, and Elyse Zucker. The epilogue has benefited from the perceptive comments of Mayer and Knowles, and the book proposal was carefully evaluated by Alexa Huang, Esther Kim Lee, and another reader chosen by Routledge, all of whom made judicious suggestions.

Here I thank Liz Levine, Commissioning Editor of Routledge Research, who, with prudence and attentiveness, has guided me through the process of explicating my research and its relationship to relevant fields of scholarship. I also thank Nancy Chen, Editorial Assistant at Routledge, who has offered her help with promptitude and professionalism.

Chapter Four, in a condensed form, was published earlier as "Proximity and the Demarcation of the Other: Three 'Chinese' Productions on the Early-Twentieth-Century London Stage" in *Querying Difference in Theatre History* (2007). I am very grateful to Cambridge Scholars Publishing for its permission to adapt the article for this book, as well to Scott Magelssen, coeditor of *Querying Difference*, for editorial and conceptual sharpening of the article.

I am grateful for the opportunities that I have had over the years to present papers related to this project at various national and international conferences. I would like to thank in particular the Department of Drama and Theatre at National Taiwan University, which hosts the bi-annual International Theatre Conference; Anne Witchard of the "China in Britain" project; and Liang Luo of the KFLC Languages, Literatures, and Cultures Conference for both the scholarly exchange and networking and the warming hospitality they offered. At the "Race, Nation and Empire on the Victorian Stage" Conference organized by Kate Newey and Peter Yeandle, who connected me with Witchard, I met wonderful British theatre scholars, among whom Simon Sladen introduced me to the Pantoland. The epilogue would not have been possible without his initiation.

Throughout the years, this project has received generous funding from several sources in addition to from Hunter and CUNY: two Research Awards from the Society for Theatre Research (U.K.), a Dissertation Fellowship from the Chiang-ching Kuo Foundation for International Scholarly Exchange, and the Elaine Brody Fellowship in the Humanities from the Graduate School of Arts and Science at New York University (NYU). I thank Richard Schechner for his writing of strong letters of support that helped secure funding for the project at its dissertation stage.

The staff members at the libraries listed below in addition to those at the Stephen A. Schwarzman Building of the New York Public Library have offered much-appreciated assistance for my project: The Department of Manuscripts at the British Library; the former Theatre Museum in London;

its current home, the Theatre and Performance collection at the Victoria and Albert Museum; the Bodleian Library at Oxford University; the Special Collections of University College London; the New York Public Library for the Performing Arts; the Folger Shakespeare Library; the Harvard Theatre Collection at Harvard University; and the Fales Library and Special Collections and Interlibrary Loan at NYU.

Assistance with this project has also come from the following individuals: Dr. Min-sun Chen, who provided a complimentary copy of his monograph on Sino-Western contacts in relation to the Jesuit missions in China; Dr. Isabelle Duchesne, a dear teacher and friend, who proofread my English translations of French texts; Holy Chang, who played through the score of *A Chinese Honeymoon* and reconstructed its music and singing; Edwina Ashie, who double-checked my transcriptions of several play scripts kept in the British Library; and Bru Dye, a trustworthy friend and rigorous editor, who worked with me as I wrote the dissertation form of this project.

On a personal note, I have been blessed with moral and social support from Helen Moss, Deborah Klens-Bigman, Liana Chen, Xiaoming Chen, Lucy Yeh, Meiying Huang, Yurong Xin, Victoria Huynh, Andy Yen, Matthew Morrison, and my siblings and their loved ones in Taiwan: Shu-hui Chang, Shu-nuan Chang, Dong-meau Chang, Yi-ling Chang, Ying-ping Wang, and Hui-chuan Chang. I would not have been able to complete the project without the love, patience, and support, throughout the years and on each and every page, of my partner, Charles Starks.

This book is dedicated, with much love, to my parents, Hsiu-chen Lai and Pai-hsi Chang, for giving me a chance to experience this miraculous world.

Introduction
From Orientalism to Intercultural Performance

In 1675, the Dorset Garden theatre in London presented *The Conquest of China by the Tartars*, a play that depicts a dynastic change in which the disintegrating Chinese court is overthrown by the Tartars, and the Tartar prince Zungteus marries the valiant Chinese queen Amavanga, declaring his intention to maintain China's customs and culture while strengthening its military force. In this play, the first work that I examine in this book, the identity of China can be read as feminized, but its femininity, as represented by the female warrior Amavanga, does not correspond fully to the conventional depiction of the gender, nor does it conform completely to the orientalist correlation between race and gender. As I argue in Chapter One, it is Amavanga who saves and accepts Zungteus, demonstrating a mental toughness that is stronger, or more masculine, in the playwright Elkanah Settle's depiction, than her Tartar conqueror. Compared with its enemy, China is portrayed as a militarily weaker but culturally stronger political entity. The invading Tartars may end its sovereignty, but they accept and absorb its cultural practices.

In 1913, the Strand theatre in London presented *Mr. Wu*, a dark melodrama set in contemporary Hong Kong that dramatizes devious plans plotted by the eponymous character, a formidable Chinese villain, to take revenge on and ruin an English family. This last example in my study, which I analyze in Chapter Four, cautions the British about the possible dangers of an intercultural environment, the colony, created by the expansion of the British Empire and reflects paranoia about the possibility that a wicked, colonized subject could abuse his power. In this case, the identity of China, in the character Mr. Wu, can be read as perversely and destructively masculinized, while the British have replaced the Tartars in the dramatization of an interracial conflict with the Chinese.

Framed by *Conquest of China by the Tartars* (1675) and *Mr. Wu* (1913–1914), the four chapters of this book examine in chronological order a selection of historical London productions and analyze how, in each case, the identity of China was *interculturalized* as a combination of China and Britain (the West); how the plays contributed to the evolving, *intercultured* depictions of China as a feminized and material attraction; and how the *Chinaface* style became the most prominent staging approach to representing

China. By *interculturalize*, I mean the act of creating a relationship between elements that belong to disparate cultures; by *interculturation*, I mean the ongoing process in which disparate cultural elements are interculturalized over a substantial period of time; and by *Chinaface*, I mean the creative choice to represent China on a visual, formal level as opposed to a textual, conceptual level. The character Amavanga from *Conquest of China by the Tartars*, for example, manifests the interculturalization of Chinese historical figures and the Amazons, in both her name and her warrior deeds. The performance of the eponymous character from *Mr. Wu*, on the other hand, demonstrates the use of Chinaface mannerisms to create a believable Chinese character in appearance who is unmistakably a conventional melodrama villain, a depiction that counters the interculturated, feminized depiction of the Chinese.

In this book, I argue that the Chinese identities represented in the historical London productions of my study were inherently interculturalized, being informed by English (British)[1] knowledge about China, Anglo-Chinese relations, English (British) dramatic and theatrical practices, and individual creative choices. The interculturalized Chinese identity in each case and the interculturated depictions of China that evolved during the historical period of my research evince the significance of Jesuit writings, Britain's expanding material interest in China, the presence of British imperial power in Asia, and the establishment of diasporic Chinese communites, all of which in turn critically influenced the stage representations of the country. These instances of interculturalization and interculturation reflect how a range of contemporary and topical concerns about England (Britain) were dramatized through the subject of China, including royal succession, anti-French protests, China's increasing material presence and influence, and the expansion of the British Empire. What came out of these historical precedents was the development and establishment of what I call Chinaface satire, in which Britain's social and cultural foibles were ridiculed in a highly artificial Chinese setting with Chinese characters that were played by English (British) performers who made explicit their English (British) identities. In the Epilogue, I analyze how the Christmas *Aladdin* pantomimes I have attended in recent years represent lively, twenty-first century examples from this long tradition that continues to thrive today.

The framework and focus of my study are informed by and intended to contribute to two related fields of scholarship, Orientalism and intercultural performance. In his landmark work, *Orientalism* (1978), Edward W. Said uses a theatrical metaphor as an analogy to describe the authority that Anglo-French-American discourse has had on the Arabs and Islam. This authority, as Said emphasizes, is informed by the imbalanced power dynamics and relationships between the strong, dominating Western empires and the weak, dominated Orient. "Orientalism," in short, is "a Western style for dominating, restructuring, and having authority over the Orient"; an orientalist discourse makes the Orient "a closed field, a theatrical stage affixed to Europe" on which "a set of representative figures, or tropes" is to the actual Orient, or Islam, as "stylized costumes are to characters in a play."[2] According to Said, the Orient is made into a field of study, a created body of theory and practice, through generations of continued, institutionalized, and systematized material investment. The field of the Orient is closed or clearly demarcated on the basis of an ontological and epistemological distinction made between the European Self and the Oriental Other. The field is closed also in the sense that the European vocabulary and imagery of the Orient, as a result of orientalist discourse, are theatrical but limited; Europe has constructed and perpetuated a repertoire of representative Oriental figures, in their stylized costumes, that have been confined to, for example, monsters, devils, and heroes, characterized by their Oriental backwardness, aberrant mentality, degeneracy, and sensuality, and projected with terrors, pleasures, and desires.[3] Said is very aware that by limiting his study of Orientalism to the Arabs and Islam he has eliminated a large part of the Orient—India, Japan, China, and other sections of the Far East. Said also focuses his study on the time period from the late eighteenth century onward, taking Napoleon's failed occupation of Egypt as the critical historical progenitor of what he calls modern Orientalism.[4]

As one of the many projects informed by and indebted to Said's seminal work, my study set out to explore the existence and operation of Orientalism and Saidian orientalist discourse in London's stage representations of China during the historical period of the Qing Dynasty (1644–1911), China's last monarchy. I also took the reading of Said's theatrical metaphor and analogies offered by Angela Pao, who examines the depictions of the Orient in nineteenth-century French popular theatre, as the premises of my own critical inquiry. According to Pao, Said's metaphor stresses the total and unidirectional control held by the Western theatre participants, from the playwright to the audience, over the stage representation of the Orient, and the inherent reductionism in staging the Orient. Pao also highlights the long and dynamic relationship between the Orient and European theatre in Said's analogies. In each historical period, Pao observes, the presence of the Orient in European drama takes a different shape. But whatever the changes, Pao argues, its representations are always framed by "the triple context" of the historical and material relations between the two regions; the prevailing social, political, and intellectual concerns in the Western country (France in her study); and, last but not least, the dominant theatrical practices and dramatic conventions of the time.[5]

For each work of my study, I highlight the prominent factors of this "triple context," as well as other considerations, that informed and impacted the stage representation of China. Chapter One examines *Conquest of China by the Tartars* (1675), a heroic play, that dramatizes the so-called Manchu Conquest, which established the Qing Dynasty in China, and incorporates accounts reported by the Jesuits. Chapter Two analyzes *The Chinese Festival* (1755), a dance entertainment, and *The Orphan of China* (1759), a tragedy, both of which manifest Britain's keen material interest in China, its so-called "China-mania," and its anti-French antagonism in the mid-eighteenth century. Chapter Three explores how the literary works of John Francis Davis (1795–1890), who worked for the East India Company and served as Hong Kong's governor, and *The Chinese Sorcerer* (1823), an Easter holiday spectacle, demonstrate the dual and parallel development of British literary and theatrical output about China and the up-to-date views of the country in the early nineteenth century, which were informed by the British embassies' visits and the Anglo-Chinese trade. Chapter Four compares and contrasts three early twentieth-century London productions: *A Chinese Honeymoon* (1901–1904), an "escapist" musical comedy; *The Yellow Jacket* (1913), a fable about a young hero; and *Mr. Wu* (1913–1914), a gruesome melodrama of Anglo-Chinese conflict, and probes how they represent three distinct Chinaface fashions and reflect the development of intercultural contact between Chinese and Westerners during the last decade of the Qing court and immediately after its fall.

In each historical period of my research, the presence of China on the London stage indeed took a different shape, to use Pao's words. However, these Chinese shapes were not completely different; they shared similar traits, but they also evolved. Furthermore, the productions that manifested these shapes revealed, either explicitly or implicitly, as much about China as Britain, as they were conceived and performed by and for the English (British). Most significantly, the Chinese shapes did not always confirm, and sometimes even contradicted, the direct correlation between power and representation articulated by the theory of Orientalism. In these findings I argue that the representations of China on the historical London stage were not reductionist in the Saidian sense, but were in fact intercultural in their making, as manifested by the instances of interculturalization I identify and the process and phenomenon of interculturation I observe. Through continued interest and investment by generations of theatre practitioners and writers, the English (British) vocabulary, imagery, and repertoire of representing China have inherited historical practices but have also been open to new influences. Through the dramatization and stage representation of the Chinese Other, the ontological and epistemological bases of the English (British) Self have been put in sharp relief, questioned, and even satirized.

My reading and findings, which have departed from my initial intention to engage the theoretical framework of Orientalism as the analytical basis for this project, have been fundamentally shaped, throughout the course of research and writing, by considerations of the geographical distance of China from Britain (the West), by the historical period of my inquiry, and by my interest in probing whether the concept and practice of intercultural performance are applicable to these historical examples on the London stage. China, situated in the European conception of the Far Orient/East, is geographically much farther away from Europe than the Biblical lands or the Near Orient/East. The imbalanced power dynamic between the dominating West and dominated Orient, and the challenge, threat, and fear caused by the immediate proximity of Europe and the Near Orient, which are central to Said's work, do not often apply well to the relationship between England (Britain) and China. During the historical period covered in this book, from the late seventeenth century to the early twentieth century, the power dynamics between the two countries went through a reversal, with both at one time the stronger, and at another time the weaker partner, in their relations. That is, the imbalanced power dynamics were not unidirectional.

In terms of Orientalism, the time frame of my study covers both the period of what Chi-ming Yang calls early modern orientalism, in which China seemed superior to England (Britain) and other Western countries, and the period of Said's modern Orientalism, in which China was subjected to British and other imperial invasions and demands. In her study of China as "an exemplary and controversial model of empire" to early modern Europe, focusing on eighteenth-century England, Yang points out that recent scholarship has argued that China was never colonized and hence cannot be made to fit into "the type of ideological East-West dynamic" theorized by Said. Yang characterizes early modern orientalism as "a structure of ambivalence," which resulted from the British's desire for East Indies markets and the encounter with their superior "moral *and* economic example," China.[6]

The moral and economic superiority China assumed in early modern European (Western) perceptions was informed by both Jesuit writings and trade activities. Members of the Roman Catholic order of the Society of Jesus (Jesuits) arrived in China beginning in the late sixteenth century for their Christian mission. They assumed the manner and dress of Chinese scholars, befriended the literati, studied and translated Chinese classics, and provided their expertise in astronomy, cartography, and mathematics to the Chinese rulers. During their stay, the Jesuits sent back to Europe annual letters and reports on contemporary China, manuscripts on its history and geography, and translations of its classical teachings, especially those of the Chinese philosopher Confucius.[7] At the same time, European merchants brought goods from China, such as silks, herbs, paintings, and porcelains. The Jesuit writings were translated into several European languages and widely circulated; the Chinese imports, together with other "curiosities" taken from Asia, were collected and prized as treasures.[8] In response to these influxes, Europe in the seventeenth and eighteenth centuries perceived China as a country of high culture, superior morality, and good government. At the same time, goods imported from China and Asia inspired the fad of *chinoiserie*, as European craftsmen applied their interpretations of Chinese styles to various decorative arts.[9]

England (Britain) began to compete for Asian trade in the early seventeenth century. Although they arrived a century later than the pioneering Portuguese, the English merchants gradually came to dominate the scene as the East India Company established its base in India and expanded its trade into neighboring countries. Prompted by accelerating trade volumes and demand for Chinese goods, the British governments dispatched official embassies to the country, and the 1792–1794 Macartney embassy, known for Macartney's refusal to *kowtow* to the Qianlong emperor (see Chapter Three), brought home views of China that revised and reversed the Jesuits' admiring depiction. The first Opium War (1839–1842), fought over British importation of opium into China, led to the concession of Hong Kong and marked the key turn in Sino-Western power dynamics.[10]

The examples in my study, from the periods of both early modern orientalism and modern Orientalism, suggest that the interracial power dynamic between England (Britain) and China was not the fundamental and decisive factor that determined London's stage representation of the country. Instead, as I have identified earlier, it was the Jesuit writings and Britain's expanding material interest in China that conditioned its evolving stage depictions. The Jesuit writings gave rise to the persistent, interculturated dramatization of the Chinese-Tartar conflict in which the Tartars were conceived as China's perennial enemy, its political and cultural other. Britain's material Chinese interest motivated theatre practitioners to present Chinese goods, dress, architecture, and locales as visual attractions, establishing the Chinaface style of stage representation. In the examples discussed in this book, by the early twentieth century the Tartars had been replaced by the British (Westerners) in dramatizations of interracial conflict, while the Chinaface style continued to expand and multiply.

Within the examples of Chinese-Tartar or Anglo-Chinese conflicts discussed in this book, the identity of China can evidently be read as gendered and feminized, as the conflicts usually involve romantic interests between a female Chinese and a male Tartar (British). The distinct feminization of China in each case and the discernible changes in these depictions over the historical period reflect the intercultural formation of China's femininity and the trend toward trivialization and exoticization. The character Amavanga from *Conquest of China by the Tartars* (1675), cited earlier, embodies warrior characteristics informed by portrayals of both the Amazons and a Chinese female general. While the play's dramatization of the Tartar conquest of China corresponds with the historical Manchu Conquest, in which the Manchus, a nomadic people, overthrew the Chinese Ming Dynasty (see Chapter One), the Tartar prince Zungteus's "rescue" by Amavanga and his declaration that he would maintain China's customs and culture demonstrate the influence of the Jesuit characterization of the country as continuing its ancient civilization despite dynastic changes. China's femininity, in this case, is associated with female bravery and cultural power.

Orphan of China (1759), written by Arthur Murphy, dramatizes another Chinese-Tartar conflict, in which Mandane, wife of the loyal mandarin Zamti, rejects outright the romantic advances of the Tartar emperor Timurkan and devotes herself completely to the patriotic, anti-Tartar cause. Murphy's desexualized depiction of Mandane intentionally eliminates the interracial romance in the play's immediate French inspiration, Voltaire's *L'Orphelin de la Chine* (1755), and brings the play, in terms of the theme of justice and revenge, closer to its Chinese inspiration, Ji Junxiang's *Zhao Shi Gu Er* (*The Orphan of the House of Zhao*), which had been trans- lated, albeit incompletely, by a Jesuit friar. In her delivery of the epilogue, which Murphy presumably intended as a lighthearted coda to offset the moral high tragedy that had just been performed, the actress Mary Ann Yates, who played Mandane, engaged in small talk with her female audi- ence, gossiping, in her fashionable Chinese dress, about the strange Chinese aesthetic standards that deemed women with broad foreheads, pig eyes, and crippled feet as beauties, and revealing that Chinese women would cheat just as Englishwomen did. Murphy's feminization of China increased China's material appeal and trivial exoticness and diminished Voltaire's idealization (informed by the Jesuits) of Chinese culture, which Voltaire personified as a beauteous lady who conquers the invading Tartar con- queror by her virtue.

In *Chinese Honeymoon* (1901–1904), the princess Soo Soo appears naïve, as do the other Chinese girls, whose "pretty little faces," "dainty little feet," and "fetching little ways" Mr. Pineapple, a British vacationer, cannot resist. Soo Soo is attracted to Tom, Mr. Pineapple's nephew, and his attractiveness partly comes from her fantasy about his imperial mili- tary position in China, which he gives up to pursue her. A similar Anglo- Chinese romance is depicted in *Mr. Wu* (1913–1914), in which Nang Ping, Mr. Wu's innocent daughter, falls for Basil, a womanizing British young man sojourning in Hong Kong for his family business, and is killed by her father for transgressing what he considers a social taboo. In these last two examples of dramatization in the early twentieth century, China's feminin- ity has lost its former cultural allure and operates via exotic and childlike physical attraction.

In the epilogue delivered by Yates, cited above, her comments on strange Chinese cultural and social practices indirectly mock the British's foibles; Yates herself, in trendy Chinese dress, serves as a visual proof of Britain's fascination with China and its material goods while trying to make light of this obsession. This is an early instance of what I call China- face satire, which made social commentary on the contemporary British society through the Chinese appearance and developed into a distinct and established British theatre practice. In Chinaface satire, the Chinese appearance is a façade, and the British themselves are ridiculed. In one of the story lines in *Chinese Sorcerer* (1823), the characters Pe-Kin and Bri-Ti may be read as personification of China and Britain. Their relationship, strained by Bri-Ti's ever growing material appetite for grander dwellings in Chinese architectural style, very likely references both the British embassies' visit to China and the swift changes in London's landscape propelled by the prospering China trade, including trendy Chinese-style residences. In *Chinese Honeymoon*, cited above, the naivety of Soo Soo and other Chinese girls heightens Tom's romantic inclination and Mr. Pineapple's lasciviousness, as the British males' speech bears undertones of sexual innuendo, and they are attracted by the Chinese women's exotic appeal. The play also satirizes British social and cultural practices, such as church attendance, public meetings, male privilege, and power relations between the sexes in the workplace. The Christmas *Aladdin* pantomimes I have attended (see Epilogue) represent contemporary examples of Chinaface satire. In a nominal Chinese setting with nominally Chinese characters, the *Aladdin* pantos (as they are usually called in Britain) are not really about China at all, but rather utilize the clearly artificial Chinaface look to joke, share, and commiserate as an intimate community in a comic, holiday spirit. Through the making and use of the Chinaface satire, the British questioned why they were so obsessed with China, ridiculed their own idiosyncrasies, and discerned their own selves, which demonstrates the fact that China had entered and become part of the British identity.

The Chinaface satires I describe above, as well as other examples discussed in the following chapters, can be read as historical examples of intercultural theatre and performance, which, in a definition offered by Ric Knowles, is "a site for the continuing renegotiation of cultural values and the reconstitution of individual and community identities and subject positions."[11] From this perspective, the study presented in this book is about the continuing renegotiation of British cultural values and identities that I see in London stage's historical and contemporary representations of China. In addition to Knowles's definition, intercultural performance is generally described as performance that intentionally incorporates elements from disparate cultures as an approach to artistic creation. In both its conception and practice, intercultural performance has continued to draw scholarly interest in and reconsideration of what it is, how it works, and what it achieves as it has sparked and informed a growing field of critical inquiry beginning in the late twentieth century.[12] While acknowledging the wide-spread, conscious practice of intercultural performance and its theorization in the western world in the twentieth century, Knowles, citing examples from the indigenous peoples of the world, argues that theatre "has always been intercultural," and he uses this position as the basis of his survey of intercultural performance.[13] My examples from both pre-twentieth and early twentieth-century English (British) practice can be read as supporting Knowles's claim.

More specifically, my coinage of interculturalization, interculturation, and Chinaface is intended to create tools for critical analysis that may help clarify and explore answers to the "temporally specific and normative" question Una Chaudhuri asks about interculturalism: "What has interculturalism been, and what might it—should it—be, now and in the future?"[14] If theatre has always been intercultural, I define and use interculturalization, the act of creating a relationship between disparate cultural elements, to identify where the act occurs in a work and how the work is made intercultural. If interculturalism has been an aspect of theatre practice, I define and use the concept of interculturation, the ongoing process in which disparate cultural elements are interculturalized over a substantial period of time, to observe and characterize the diachronic impacts and effects of historical practices, and postulate, in the example of China on the London stage, what interculturalism might be or should be, now and in the future.[15] My interest in observing the process and phenomenon of interculturation is inspired by Joseph Roach's approach to examining what he calls circum-Atlantic performance through the three-sided relationship of memory, performance, and substitution,[16] and Marvin Carlson's inquiry into the relationship between theatre and memory through his conception of *ghosting*, as "the identical thing" encountered before returns to the stage in a different context.[17] Instead of examining how the various candidates in different situations perform by "standing in" for the presumed originals, as Roach conceives in his critical inquiry,[18] in my case I observe that many of the historical stage depictions of China, the "various candidates," did not intend to "stand in" for China, but to create and present the temporally specific Chinafaces of the British identities. While there were seemingly "identical things," in dramatic texts and the means of performance (in costuming and scenery, for example), which continued to return and represent China on stage, my interest is in identifying how, through the process of interculturation, they became differentiated at various historical moments, and what factors from what Pao calls "the triple context" and beyond caused their evolution and transformation.

The examples I study suggest that the act of interculturalization can occur on various levels: conceptual (the Tartars, the deist depiction of Confucian philosophy, dramatic convention and theatre practice), textual (Chinese material written into a heroic play, a tragedy, or a fairy tale), linguistic (names), behavioral (mannerisms and cultural customs), visual (court ritual and scenery), spatial (inclusion of various peoples in one place), and material (costume cut and design)—and that it can operate in different ways through merging, adding, simplification, and juxtaposition. English (British) theatre practitioners, that is, amply demonstrated their creativity in the myriad ways they created intercultural performance. Yet through the ongoing process of interculturation, what were retained in the early twentieth century (the last period in my study) from the earlier instances of interculturalization were the visual Chinaface attractions in costumes and scenery and the trivial and exoticized depiction of Chinese women (see earlier discussion on *Chinese Honeymoon*). *Yellow Jacket* (1913) and *Mr. Wu* (1913–1914), the other two examples examined together with *Chinese Honeymoon* in Chapter Four, manifest the participation and contributions of diasporic Chinese, which, as I argue in the chapter, served only to enhance the formal, more authentic-looking Chinaface appeal of the two productions.

Although the long-lasting, interculturated use of material and visual representations of China on the London stage may be explained by the reliance of theatre, a sensory art, on visual and aural means to create, express, and clearly mark the distinct features of an entity, in this case China, I conjecture that there are two epistemological reasons that may help explain this sustained phenomenon. First, throughout the course of the historical period of my study, Britain continued to increase its trading activities in China, which might have reinforced the close association of China with material goods and lessened Britain's interest in the country's cultural and literary output. The second reason concerns the lack of translated Chinese dramatic texts, and the associated lack of understanding of Chinese theatre, which resulted in a situation in which British theatre practitioners could not have drawn on Chinese dramatic literature and aesthetic principles for textual and conceptual inspiration even if they had wanted to. My conjectures are based upon my analysis of the literary works of John Francis Davis (see Chapter Three). During his formative years with the East India Company, Davis wrote extensively on Chinese language and literature, including drama and theatre, advocating linguistic and literary approaches to understanding the country and its people. He translated two Chinese plays and made great efforts to identify comparable theatre conventions, in terms of dramatic structure and staging, that could be found in both Chinese and British (Western) traditions. Davis's efforts, while laudable, nevertheless evince his ultimate incapability to overcome an epistemological barrier which prevented him from recognizing Chinese theatre as an art form that is ontologically different from Western theatre. His translations, which contrast with each other in terms of both subject and completeness, seem to have had no impact on contemporary British theatre's depictions and representations of China. His literary output on Chinese drama and theatre, that is, remained parallel to and outside of the realm of British theatre.

To return to the question Chaudhuri asks about interculturalism, in the following chapters I provide my reading of what intercultural performance has been in the examples I study. As for what it might or should be, now and in the future, I see two areas of great potential that could engage China beyond the historical visual and formal Chinaface approach: one is the textual inspiration I identify above as missing, and the other is the participation of the British Chinese community. Since the early twentieth century, Chinese theatre has been characterized by and drawn interest in the West for its visual performing and staging characteristics, but largely not for its texts. The most notable inspiration taken from Chinese theatre by a Western theatre practitioner in the twentieth century has been Bertolt Brecht's theorization of the alienation effect through his observation of Chinese acting, which exemplifies the formalist, Chinaface approach to Chinese theatre. As of the early twenty-first century, Ji's play, *Zhao Shi Gu Er*, remains the most visible (or perhaps the only) example of a Chinese play that has continued to receive significant Western attention and intercultural exploration of both its text and staging. The textual well and emotional depth of Chinese theatre remains to be probed, felt, and understood.

When I attended the *Aladdin* pantos, I was very aware of being an outsider, as I was from out of town, as well as one of the few Asian faces in the audience. I reason from my own experience that it might take some time for newer British audiences, including the British Chinese community, who may be unaware of or unfamiliar with the panto tradition, to get to know and take part in it. One of the productions I viewed featured a Chinese lion dance, which suggests a contribution from the local Chinese community. Although it could be characterized as another brief Chinaface moment in the production, it also led me to imagine that more fruitful and engaged collaboration might move the *Aladdin* pantos beyond their current Chinaface approach. As British Chinese enter the sites of British intercultural performance, I envision how they will, in the words of Knowles, take part in the continuing renegotiation of British cultural values and the reconstitution of their individual and community identities and subject positions in Britain.

NOTES

1. As my inquiry covers a historical period dating before the establishment of the United Kingdom of Great Britain in 1707, and the theatrical productions to be discussed were staged in London, England, I use England (English) and Britain (British) interchangeably. However, a conscious choice is made to use Britain (British) when describing its imperialism that intruded into China beginning in the 1830s.
2. Edward W. Said, *Orientalism* (New York: Vintage Books, 1979), 3, 40, 63, 71–72.
3. Ibid., 2, 6, 60, 63, 205.
4. Ibid., 3, 16–18, 22, 87.
5. Angela Pao, *The Orient of the Boulevards: Exoticism, Empire, and Nineteenth-Century French Theater* (Philadelphia: University of Pennsylvania Press, 1998), 1–2.
6. Chi-ming Yang, *Performing China: Virtue, Commerce, and Orientalism in Eighteenth-Century England, 1660–1760* (Baltimore: The Johns Hopkins University Press, 2011), 1, 23, 25.
7. For the Jesuit mission and activities in China, see, for example, David E. Mungello, chap. 2 in *The Great Encounter of China and the West, 1500–1800* (Lanham, MD: Rowman and Littlefield, 2013); *Curious Land: Jesuit Accommodation and*

the Origins of Sinology (Honolulu: University of Hawaii Press, 1989); Yulie Lou and Zhigang Zhang, chaps. 5 and 6 in *Zhong Wai Zong Jiao Jiao Liu Shi* [A Chinese-Foreign Exchange History of Religion] (Changsha Shi: Hunan Jiao Yu Chu Ban She, 1998).

8. See, for example, Donald Lach, *Asia in the Making of Europe*, chap. 9 in vol. 1, bk. 2; chap. 1 in vol. 2, bk. 1; chaps. 10 and 11 in vol. 3, bk. 4 (Chicago: University of Chicago Press, 1965–1993).

9. See, for example, Hugh Honour, *Chinoiserie: The Vision of Cathay* (London: J. Murray, 1973).

10. See, for example, Mungello, chap. 5 in *Great Encounter*; Hosea Ballou Morse, *The International Relations of the Chinese Empire*, 3 vols. (Shanghai: Kelly and Walsh, 1910–1918); Tingyi Guo, ed., *Jin Dai Zhongguo Shi* [History of Contemporary China] (Taipei: Taiwan Shang Wu Yin Shu Guan, 1971); Maochun He, *Zhongguo Wai Jiao Tong Shi* [General History of the International Relations of China] (Beijing: Zhongguo She Hui Ke Xue Chu Ban She, 1996).

11. Ric Knowles, *Theatre & Interculturalism* (Basingstoke: Palgrave Macmillan, 2010), 4–5.

12. See, for example, Erika Fischer-Litche, Josephine Riley, and Michael Gissenwehrer, eds., *The Dramatic Touch of Difference: Theatre, Own and Foreign* (Tübingen: Gunter Narr Verlag, 1990); Bonnie Marranca and Gautam Dasgupta, eds., *Interculturalism and Performance: Writings from PAJ* (New York: PAJ Publications, 1991); Patrice Pavis, *Theatre at the Crossroads of Culture*, trans. Loren Kruger (London: Routledge, 1992); Rustom Bharucha, *Theatre and the World: Performance and the Politics of Culture* (London: Routledge, 1993); Patrice Pavis, ed., *The Intercultural Performance Reader* (London: Routledge, 1996); Christopher Balme, *Decolonizing the Stage: Theatrical Syncretism and Post-Colonial Drama* (Oxford: Clarendon Press, 1999); Julie Holledge and Joanne Tompkins, *Women's Intercultural Performance* (London: Routledge, 2000); Jacqueline Lo and Helen Gilbert, "Toward a Topography of Cross-Cultural Theatre Praxis," *The Drama Review* 46, no. 3 (2002): 31–53; Penny Farfan and Ric Knowles, eds., "Rethinking Intercultural Performance" Special Issue, *Theatre Journal* 63, no.4 (2011); and Erika Fischer-Lichte, Torsten Jost, and Saskya Iris Jain, eds., *The Politics of Interweaving Performance Cultures: Beyond Postcolonialism* (New York: Routledge, 2014).

13. Knowles, 6.

14. Una Chaudhuri, "The Future of the Hyphen: Interculturalism, Textuality, and the Difference Within," in *Interculturalism and Performance: Writings from PAJ*, 192.

15. Technically, interculturation is not my coinage, as Chaudhuri has coined and used it in her essay. My definition and use of the term, nevertheless, differ from hers. See Chaudhuri, 192–193. I must admit that as I have formulated these tools of critical analysis and further differentiated between interculturalization and interculturation, what I defined as interculturation in one of my earlier publications would now be re-defined as interculturalization. See Dongshin Chang, "*Antigone* Intercultured in Tainan of Southern Taiwan," in Antigone *on the Contemporary World Stage*, eds. Erin B. Mee and Helene P. Foley (Oxford University Press, 2011), 148, fn. 4. This contradiction in my own definitions and usages of the term will mark the trajectory and revision of my continuing inquiry into intercultural performance.

16. Joseph Roach, *Cities of the Dead: Circum-Atlantic Performance* (New York: Columbia University Press, 1996), 2.
17. Carlson, Marvin Carlson, *The Haunted Stage: The Theatre As Memory Machine* (Ann Arbor: University of Michigan Press, 2003), 7.
18. Roach, 3.

REFERENCES

Balme, Christopher. *Decolonizing the Stage: Theatrical Syncretism and Post-Colonial Drama*. Oxford: Clarendon Press, 1999.

Bharucha, Rustom. *Theatre and the World: Performance and the Politics of Culture*. London: Routledge, 1993.

Carlson, Marvin. *The Haunted Stage: The Theatre As Memory Machine*. Ann Arbor: University of Michigan Press, 2003.

Chang, Dongshin. "*Antigone* Interculturated in Tainan of Southern Taiwan." In *Antigone on the Contemporary World Stage*, edited by Erin B. Mee and Helene P. Foley, 147–155. Oxford University Press, 2011.

Chaudhuri, Una. "The Future of the Hyphen: Interculturalism, Textuality, and the Difference Within." In *Interculturalism and Performance: Writings from PAJ*, edited by Bonnie Marranca and Gautam Dasgupta, 192–207. New York: PAJ Publications, 1991.

Farfan, Penny, and Ric Knowles, eds. "Rethinking Intercultural Performance" Special Issue. *Theatre Journal* 63, no.4 (2011).

Fischer-Lichte, Erika, Torsten Jost, and Saskya Iris Jain, eds. *The Politics of Interweaving Performance Cultures: Beyond Postcolonialism*. New York: Routledge, 2014.

Fischer-Litche, Erika, Josephine Riley, and Michael Gissenwehrer, eds. *The Dramatic Touch of Difference: Theatre, Own and Foreign*. Tübingen: Gunter Narr Verlag, 1990.

Guo, Tingyi, ed. *Jin Dai Zhongguo Shi* [History of Contemporary China]. Taipei: Taiwan Shang Wu Yin Shu Guan, 1971.

He, Maochun. *Zhongguo Wai Jiao Tong Shi* [General History of the International Relations of China]. Beijing: Zhongguo She Hui Ke Xue Chu Ban She, 1996.

Holledge, Hulie, and Joanne Tompkins. *Women's Intercultural Performance*. London: Routledge, 2000.

Honour, Hugh. *Chinoiserie: The Vision of Cathay*. London: J. Murray, 1973.

Knowles, Ric. *Theatre & Interculturalism*. Basingstoke: Palgrave Macmillan, 2010.

Lach, Donald F. *Asia in the Making of Europe*. 3 vols. Chicago: University of Chicago Press, 1965–93.

Lo, Jacqueline, and Helen Gilbert. "Toward a Topography of Cross-Cultural Theatre Praxis." *The Drama Review* 46, no. 3 (2002), 31–53.

Lou, Yulie, and Zhigang Zhang. *Zhong Wai Zong Jiao Jiao Liu Shi* [A Chinese-Foreign Exchange History of Religion]. Changsha Shi: Hunan Jiao Yu Chu Ban She, 1998.

Marranca, Bonnie, and Gautam Dasgupta, eds. *Interculturalism and Performance: Writings from PAJ*. New York: PAJ Publications, 1991.

Morse, Hosea Ballou. *The International Relations of the Chinese Empire*. 3 vols. Shanghai: Kelly and Walsh, 1910–18.

Mungello, David E. *Curious Land: Jesuit Accommodation and the Origins of Sinology*. Honolulu: University of Hawaii Press, 1989.

———. *The Great Encounter of China and the West, 1500–1800*. Lanham, MD: Rowman and Littlefield, 2013.

Pao, Angela. *The Orient of the Boulevards: Exoticism, Empire, and Nineteenth-Century French Theater*. Philadelphia: University of Pennsylvania Press, 1998.

Pavis, Patrice, ed. *The Intercultural Performance Reader*. London: Routledge, 1996.

———. *Theatre at the Crossroads of Culture*. Translated by Loren Kruger. London: Routledge, 1992.

Roach, Joseph R. *Cities of the Dead: Circum-Atlantic Performance*. New York: Columbia University Press, 1996.

Said, Edward W. *Orientalism*. New York: Vintage Books, 1979.

Yang, Chi-ming. *Performing China: Virtue, Commerce, and Orientalism in Eighteenth-Century England, 1660–1760*. Baltimore: The Johns Hopkins University Press, 2011.

1 "History and Truth"

The Conquest of China by the Tartars (1675)

... the insipid ass [Elkanah Settle] Would needs write on; and told me that his
Muse Had History and Truth for her Excuse.
—Epilogue to *The Conquest of China by the Tartars*,
spoken by Mary Lee

In 1644, the Ming Dynasty of China ended in chaos. Li Zicheng (李自成),[1]
with his troops of bandits, sacked numerous cities in the provinces and
attacked the capital Peking (Beijing). The Chongzhen (崇禎) emperor,
unwilling to yield and unable to escape, committed suicide. The Manchus, a
nomadic people living beyond the Great Wall who had developed a formidable
military organization, were pressing in from the northeast. Allied with the
Ming general Wu Sangui (吳三桂), the Manchus engaged in an intense battle
with Li and his followers. After Li was defeated and driven away from the
capital, the Manchus, led by the regent Dorgon (多爾袞), took control of
Peking and established the rule of their dynasty, called the Qing, over China.[2]

The drastic change of dynasties, now called the Manchu Conquest,
shortly became known in Europe through the letters of the Jesuit fathers and
the reports from China of European trading companies such as the Dutch
India Company. According to Edwin J. Van Kley, the defeat of the Ming was
the first major Chinese historical event ever reported in the Western world.[3]
The news of disorder, rebellions, and wars uncovered a contemporary
China in turmoil and quickly caught the attention of the Europeans; various
historical, literary, and dramatic writings on the Manchu Conquest were
published in several European languages in the late seventeenth century.[4]
These works were inspired by recent news about China.

Of the dramatic works, *The Conquest of China by the Tartars* (hereafter
shortened as *Conquest*) by Elkanah Settle (1648–1724) was the first
actually performed on the stage.[5] On May 28, 1675 (the earliest traceable
performance date and not necessarily the premiere), it was acted before King
Charles II by the Duke's Company at the Dorset Garden theatre in London.[6]
The script was published the next year, 1676.

This chapter examines Settle's *Conquest* and identifies its interculturalized
depiction of the Chinese-Tartar conflict and the Chinese female warrior
Amavanga as the defining factors that inform its ambiguously gendered

and gorily sensualized representation of China. *Conquest* depicts a Chinese empire besieged by both a foreign invasion of the "Tartars" and an inner turmoil of civil uprisings and usurpation schemes; a new regime, ruled by the Tartars but supported by the Chinese, eventually emerges out of disorder and excessive manslaughter. Among the characters, Amavanga, a Chinese female warrior, stands out for her valor and courage; her surprise appearance at the end, as she was presumed dead after a duel with the Tartar prince Zungteus on the battlefield, brings the play to conclude with nuptial and coronation celebrations as she accepts the hand of Zungteus, now the new king of China.

In depicting a disintegrating Chinese empire both lost to and continued by the Tartars, and in portraying Amavanga as both masculine in fighting and feminine when facing Zungteus, Settle's *Conquest* exhibits traits that conform to and yet simultaneously defy a Saidian, orientalist reading of power correlations between race and gender. Indeed, China's final submission to Tartary is symbolized in that of Amavanga to Zungteus, and by conflation and extension, of feminine China to masculine Tartary. However, Amavanga's submission is rather a rescue, as Zungteus attempts suicide after supposedly killing her despite his military conquest of China. The Chinese throne he now claims, as Zungteus declares at the end of the play, pays homage to Amavanga's feet; his "rougher" Tartary needs China's finer civilization. In other words, the play ultimately ends with the conquering, masculine Tartar rescued by and voluntarily submitting to the culturally stronger, feminine China. This depiction reflects the European perception of and respect for China as a country of high civilization during Settle's time, a perception that would persist over the next century. If China is depicted as feminine, its femininity, by its association with culture, is nevertheless not equated with weakness and decadence, nor is it seen as disadvantageous in power relations.

As performed before Charles II, Settle's *Conquest* also offers a political allegory about royal succession for the English king's entertainment. In depicting the Chinese king who wills his sovereignty to the Tartar invader as his legitimate successor after his throne is usurped by a villainous Chinese prince, the play suggests that blood lineage need not rank as the top priority in royal succession. Similarly, the heightened agency and courageous acts of women, exemplified by Amavanga and others, demonstrate how Settle capitalizes on the king's sanction of actresses on stage, exploiting their novel presence and appearance. Last but not least, the accentuated violence and gore Settle depicts in the play, when compared with that in his other works and those of his predecessors and contemporaries, demonstrates Settle's artistic inclination toward resorting to "show" or "scene," contemporary terms for stage spectacle, to appeal to his audience. In all, Settle's *Conquest* was conceived and written as a sexy, gory political spectacular for his special audience.

In his depiction of the Chinese-Tartar conflict, Settle inherited the interculturalized conception of the Tartars from Jesuit writings, which inspired him to depict the people as China's perennial northern enemy, its political and cultural opposite. Settle's portrayal of Amavanga's deeds interculturalizes the acts of the Amazons with those of a brave Chinese female general; in his creation of her name, Settle interculturalizes multiple linguistic and cultural references. Further, Settle's design of the Chinese royal courtship ritual interculturalizes a Chinese court practice as described by the Jesuits with an English court entertainment. These examples represent the various levels—conceptual, textual, linguistic, behavioral, and visual— on which interculturalization (the act of creating a relationship between elements that belong to disparate cultures) could occur and the different ways—merging, adding, and juxtaposing—in which it could operate. These instances of interculturalization prefigure those in the later London productions to be discussed in the following chapters. Most notably, the depiction of the Chinese-Tartar conflict has proven to be long-lasting and becomes the basis upon which further interculturation (the ongoing process in which disparate cultural elements are interculturalized over a substantial period of time) takes place.

Overlooked by modern scholarship and, when examined, typically treated as an inferior, deviant imitator of the prominent Restoration literary figure John Dryden (1631–1700),[7] Settle was actually a highly promising young playwright from Oxford in the 1670s. He received court patronage and his popularity overshadowed that of more senior and established talents.[8] He was encouraged to write his first play, *Cambyses King of Persia* (*Cambyses*, 1670–71), by the Duchess of Monmouth.[9] His next play, *The Empress of Morocco* (*Morocco*, 1673), was a sensational success, performed both at court and in public; its script was published with engravings ("sculptures"), a rarity in the English theatre of that age.[10] *Conquest*, following *Morocco*, was staged in public in 1675, as already mentioned, and attended by Charles II.

Quite noticeably, the first three plays of Settle are set in the distant, oriental lands of Persia, Morocco, and China. Written in rhymed couplets, they depict political crises that involve and clash with the characters' romantic pursuits. These general features, in terms of story setting, dramatic conflict, and language, demonstrate the plays' indebtedness to the conventions of rhymed heroic plays, a genre of Restoration drama that was advocated and popularized by Dryden. Considering his court patronage and his investment in the conventions of heroic drama, I anchor my examination of Settle's *Conquest* in the exploration of "history and truth" he claimed for the play (see epigram of the chapter).

In a mocking, self-deferential manner, addressing himself as "the insipid ass" in the play's epilogue, Settle claims that "his Muse had History and Truth for her Excuse."[11] This claim is in response to the epilogue's opening statement: "Well, a Romantick and a Slaught'ring Lass / With th'Hectours in the Pit, will never pass." The statement draws attention to the actress Mary Lee, who delivered the epilogue and played the role of Amavanga, described as "a Queen of a Province in China, in the Disguise of a Souldier" in the script's listing of characters. Settle is referring to the role's reception by the

"Hectors/hectors," boorish male audience members in the pit of the theatre. Through Lee, he defers to "history and truth" to justify his conception of a female character who is both romantic and valiant ("slaughtering"), cross-dressed as a male soldier.

Settle's remark shows his awareness that Amavanga was not what the (male) audience expected in a heroic play when compared with those of Dryden, who popularized and set the standards for the genre. In his often-quoted definition of heroic plays, prefaced to *The Conquest of Granada, Part I* (*Granada*, 1670–71),[12] Dryden states that "an Heroick Play ought to be an imitation, in little of an Heorick Poem: and, consequently, that Love and Valour ought to be the Subject of it."[13] Dryden then uses his delineation of the genre to defend his depiction of Almanzor, the hero in *Granada*, as both passionate and brave. To an audience used to seeing heroic male characters like Almanzor being romantic and slaughtering, Amavanga, a female counterpart, could appear unfamiliar and therefore provoke protests against her claim to embody the same qualities.

In his preface to *Granada*, Dryden acknowledges Achilles in Homer's *Iliad* as his inspiration for Almanzor.[14] As cited earlier, in the epilogue to *Conquest*, Settle calls the raucous male audiences in the pit "Hectours," a reference to the Trojan hero Hector in Homer's *Iliad*. Settle's use of the word therefore bears a Greek reference and invites the association of Amavanga with the Amazons, the legendary female warriors and enemies of ancient Greece. Like the Amazons who fought the Greek male soldiers, Amavanga goes on the defensive against the disapproving male hectors. By "history and truth" I suspect that Settle refers to classical literature as his defense; his take from the female, Amazonian perspective is parallel and contrary to Dryden's male, Greek angle. A few other critics have identified contemporary European writings on the Manchu Conquest and China as the "history and truth" in this passage.[15] I would argue that both western classical literature and these contemporary historical accounts constitute the "history and truth" that inspired Settle to write the character Amavanga, and by extension the play as a whole. Settle's handling of these sources and his deliberate deviations from Dryden's model for heroic plays are crucial to the occurrences of intercultualization in his play and the distinct ways that it represents China.

In the preface to *Ibrahim, the Illustrious Bassa* (1677), Settle stated:

> For that *Conquest* was written before *Morocco*, though it happened to lye so long by me: And *Morocco* which had been made a year and a half before it came upon the Stage, was Acted in less than three years after *Cambyses*.[16]

This short passage explains the sequence of writing and producing these earlier works. According to *London Stage* and other scholarly research, *Cambyses* premiered in 1670–71 and a public performance of *Morocco* was recorded in July 1673.[17] Since *Morocco* "had been made a year and a half before it came upon the Stage," the script was very possibly completed some time in late 1671 or early 1672. *Conquest*, "written before *Morocco*," therefore, was probably finished no later than early 1672. This dating clarifies its proximity to contemporary English publications on the Manchu Conquest.

Between 1644 (the date of the Manchu Conquest) and 1672, there were two main English sources about the history of the Chinese event. One is *Bellum Tartaricum* written by the Italian Jesuit friar Martino Martini (1614–1661),[18] translated from the Latin original *De bello Tartarico historia* into English in 1654.[19] The following year a newer and slightly different edition[20] of *Bellum Tartaricum* was appended to *The History of that Great and Renowned Monarchy of China*, which was written by the Portuguese Jesuit friar F. Alvarez (Alvaro) Semedo (1585–1658) and translated into English based on an Italian version of the Portuguese original.[21] The other available English account is *The History of the Conquest of China by the Tartars*, which was compiled by the Spanish bishop Juan de Palafox y Mendoza (1600–1659) and translated into English in 1671 based on a French version of the Spanish original.[22] The number of European languages— Latin, Italian, Portuguese, French, Spanish, and English—involved in circulating and disseminating this information demonstrates Europe's huge interest in the historical event of the Manchu Conquest and the country of China in the late seventeenth century.[23]

The composition, coverage, and spelling of Chinese proper names differ in the accounts provided by Martini and Palafox y Mendoza. For the Jesuit mission, Martini arrived at Hangzhou, China, in 1643, and personally experienced some of the conquest's progressions. In 1650, he was sent to Europe to see the pope in order to defend the Jesuits' accommodative approach to disseminating Christianity in China.[24] When Martini eventually arrived in Europe in 1653 after a hazardous journey,[25] he had finished several books about China, including *De bello Tartarico historia*. By contrast, Palafox y Mendoza never went to China. While serving as an archbishop in Mexico, Palafox y Mendoza received, compiled, and edited information about the Manchu Conquest that he received from the Philippines. After his death, his kinsman had the manuscript published.[26] While Martini described the rise of the Manchus, their conflicts with China, the rebellious disturbance within China, the fall of Peking, and the Manchus' subsequent control of the capital, Palafox y Mendoza focused on the Manchus' suppression of resistance in southern China, which is not covered by Martini. To the reader's disadvantage, Martini and Palafox y Mendoza used different spellings or names when addressing the same historical figures or geographical locations.[27]

The opening scene of *Conquest*, set in the Tartar camp, is indicative of the ways in which Settle makes use of the various sources of "history and truth." Prince Zungteus exalts the intrepidity and exploits of the Tartar army, which is fast approaching China under the command of his father, the Tartar king Theinmingus: "Yet those strong Bars [of snow and ice] have not your Arms with-stood; / The Gods that froze your Climate, warm'd your blood"; "Our Armes the News of our success out-fly: / We give our Foes but time to stare and dye. ... And where the Winter does our passage stay, / We burn down Citys till we melt our way" (I.i.; 1, 2).[28] To his son's commendation of their achievements, Theinmingus replies that their honor calls for further and greater action: to reach the wall of Pequin, i.e., Peking, the capital of China, and have Chinese "Imperial Heads in Blood, and Thrones in Dust" to avenge the murder of his father (I.i.; 2). Soon an ambassador of the king of China arrives, the disguised Amavanga in man's dress. Introduced by trumpets, she is accompanied by her confidante Vangona, who is also in disguise, and attendants. In an aside, Amavanga reveals that she has falsely claimed herself as the king's ambassador because the invading Tartars' victory has cast on him the name of coward. Her false claim is for his "wrong'd Honours sake" to "give check to the proud *Tartars* Pride" (I.i.; 3). Furthermore, her challenge of Zungteus, whom she loves, to "meet in Arms" is "To try his Courage, and his Gallantry, / The only merit that can Conquer Me" (I.i.; 4, 6).

The scene sets up the Chinese-Tartar conflict caused by the murder of the former Tartar king. For honor and revenge, the Tartars have invaded China, which provokes Amavanga to stop their sweeping progression. The challenges she poses to the enemy in public, nevertheless, also involve a private, personal wish to test Zungteus's valor and prove that he is worthy of her love. Her challenges thus create a dilemma, a head-on clash between her and Zungteus's pursuits of both honor and love.

The defining characteristics of heroic plays as delineated by Dryden are apparent in the scene's depiction of the Chinese-Tartar conflict: the subjects of love and valor, the use of rhymed couplets, the use of music (sounding of trumpets) to enhance the warring situation.[29] However, much more prominent are the Settle's departures from Dryden's model: the emphases on female agency and gore. Ultimately it is Amavanga's decision to check the Tartars' progression that engenders the dramatic conflict of the play. Her cross-dressing act, false claim to be a Chinese ambassador, and desire to test Zungteus all demonstrate her boldness and will against the odds. The female agency seen in Amavanga is not a lone example; other female characters in *Conquest* also incite conflicts and actions. But even more prominent is the depiction of gore. In a stilted, lofty style, Zungteus in rhymed couplets depicts the Tartars' conquering victories as fervent and fiery; with their warmed blood they killed the Chinese and set their cities aflame. Theinmingus also speaks of blood, in a more literal sense of the word, as he seeks the deaths of the Chinese royal family, with their "heads in blood." The gore evoked in Zungteus's and Theinmingus's speeches operates on an illocutionary level; applying J. L. Austin's definition of illocution,[30] their words have a direct performative force, one of killing, burning, and destroying. Later in the play the gore extends from the spoken acts to physical acts of suicides and the visual display of mutilated bodies. These gory acts, with their aural and visual shocks, overwhelm and overshadow the heroic drama focus on love and valor.

In *Conquest*, the Tartars, not the Manchus, are depicted as the deadly, destructive enemy of China. In both Martini and Palafox y Mendoza the Manchus were called the Tartars. At the opening of his *Bellum Tartaricum*, Martini defined what he meant by the Tartars:

The most ancient Nation of *Tartars* in *Asia*, the Parent of many
Nations, hath been an Enemy to the Empire of *China* above four
thousand years. ... I call that Nation, *Tartars*, which inhabiteth the
Northern parts, behind that famous Wall [the Great Wall], hath ever
served for a Rampart to hinder their irruptions into the said Empire. ...
The Country the *Chinese* having a defect of the letter R anciently
called *Tata*: comprehending under this name, not only the occidentall,
but the Oriental *Tartars*. ... (255)[31]

Martini used Tartars as a generic term for various nomadic peoples
("nations"), denoting what he believed to be their shared ancestry and conflict with China. Martini was aware of the Chinese term Tata which he,
interestingly, interpreted as a diminutive form of Tartar due to the Chinese
difficulty in pronouncing the letter *r*. In Chinese accounts, however, Tata
designates specifically one of the Mongolian tribes.[32] Through his interpretation of the missing letter and sound of *r*, Martini drew an imperfect parallel between Tata and Tartar and, to apply one of the key concepts of my
argument, interculturalized them to justify the term's validity. In Martini's
accounts, and further in Settle's *Conquest*, the Tartars have become China's
perennial northern enemy; the Manchu Conquest is the latest manifestation
of the conflicts between the two countries.

Martini's usage recalls writers of his time who used the term *Tartar* in a
similar manner and even a broader sense to designate a distinct political and
cultural entity that was the contrary and enemy of culture and civilization.
To use a Saidian analogy, these writings told of Tartarism, the Tartar other. In
his *History* to which Martini's *Bellum Tartaricum* is attached, Semedo also
made no distinction between the Mongolians and the Manchus, calling them
the Tartars who had warring conflicts with the Chinese at both the beginning
and ending of the Ming Dynasty (1368–1644).[33] Peter Heylyn (1600–1662),
an Oxford-educated Anglican clergyman and historian of noted writings on
world geography and nations,[34] described the Tartars as "a puisant [puis-
sant] and mighty people," "a Ruder and more Northern brood of Scythians"
whose vast territory stretched between China, Russia, Persia, the Caspian Sea,
and the Caucasian Mountains. Heylyn further identified Cingis under whose
leadership all the Scythian nations were united in the name of Tartars.[35]

Heylyn's accounts demonstrate how the term *Tartar* could operate across
space and time and create an ultimate other in the broadest possible way. He
regarded the Tartars as descendants of the Scythians, an earlier generic term
for the various nomadic tribes in the north and east outside the realms of
ancient Greek and Roman civilizations.[36] His identification of Cingis (i.e.,
Genghis Khan) as founder of the vast Tartar empire, on the other hand,
shows that by the Tartars he also meant the Mongolians who had swept
across Central Asia and reached Europe in the early thirteenth century
and established the Yuan Dynasty (1206–1367) in China. The Tartars in
Heylyn's usage were thus an immense political and cultural other, uncouth

and militarily mighty, extending both geographically and temporally from border to border between China and the West.[37]

Along with the writings of Martini, Palafox y Mendoza, Semedo, and Heylyn, Settle's depiction of the Chinese-Tartar conflict in *Conquest* was part of this literary tradition of binary opposition: at the end of the play Zungteus wins Amavanga in marriage and becomes king of China. In return, Zungteus offers the Chinese prince Quitazo the Tartar crown, "Your Milder Presence will auspicious be, / And Civilize my Rougher *Tartary*. / And whil'st the *Chinans* pay Allegeance here: / I'le Teach their softer Natures Arms and War" (V.ii.; 67).[38] The "rougher" Tartars eventually conquer the "milder," "softer" Chinese, but the two peoples will benefit from acquiring each other's strength. This ending could easily be interpreted as gendered, pitting the "rougher," masculine Tartars against the "softer," feminine Chinese. However, the character Amavanga and the ways in which she and Zungteus deal with the conflict between love and valor complicate the seemingly straightforward contrast.

Amavanga is depicted as patriotic, quick to act, opting for valor as proof of love. She stops the Tartars because, cited earlier, their success has cast the name of coward on the king of China, which is "An Infamy so loud, as would awake / A Womans Rage" (I.i.; 3). Zungteus recalls that during a civil war Amavanga escaped her father's court in "a Masc'line shape" and flew into the thickest dangers where she avenged the death of her brother on the rebel Chanquincungus in one stroke and overthrew his army (I.i.; 7). Upon hearing that the Tartars have chosen Zungteus as her opponent in the duel, Amavanga wavers, for a moment, and refuses to fight. Her reasons—she fears that, as a woman, she will be unable to match "a manly hand," and she hesitates to fight with a lover—quickly dissolve after her confidant Vangona calls her a coward. "I'le shew that I can Love, 'cause I dare Fight," Amavanga declares, her sense of honor re-charged (III.ii.; 25, 26). After being mortally wounded in the duel (so we think), Amavanga explains to Zungteus, "Nothing but Loyalty and Honour's Laws / Engag'd me in this Great but Fatal Cause." As for love, it must remain a distant affair, of loss and reminiscence: "And when I'm there [Heaven]; if Love so far can view / Look up to me; as I'll look down to you" (IV.i.; 39).

Compared to Amavanga, Zungteus is depicted as more love-stricken and passive in the fight to defend his honor. Having ascertained that Amavanga will be in the battle, he intends to disobey his father and quit the war so that he may avoid becoming his mistress's murderer. Palexus, his confidant, calls his plan of retreat "unmanly" and convinces him that Amavanga will only be won through honor and victory (I.i.; 8–9). In the duel Zungteus kills Amavanga as he feared that he would (or so he thinks); heartbroken and distressed, he plans to kill himself. His father Theinmingus scolds him; his suicide plan, "an Effeminate design," will disturb his "more Masc'line mothers Ghost." Zungteus eventually chooses duty over love, for he cannot bear the blame of betraying his father, a king, and "break[ing]. ... Duty, Honour, Nature's Laws; / and from a Conqueror turn[ing] a Womans slave" (IV.i.; 43–44). After helping Quitazo defeat the usurper Lycungus, Zungteus again attempts suicide, for he wants to "resign Life and Crown" for Amavanga. His stabbing himself is stalled by the miraculous appearance of Amavanga who, helped by "a God that smil'd on Love," has witnessed how he has his "Love and Honour try'd" and at last accepts him by "Fate and Justice" (V.ii.; 66–67).

By having Palexus and Theinmingus respectively call Zungteus's plans of retreat and suicide for love unmanly and effeminate in order to prod him into fighting, Settle appears to contrast love as womanly or effeminate with valor as manly or masculine. A love-stricken Zungteus is less masculine than the honor-driven, patriotic women Amavanga and his own deceased mother, though they may not possess his physical prowess. Read in this way, the play actually ends with the more masculine, miraculously revived Amavanga coming to the rescue of the more effeminate, suicidal Zungteus. His declaration that the conquest will civilize the "rougher" Tartars and toughen the "softer" Chinese may be diplomatic rhetoric that plays down his loss of masculine valor at those emotional moments.

Nevertheless, Amavanga claims that it was a god smiling on love who restored her to life. Zungteus lays the Chinese throne he wins at Amavanga's feet for her love of him (V.ii.; 67). Love ultimately brings Amavanga and Zungteus to a reunion, in which Zungteus dedicates his military achievements to her. Settle's exaltation of love in the play's conclusion may be in accord with Dryden's English model of tragedy in heroic plays, which differs from the classic Greek ideal:

> ... If this be true [that Tragedy is to reform Manners by delightful Representation of Human Life in great Persons, by way of Dialogue], then not only Pity and Terror are to be mov'd as the only Means to bring us to Virtue, but generally Love to Virtue, and Hatred to Vice, by shewing the Rewards of one, and Punishments of the other; at least by rendring Virtue always amiable, though it be shown unfortunate; and Vice detestable, tho' it be shown Triumphant.[39]

By this moralist model, Dryden proposes love, "an Heroique Passion," as fit for tragedy when its proper end is "to reform manners," with "the Encouragement of Virtue, and Discouragement of Vice."[40] In *Conquest*, love inspires Amavanga to valor ("I'le shew that I can Love, 'cause I dare Fight") and brings her into direct conflict with Zungteus. Their "amiable" virtues of honor and duty are shown as "unfortunate" while the two countries are at war, but are eventually rewarded with title and marriage. Dryden's proposal of "Love to Virtue" helps explain the highly contrived ending of *Conquest* with its poetic justice. "Hatred to Vice" is seen in Settle's depictions of the love triangle between the Chinese princess Orunda, the Chinese prince Quitazo, and Quitazo's mistress Alcinda, as well as in the usurpation scheme of Lycungus. The vices involved in these plot developments, to be discussed shortly, are indeed shown as both detestable and triumphant, albeit with copious violence and gore that was probably beyond Dryden's ideal.

While Dryden's model informs the structural framework of Settle's *Conquest*, passages from Martini and others have been identified as inspiration for Settle's depictions of character and plot. As already stated, I see in the play's epilogue a possible inference to the Amazons, in Amavanga's challenge to the Hectors in the pit. Martini actually compared a brave Chinese woman commander to the legendary female warriors: "[T]here was one *Heroick* Lady," he wrote, "whom we may well call the *Amazon* or *Penthesilean* [Penthesilea] of China" who joined the war against the Tartars in her son's place and brought along three thousand female soldiers carrying "not only Masculine minds, but mens habits also, and assuming Titles more becoming men than women" (261, Figure 1.1).[41] In addition, Martini explained that the reason the Tartars invaded China was to avenge the wrongful death of the father of the Tartar king Theienmingus[42] (257–259, Figure 1.2). Zungteus, the Tartar prince, was sent to China at a young age to learn "*China*'s Manners, Doctrine and Language" (266).

Figure 1.1 Illustration of female warrior and Chinese emperor, from Martini, *De bello Tartarico historia* (1655). Rare Books Division, The New York Public Library, Astor, Lenox and Tilden Foundations.

Figure 1.2 "The Lively effigies of Theinmingus," from Semedo, *History of that Great and Renowned Monarchy of China* (1655). Rare Books Division, The New York Public Library, Astor, Lenox and Tilden Foundations.

Settle clearly made use of the names of the historical figures and incidents reported by Martini. For example, *Conquest* depicts the death of Theienmingus's father as the cause for the Tartar invasion of China. Settle also appears to have taken inspiration from Martini's accounts about Zungteus's sojourn in China and the Chinese heroic lady's deeds to concoct a romantic relationship between them.[43] Martini's comparison of the Chinese woman commander to Penthesilea, the Amazon queen who was killed by the Greek hero Achilles, very possibly provided further inspiration for Zungteus's killing of Amavanga in the play.

Settle's character Amavanga offers an interesting case of interculturalization in her gender-crossing deeds and name. Her valor embodies qualities of the Amazons and the Chinese female commander and soldiers; her name, as analyzed by Adrian Hsia and Chi-ming Yang, combines the words Amazon and Amavang used in Martini's descriptions.[44] While Amazon comes from Martini's analogy, Amavang is a Chinese approximation, in Martini's Latinized spelling, of the Tartar (Manchu) term Amahan, "Father

King," given to Zungteus's brother Dorgon who was an able and respected regent-uncle and ruled on behalf of his underage nephew (278).[45] In adding the feminine ending "a" to his endearing title Amavang, as Yang observes, Settle "re-gendered" the historical male Manchu figure and created a female heroine whose name bears Greek, Latin, Chinese, and Manchu cultural significations.[46] The act of adding the extra "a," in other words, interculturalized the various linguistic and cultural references in Settle's coinage of the name.

This interculturalization of the name Amavanga clearly operates along the gender line and may, similar to the case of the Chinese-Tartar opposition, prompt an orientalist, gendered reading of it as an act of effeminizing China; it, nevertheless, can evoke multiple and complex readings. Like her Amazon and Chinese sisters, Amavanga is depicted as owning exceptional valor and martial skills comparable to those of men. Amavanga may represent China, but she is depicted as a strong-willed, physically capable woman who does not conform to an orientalist or even conventional depiction of femininity. Yet, in imitation of her Chinese compatriots, she needs to disguise her sex and assume "masculine" habits and mannerisms in order to fight the invading male Tartars. Signs of her femininity are subjugated in order to highlight acts of valor and bravery that are associated with masculinity. Furthermore, although Amavanga may be compared to the Amazon queen Penthesilea, Zungteus, as a Tartar/ Scythian prince, does not correspond with the Greek hero Achilles because Zungteus is analogously also an outsider, not a Greek. The analogy would turn the Chinese-Tartar conflict into the Amazons against the Scythians, two barbarian states warring against each other outside of civilization. If Settle effeminizes China by the character Amavanga, her interculturalized, Amazonian femininity defies a typical orientalist conception even though it still operates under the feminine–masculine binary system. Reading her as a Chinese Penthesilea also calls into question Zungteus's contrast between his "rougher" Tartars and the "softer" Chinese. Perhaps another possible reading of Zungteus's declaration is that his "softer" Chinese refers to Quitazo and other Chinese men in attendance, "the *Chinans* [who] pay Allegeance here" (V.ii.; 67), not including his Amazonian queen who has tried his love and honor and conquered him.

Quitazo first appears among twelve Chinese princes who, in masquerade, perform a "Maskal [Masked] Dance"[47] (II.i.; 10). This "Royal Scene of Love," as the king of China calls it, is a practice of "the *Chinan* Laws" (II.i.; 9) in which Orunda, the king's only child, has to publicly declare her two choices for her eventual mate, one of whom will be selected for her by her father. After she futilely protests this practice, among the princes who unmask after the dance, Orunda picks Quitazo, whose "modesty" and "softer looks" appeal to her, and says, in an aside, Lycungus is the only man she would refuse due to his "dark, Harsh, and ill featur'd look" (II.i.; 11). Orunda anticipates that her father would see Quitazo as the obvious choice, which, unfortunately, he does not. With the Tartars approaching, the Chinese king divides his power between Quitazo and Lycungus, who he expects will rise to the occasion and prove their worth. His decision gives Lycungus the opportunity to scheme and usurp the Chinese throne. Orunda further discovers the secret love affair between Quitazo and Alcinda, a Chinese lady; infuriated, she plots a murder of Alcinda that inadvertently leads to her own death.

In the eyes of Orunda, Quitazo's softer looks impart romantic charms, and Lycungus's look suggests more "the Mark [o]f Policy"(II.i.; 11) than love. Her judgment foreshadows the following actions of these two male characters: Quitazo is torn by romantic affairs, and he uses his military assignment to delay his marriage with Orunda in the hope of reuniting with Alcinda; Lycungus places himself at the service of Orunda and the king in order to win their trust and attain his political ambitions. Quitazo's loyalty to the court contrasts with Lycungus's treachery; his inferior martial skills make him a prey to Lycungus, whom he eventually seeks help from Zungteus to defeat. As Zungteus awards the Tartar crown to the "milder" Quitazo, his declaration to teach the "softer" Chinese arms and war may be informed by Quitazo's lack of military competency.

The inner strife within the Chinese court and its consequent disintegration constitute the other half of Settle's *Conquest*. Triggered by Orunda's willful and miscalculated act of picking Lycungus as one of her marital choices, the sequence of events may be regarded as demonstrating Dryden's principle of "Hatred to Vice." After the public marital selection, Orunda has doubts about Quitazo and asks Lycungus to investigate his "native Virtues" (II.i.; 18). Thereafter Lycungus plays the villain and creates tension and confusion. After spotting Quitazo's secret tryst with Alcinda, Lycungus reports it to Orunda who, enraged, plans to have Alcinda poisoned. However, the villains hired by Lycungus mistakenly force Orunda to drink the poison. This murderous ending to the love triangle shows Orunda "punished" for her vicious plot against Alcinda. Lycungus then arrests Quitazo and Alcinda and presents them as murderers of Orunda to the king, who strips Quitazo's power and command of the army and awards them to Lycungus. Taking advantage of the king's complete trust and bestowal of power, Lycungus proclaims himself king, besieges the palace, and causes the royal family to commit mass suicides. Lycungus thus succeeds in realizing "detestable" yet momentarily "Triumphant" schemes, in Dryden's terms, before he is eventually killed ("punished") by Zungteus at the end of the play.

The characters Lycungus and Quitazo are also inspired by the accounts of Martini and Palafox y Mendoza: Lycungus recalls the bandit Licungzus (Licungz, or Ly), i.e., Li Zicheng, who sacked the capital of Peking, and Quitazo, the Chinese general Usangueius (Vsanguè), i.e., Wu Sangui, who sought help from the Manchus in order to drive out Li.[48] The characters Orunda and Alcinda, on the other hand, appear to be Settle's inventions.[49]

Orunda, notably, differs much from the reports of Martini (278) and Palafox y Mendoza (27–28), who state that before Licungzus/Ly entered the court the Chinese emperor killed his daughter, an act to which she did not object or perhaps even willingly subjected herself in order to preserve her honor (Figure 1.3). In *Conquest*, Orunda dies of her own wrongdoing in the poison scheme. Furthermore, the "*Chinan* Laws," by which Orunda and the Chinese princes are required to abide in *Conquest*, as Bridget Orr says, recall Semedo's account of Chinese royal courtships and marriages in his *History*.[50] Whereas in Semedo the Chinese princess chose two out of the twelve young men without being seen, Settle's Orunda declares her choices in public. Settle's creation of Orunda as an outspoken, willful, and vengeful character is a far cry from the voiceless, obedient, and hidden princess who was at the mercy of her emperor father in the accounts of Martini, Palafox y Mendoza, and Semedo. Next to Amavanga, she is the female character Settle depicts with the most heightened agency in deciding her own fate.

Figure 1.3 Illustration of Chinese emperor killing his daughter, from Martini, *De bello Tartarico historia* (1655). Rare Books Division, The New York Public Library, Astor, Lenox and Tilden Foundations.

In Semedo's description of the Chinese royal courtship ritual it is unclear how the chosen Chinese princes were dressed and what they did while being viewed by the hidden princess. In *Conquest*, Settle has the princes perform in a masked dance before Orunda. Originating in European carnival tradition, this form of masquerade entertainment appeared in England in the sixteenth century and Charles II and his court were reported to be fond of it.[51] "The *Chinan* Laws" of royal courtship in *Conquest* were thus enhanced by a European/English cultural and performance tradition. In this case, as with Settle's coinage of the name Amavanga, interculturalization occurs in an additive manner that links together two disparate cultural practices and creates a dramatized, intercultural form of the ritual.

After Orunda's death, the Chinese court quickly deteriorates, shaken by Lycungus's schemes and suffering various kinds of violence and gore. When the king of China learns of the secret meeting between Quitazo and Alcinda, he, in furor, announces that he will "punish his [Quitazo's] Affront on his whole Race" and have Alcinda strangled, using her blood to expiate her sin. He will also "pluck out all / Their Eyes, that shed a Tear to see her fall" (III.ii.; 28).[52] After Lycungus presents Quitazo and Alcinda to him as murderers of Orunda, the enraged king declares, "These Lovers shall be both together rackt," and he hopes Orunda in Heaven will see that "Vengeance which attends my frown" (IV.ii.; 54). Although none of the above acts of cruelty planned by the king is realized, his impassioned, performative speeches evoke in the mind's eye highly graphic imagery of homicide and various kinds of torture exerted on the human bodies.

The king's speeches anticipate the onslaught of mass bloodshed that is recounted and presented in the final scene of the play. Before he enters the palace to take the life of the king, Lycungus is reported to have killed eight chief Chinese princes, burned alive sixteen thousand students of law, and set their school on fire (V.ii.; 58). At the king's request, which he retracts a moment too late, the Chinese queens commit group suicide, an act presumably depicted in the scenery (for it would have required a huge cast of women merely for this scene if actual actresses were used) as a scene of shock and horror:

> The Scene opens, and is discovered a Number of Murdred Women, some with Daggers in their Breasts, some thrust through with Swords, some strangled, and others poyson'd; with several other Forms of Death. (V.ii.; 60)

Inspired by his queens' courage in taking their own lives as their ultimate sacrifice for him, the king asks his attendant lords, "Honour forbids, that we on Earth should stay, / When thus a Female Trayn has led the way. / In Death above their Sex they have a Courage Shown; / And shall We be less Manly in our own?" He then "Stabs himself in the Left Arm. Sits down, and writes in the Blood." In the letter the king bequeaths the throne to the Tartar prince Zungteus, who he wishes would defeat Lycungus for "Just Revenge." Legozun, a Chinese prince, responds to this decision, "Nobly Resolv'd. / A monarch should bestow / His Empire rather on a Forriegn Foe, / Than on a Traytor." When the letter is finished, the King and several Chinese princes "all fall on their Swords" and "Dy Omnes" (V.ii.; 61).

After causing the two suicides, and all the other deaths, Lycungus defeats Quitazo and pronounces his plan of execution: he will catch a full draught of Alcinda's hot blood, mix it with the worst kind of poison, and force the mixture down Quitazo's throat. "Then whil'st the Poyson's Tortures do begin, / And on his burning Entralls feed within, / His flesh without from his rack'd body tear, / And every wound with burning Irons Sear" (V.ii.; 64). Lycungus's sadistic fury, a maddening culmination of bloodshed, poisoning, and torture, is eventually extinguished by Zungteus, who comes to Quitazo and Alcinda's rescue. Lycungus's fall marks the end of the "Hatred to Vice" progression as his dead body adds to the carnage he caused. Settle's depiction of his irrational mass slaughter may represent a Restoration imagination of the brutal "Asiatic" deed, an orientalist and problematic analogy by the German historian Ernst Nolte, who used it to characterize Stalin's communist atrocities as the ultimate cause of the genocidal violence of the Holocaust and provoked the heated *Historikerstreit* (Historians' debate) among German historians about the legacy of the Third Reich in the late twentieth century.[53]

The violence and gore depicted in the disintegration of the Chinese court are shocking, but they do have roots in the accounts of Martini and Palafox y Mendoza. Lycungus's killing of Chinese princes and thousands of students recalls the cruelties of Changhienchungus (i.e., Zhang Xianzhong, 張獻忠), another rebel, as vividly described by Martini (298–301).[54] Martini's and Palafox y Mendoz's accounts of the final moments of the Ming court's fall differ in details and sequencing. According to Martini, after writing the letter with his own blood, the Chinese emperor killed his unmarried daughter and ended his life by hanging himself. The emperor's example, Martini continued, was followed by the queen, the lord marshal, faithful eunuchs, and multiple citizens who via suicide expressed "the highest point of fidelity" toward their deceased king (274). In a much longer passage by Palafox y Mendoza (24–58), the Chinese emperor first killed his daughter and then chose his empress from among his queens for a double suicide. After the empress hanged herself, the emperor wrote the letter with his own blood before following her example. The mandarins ended their lives in "divers sorts of violent deaths" as they manifested, belatedly, their allegiance to the emperor (28, 34–37, 43–44).

Settle's dramatization in *Conquest* approximates Palafox y Mendoza more closely than Martini, albeit with increased magnitude. As described earlier, at the king's request a number of Chinese queens, not just the empress, commit group suicide. Instead of biting his finger as Palafox y Mendoza described (36), the king in Settle's *Conquest* stabs his arm, an act that recalls Marlowe's Doctor Faustus, to obtain blood for the letter. The emperor's solitary suicide in the accounts of Martini and Palafox y Mendoza is replaced with a communal one, together with his lords, inspired by the example of the queens whose various forms of death were disclosed on stage.

In both Martini and Palafox y Mendoza, the emperor's suicide was precipitated by the betrayal of his commanders or mandarins, who cooperated with Licungzus, i.e., Li Zicheng, the bandit who sacked the capital Peking. In his letter the emperor expressed bitterness and despair and, according to Martini, further wished that Licungzus/Li would "take revenge of such perfidious Creatures [the commanders]" (274). In Settle's *Conquest*, as cited earlier, the Chinese king in his letter bequeaths his empire to Zungteus, the Tartar prince who he wishes would defeat Lycungus, the Chinese prince who betrayed his trust and usurped the throne, for "Just Revenge." In Settle's dramatization Lycungus embodies all the traitorous and destructive traits of the Chinese commanders and the bandit Licungzus and eventually receives poetic justice in death.

From the cross-dressing Amavanga, who orchestrates the trials for Zungteus, to the willful Orunda, whose revenge scheme goes awry, to the courageous Chinese queens who commit group suicide, Settle's creative adaptations of the conventions of heroic plays and "history and truth" noticeably accentuate female characters whose deeds and agency motivate the male characters to action. These women characters are the agents of action in *Conquest* and "emasculate" their male counterparts. On the other hand, the way these characters' bodies are exposed onstage accentuates both the "Love to Virtue" and "Hatred to Vice" progressions of the play: Amavanga's death after the duel, her final surprise appearance, Orunda's death by poison, and the queens' deaths in various forms. While heightening female agency, Settle also exploits the materiality and presence of female bodies, either real or painted, that appear to aim for sensual appeal and even allow for voyeuristic prurience. The representation of their bodies in various forms of death may represent a gory Restoration precedent to the highly controversial revel or "orgy" scene that employed a huge cast of near-naked women in Oscar Asche's *Cairo* (1921) in Brian Singleton's careful study.[55]

Along with the display of female bodies, Settle also scripts quite a few spectacular actions for visual effect: the court masked dance by the princes, the duel between Zungteus and Amavanga, the king stabbing himself to write a letter in blood, his suicide with his lords, Lycungus's defeat of Quitazo, and Zungteus's killing of Lycungus; the latter four of these events take place in the final scene. Together with the queens' mass suicide and Amavanga's surprise appearance, these actions and their visual spectacle work in rapid sequence. They elicit shock, horror, and suspense by turn, and eventually the play concludes with happy reunions. In purely theatrical terms, the festive note of the ending is completely outweighed by the amount of violence and gore that has just been presented.

In the examples of the king's and Lycungus's speeches cited above, violence and gore are also evoked in the illocutionary verbal assaults on Alcinda and Quitazo. While influences from Martini's and Palafox y Mendoza's writings on the rebels' acts of cruelty are discernible, Settle exercises creative license that amplifies and intensifies human cruelty to such a degree of madness and insanity that its detestableness almost becomes perversely alluring. From visual spectacular to language, Settle's dramatization of evil in *Conquest* is vivid and striking and hinges on shock value. By comparison, his depiction of the conflict between love and honor, the drama proper for heroic plays in Dryden's mold, is forced and insipid in its attempts to follow and complete a prescribed course of action. It is in his dramatization of evil that Settle distinguishes his kind of heroic plays from the exemplars of Dryden.

In the 1670s, Settle engaged in a series of literary quarrels with his fellow playwrights. The "notes and observations" co-written by Dryden and others attacked Settle's sensational success *The Empress of Morocco* (1673) and Settle wrote the countering "notes and observations" to defend himself and pick apart, as others had done to his work, Dryden's highly popular *The Conquest of Granada* (1670–71) and other plays.[56] These quarrels, despite their sarcasm and scathing tone, highlight the ways in which Settle differed from his peers in handling plot, character, and language of heroic plays, and help contextualize his works in relation to the London theatre world of the early 1670s.

Settle's *Morocco*, written after *Conquest*, is a tale of horror and bloodshed that reads like an expanded and elaborated version of the "Hatred to Vice" progression in *Conquest*. Two pairs of lovers—Muly Labas and Morena; Muly Hamet and Mariamne—suffer under various schemes of the villains, the evil Queen Mother Laula and her courtier Crimalhaz. In the end the valiant Muly Hamet and the virtuous Mariamne prevail. *Morocco* also features a Moorish dance performance in front of the royal family that resembles the Chinese princes' masked dance in *Conquest*. Morena's misguided stabbing of Muly Labas could parallel the Chinese king's stabbing of himself in terms of visual shock. At the end of the play the villain Crimalhaz is captured, and his body is "cast down on the Gaunches, being hung on a Wall set with spikes of Iron" to punish his treason.[57] This visual display of Crimalhaz's body is comparable to the disclosure of the mass suicide of the queens in *Conquest*. Laula's infamous claim, "I'le send such throngs to the infernal shade, / Betray, and kill, and damn to that degree, / I'le crowd up Hell, till there's no Room for Me,"[58] exhibits the same maddening fury as seen in Lycungus's illocutionary speeches.

In Dryden's appraisal of *Morocco*, he called its style "Boisterous and Rough Hewen," its rhyme "incorrigibly lewd."[59] The use of rhyme, Dryden argued, "was an help to the Poets judgment, by putting bounds [of the couplet structure] to a wilde over-flowing Fancy."[60] Dryden suggested, "That little Talent which he [Settle] has is Fancy"[61] which, like fire, "when it is too active Rages, but when cooled and allay'd by the Judgement, produces admirable Effects." To Dryden, Settle had "this rage of Fancy" and "all the pangs and throws of a fancyfull Poet,"[62] lacking the rein of proper judgment.

In his defense, Settle gave numerous examples from Dryden's heroic plays to demonstrate that Dryden violated his own principles and also wrote with much unrestrained "fancy" or poetic imagination, a point that both their contemporaries and later commentators agree is valid.[63] What most discernibly separates the works of Settle and Dryden is the qualitative difference between the verse they produced. While Dryden's is lyrical and suggestive, Settle's, as discussed earlier, is illocutionary and performative. In the analogy of Maximillian E. Novak, their quarrel was "one of classicism against romanticism, with Settle playing the role of a progenitorial Shelley to the Commentators' T. S. Eliot."[64] This fundamental textual and literary difference informs the disparate kinds of "rage" or dramatic exaltation they scripted and accentuated in their heroic plays.

In the prologue to his *Love and Revenge* (1675), Settle uses the analogy of the contrast between "raw," plain country girls and a gay town mistress to distinguish between the "Wit" and "Object" of a play. Wit, like the country girls, appeals by its unadorned Nature, while Object, consisting of "Song, Dance, and Shew," has Art. "Yet still 'tis Object has a pow'r most strong: / Nature 'tis true delights you, but not long." "Plays without Scene, Machine, or Dance, to hit," Settle recommends, "Must make up the defect of shew, with Wit."[65]

The prologue is telling about Settle's dramaturgical and artistic preference that visual spectacle (Object) take precedence over content and writing (Wit). In another reading, the prologue may also help explain Settle's characteristic illocutionary language, as it is written as a textual spectacle of vivid action and imagery. In *Conquest*, the blood and bloodshed Zungteus and Theinmingus speak of in the opening scene are later subject to literal and heightened stage representations, in fighting, killing, and various forms of suicides. These stage acts and scenic representations, together with Amavanga's cross-dressing and the royal courtship dance, are not merely suggestive, as Dryden envisions for heroic plays, in order "to raise the imagination of the Audience";[66] they fill in for the imagination and become the featured "show" of the play. The "show," notably, is mostly of a bloody, gruesome kind, what Dryden describes as "Boisterous and Rough Hewen," that eclipses the heroic drama proper with its focus on love and valor.

According to Robert D. Hume, in the 1670s the rhymed heroic play enjoyed its protracted vogue, with its accretions of sex, horror, and spectacle. Settle was one of the playwrights who wrote what Hume calls "Horror Tragedy" or the horror form of rhymed heroic drama in which fiendish villains/villainesses dominate and far overpower the proper, heroic exemplars.[67] While *Conquest* is certainly an example of Horror Tragedy, it may also be called a proto-feminist, and also sexist, heroic play that heightens both female agency and the display of female bodies as discussed earlier. Settle's predilection in this respect appears to capitalize on the introduction of actresses on the Restoration stage granted by Charles II, a prominent and sensational change in the history of English theatre performance.[68]

Mary Lee, who played Amavanga, asked the audience in the epilogue: "Why may not Women have as Generous Ends / In Conquering Enemies, as Obliging Friends?" Here I see Lee as speaking for the character Amavanga and herself, and possibly for women audience members, to advocate active conquering rather than passive obliging as a legitimate female virtue that would lead to the same "generous ends" of approval or rewards. Amavanga as "a Slaught'ring Lass" clearly exemplifies this active pursuit of conquering, and I would argue that Orunda, the Chinese queens, and even Alcinda all exhibit, in varying degrees, female agency in their defiant courageous acts, which demonstrates what I see as the proto-feminist aspect of Settle's depiction of female characters.

Further into the epilogue, Lee posed another question to the audience: "Did not the Boys Act Women's Parts Last Age?", referring to the English performing convention before the Restoration era. As one of the first actresses who graced the London and English stage, Lee continued, "We [actresses] in pitty to the Barren Stage / Came to Reform your Eyes that went astray, / And taught you Passion the true English Way." Lee's comments reflect Settle's emphasis on the novel (pretty and reforming) sight of female bodies on stage, and his conception of Avamanga as "a Slaught'ring Lass" further exploited the novelty by having her cross-dressed as a man, an instance of a so-called "breeches" role that would reveal her female physique. Lee doubly tantalized the audience, especially the male Hectors/hectors in the pit, by being both an actress and one in a shape-fitted male dress. Settle's advocacy for female agency was therefore exploited, in a sexist manner, the physical presence of actresses and their cross-dressing acts as novel, sensual attraction.

In the above epilogue, Lee stepped out of her Chinese character Amavanga and presented herself as an English woman to her audience, but presumably she was still in her shape-fitted costume as a male Chinese warrior. Figure 1.1, taken from a publication of Martino's *De bello Tartarico historia* (1655), shows a Western depiction of the Chinese and their dress. The illustration appears to exhibit a mixture of Chinese (the Chinese emperor and his attendants on the right) and Middle Eastern (the Chinese heroic lady and the lord behind her on the left) dresses, which calls attention to the issue of stage visual representation of China. One of the heated disagreements between Settle and his detractors centered on his portrayal of Moroccans performing a "mask" (masquerade) about Orpheus's descent into hell, which was criticized as extravagant nonsense. Dryden and others wrote: "But the entertainment might pass upon the Skirts of *Atlas* [Morocco], if it could be supposed they should understand recitative Musick, and make Masks in that Countrey."[69] To this accusation Settle gave an extended reply:

> ... To follow truth exact[l]y in the representations of *forreign stories*, would be as Ridiculous as to imitate their *habits* exactly. How ill and foolish would the dressing a Roman *with naked Arms and Legs*,

be, or making a *Solyman* or an *Almanzor, and Almahide* [characters in Dryden's *Conquest of Granada*], *sit Cross Leg'd* like Taylors; or dressing *Moores* in *Bootes and Moorish Women* in *trouse[r]s.* Nay there ought to be the same care in representing *Characters* as *dresses.* .... All *Heroick* actions of *Virtue* or *Gallantry* on the Stage, being *rated* and valued by the rules of the *place* and *Age* they are presented in, not by the sense of the Age or place when and whe[r]e they were first perform'd.[70]

Settle's defense conveys his protest against "truthful representations" of foreign stories, characters, and dresses in heroic plays. To apply the arguments I make in this book, Settle is an interculturalist at heart and against the practice of Chinaface. His reasoning is intriguing: to have Roman characters costumed like ancient Romans "with naked Arms and Legs," or have Moor characters sit "Cross Leg'd" like contemporary English tailors, would make these characters improper ("ill and foolish") in the eyes of contemporary English audience. Heroic actions set in the foreign lands have to be assessed ("rated and valued") by the rules of contemporary English drama, rather than by the actual occurrence ("sense") of these actions in their original contexts.[71] According to Settle, both the stage representation of foreigners and dramatic actions set in foreign lands need to heed English aesthetic values and dramatic conventions, which will require them to be anglicized and interculturalized.

Settle's reply rationalizes the ways in which he turned the Manchu Conquest into a heroic play of the horrific and feminist kind that dramatizes the trials of love and honor and the abominable schemes of villainy. The characters are depicted as typed, into the virtuous and vicious according to the conventions of heroic plays. The examples of Amavanga and the court masked dance exemplify Settle's attempts to interculturalize the character and courtship ritual so that they may better suit the English audience. In countering his contemporaries' attack that he had deviated from or debased what the "rules" of heroic plays aimed to achieve, Settle challenged the extent and kinds of creative license the "rules" should allow. His reply also begs the question of how the "rules" encouraged the setting of heroic plays in foreign and distant lands and the reasons for doing so.

It has been observed that Restoration playwrights of serious drama, including heroic plays, tended to turn to histories of distant places and times rather than the native history of England.[72] Dryden's heroic plays are set in, for example, Peru (*The Indian Queen*), Mexico (*The Indian Emperor*), Granada (*The Conquest of Granada*), and India (*Aureng-Zebe*), and Settle's in Persia (*Cambyses*), Morocco (*Morocco*), China (*Conquest*), and Turkey (*Ibrahim*). In his dedication of *Conquest of Granada, Part I* to the Duke of York, Dryden states that princes and heroes have been the guides of poets' imitation and his play is not to dedicate to the duke the "faint representations" of his worth and valor but to restore to him "the ideas," which, in the most perfect part of Dryden's characters, Dryden has taken from the duke.[73] Similarly, Settle dedicates his *Cambyses* to the Duchess of Monmouth, saying that heroic stories of the world's past glories are offered to those who are the "Ornaments of the present."[74] His *Morocco*, on the other hand, was inspired by and dedicated to the Earl of Norwich who was ambassador to that country.[75] Last but not least, in the dedication to *The Indian Emperor*, Dryden brings the character Montezuma, the emperor of Mexico, whom he describes as his child, to the feet of his patron, the Duchess of Monmouth. Dryden asks the duchess to consider his simplicity and his story, which is "perhaps the greatest" ever represented in English theatre that includes the discovery and conquest of a new world.[76]

In performing the perfunctory duties of glorifying and thanking their patrons, these dedications suggest four possible reasons for setting the heroic plays in foreign and distant lands: to imitate or model after contemporary personalities, to present past and bygone histories of note, to respond to recent events, and to introduce novel characters and stories. Among these reasons, only the response to recent events may be regarded as bearing a neutral cultural and political outlook on the foreign other, whereas the other three exhibit a superior attitude, with foreign lands' glories depicted as faded when compared with those of the English, and the foreign characters looking up to their English models or seeking protection and understanding like primitives or children. Settle's *Conquest*, as discussed, represents a dramatic response to the Manchu Conquest, and its cultural attitude toward China may be described as mixed in its depiction of both the country's chaotic decline and the persistence of its civility and culture even as it succumbed to a foreign invader.

In explaining the frequent use of remote times and places in Restoration serious drama, Allardyce Nicoll suggests that the Oriental settings may be taken as indicating a desire to "escape from conventional surroundings to a world of unrestrained bustle and turmoil and impossible romance."[77] Similarly, Hume proposes that to free their imaginations, writers "tended to turn to distant history—distant in place or time—to avoid unwelcome restrictions."[78] Both explanations point to the need to escape restraints or avoid restrictions imposed by Restoration authorities or cultural norms, and Nicoll's comment, interestingly, could be used perfectly to describe the so-called "escapist musicals" at the turn of the twentieth century (see *Chinese Honeymoon* in Chapter Four). As Nancy Klein Maguire points out, early Restoration playwrights wrote for a partisan theatre permeated with royal connections; for example, Charles II frequently attended and supported theatre. Many, if not all, were politician–playwrights who formed a political network closely connected through families, experiences, and financial enterprises.[79] The restraints or restrictions on the playwrights most likely arose out of this highly political working environment which further informed the "rules" of heroic plays.

The dedications quoted above acknowledge not only the royal patronage Dryden and Settle received but also the political allegiance they sought from different parties, most notably the Duke of York, the future King James II, and the Duchess of Monmouth, wife of Charles II's illegitimate son who competed with James for royal succession. As their plays were acted before Charles II,[80] Dryden's and Settle's dramatizations of foreign state emergencies caused by invasions or succession crises and heroic deeds that saved the depicted countries invite allegorical readings into possible messages involving their own political contexts and circumstances, including the need to entertain their special patrons. Setting the plays in foreign and distant lands could have been a way for them to convey their political allegiances and messages without risking their patronage and political connections.

In the case of Settle's *Conquest*, the king of China is betrayed by a traitorous Chinese prince, which prompts him to designate the invading Tartar prince as his legitimate successor for the reason of just revenge. This decision is supported by one of his loyal princes who, as cited earlier, comments that forced to choose between a foreign foe and a traitor, a monarch should bestow his empire on the foe. Before he dies, the king pleads to the gods above, "Grant in my Second Reign I may Enjoy / Such secure Peace, as Treason can't destroy" (V.ii.; 61). Settle's dramatization of the king's last wish may be read as his view that loyalty to the court should be the only or utmost criterion for the legitimacy of a royal successor.

In Derek Hughes's reading, Settle belonged to the second generation of playwrights of heroic plays, who rejected the paeans to just political order in the works of the first generation after Charles II was restored to the throne and instead depicted justice and legitimate authority as flawed and even undiscoverable. In Settle's works, Hughes sees the recurrent theme of mutable authority and justice.[81] He observes that in *Conquest* the king of China uses the same vocabulary of violence as Lycungus does, and Zungteus is no less brutal than Lycungus. Justice and revenge are synonymous; heroic and base aims are justified with identical terminology and pursued with similar violence.[82] The play, in other words, fails to differentiate between the different political contestants in terms of character, language, and action; it creates confusion about who is a legitimate claimant of the throne, and stokes fear concerning those who eventually become the sovereign.

Jeannie Dalporto, on the other hand, suggests that Settle in *Conquest* attempts to allay fears about political unrest caused by competing claims to the throne. The Chinese king's bestowal of the kingdom on the Tartar Zungteus could be interpreted as Settle's reflection of a desire by the English people that Charles II name Monmouth as his legitimate successor. Zungteus's sharing of power with the Chinese prince Quitzao, whom he offers the Tartar crown, could be seen as granting authority to and recognizing the rightful position of a lawful candidate, James II. The compromise solutions Settle depicts might reassure English audiences that ultimate threats to England will not destroy the basic underpinnings of the Restoration settlement.[83] When read in this way, Settle could be considered as speaking and advocating for Monmouth, the candidate who eventually lost in the rivalry.

Dalporto's close reading of the play also credits Martini for, above all, providing an essential ideological framework which Settle could adapt to reflect the English political situation, most notably the justification of Zungteus/Monmouth, an intruder/outsider, as the legitimate ruler of China/England.[84] Although his accounts are considered fairly well balanced, Martini tended to condemn the faults of the Chinese rulers and praise the Manchu leaders as intelligent and humane, which might have been influenced by their favorable treatment of the Jesuit missionaries.[85] Martini described the founding father of the Ming Dynasty as a person of low social standing and a highwayman (256). After recounting the woeful and gory demise of the Ming court, with the last emperor ending his life by hanging, Martini inserted his interpretation, "as the [Ming] Empire was erected by a Theef, so it was axtinguished by another [Li]" (274). This passage exemplifies Martini's justification of the Manchu Conquest, Orr points out, "as an index of Providential wrath or approbation at the treatment of the Catholic missions" in China.[86] In Settle's reworking of Martini's religious interpretation, the king's final plea to the gods, as cited earlier, is to see Lycungus killed by Zungteus and secure peace against treason. Lycungus's eventual death at the hand of Zungteus suggests that wishes for political loyalty and stability indeed receive divine approval and assistance.

In her study of Restoration plays, Orr argues that while they are important for the representation and negotiation of local political issues, they can also be seen as a form of colonial discourse insofar as they contribute to shaping perspectives on non-European societies *vis-à-vis* English hopes for building and expanding their own empire.[87] At this historical moment England had not established direct contact or formal relations with China. The writings of those who had made contact, either directly or indirectly, such as Martini and Palafox y Mendoza, informed European and English writers like Settle who further developed their perspectives on the country in their own works. An example of one particular scene from Settle's *Conquest* could be used to illustrate this form of intercultural colonial discourse. This reading complements the readings presented earlier in this chapter that explore the play's manifestations of race and gender power relations, in terms of Said's conception of Orientalism (the most common trope of scholarly colonial discourse).

Immediately after the king of China and his lords commit suicide, Lycungus barges in and is disgusted by the king's bestowal of the empire on Zungteus and what he sees as the cowardly act of suicide. He rants, "*China*'s Crown has 'till my Reign been worn / By Lazy Kings, with Female Spirits born; / Guarded by Eunuch's, bred in Palaces, / Nurtur'd in Lusts, the Progeny of Peace" (V.ii.; 62). Lycungus ridicules Chinese kings/men as feminized or emasculated by nature, which brings to mind associations with lethargy, vulnerability, indulgence, and passivity. The passage reads like a disapproving exaggeration of Orunda's and Zungteus's comments on Quitazo's "softer" looks and "milder" presence as a Chinese man; it also makes explicit what I see as implicit in the queens' mass suicide, that is, that the king and his lords only act after being awakened from their passivity by the women's suicide. These points may help explain why China, governed by emasculated men, is unable to fend off the "rougher," warring Tartars. China as represented by Settle loses its sovereignty because it is undesirably and disadvantageously feminized. This phenomenon, however, is offset by the examples of Amavanga and Lycungus. Amavanga's Amazonian femininity is respected by Zungteus, who needs her presence and help in order to survive. Lycungus, the ultra-villain, appears "rougher" than other Chinese men, yet as a prince of royal upbringing he was actually raised to embody what he ridicules about the Chinese kings/men, which leads to the question of whether Lycungus was also born with a female spirit. If so, his eventual fall may be read as his failure to reconcile with his innate femininity by assuming a more aggressive, destructive masculinity. In other words, China's breeding and nurturing of femininity, in both women and men, is not completely undesirable or disadvantageous in the play.

In Yang's critical study of English writings on China in relation to the orientalism of the early modern period, she argues that both female effeminacy (gendering of women) and cultural effeminacy (gendering of empire) were "ambiguous rather than purely negative traits."[88] In Settle's *Conquest*, Yang highlights Amavanga as a notable example, and I would add Orunda and the Chinese queens as well, for they display a similar Amazonian/masculinized femininity and agency. In their power relations the perceived effeminate Chinese empire is conquered by the rougher Tartars whose own mortality, symbolized by Zungteus's suicide attempt, can only be overcome through the reunion with China's masculine females, represented by Amavanga. As Zungteus proclaims, the Tartars are also in need of China's cultural refinement, bred by her innate femininity, for his subsequent rule of the country.

Hsia's analysis of seventeenth-century Dutch and English dramas that depict the Manchu Conquest takes a very different angle. He observes that "China and the Chinese were not stereotyped," and that the characters "were just normal human beings, that is heroes and villains as they should be in any heroic play."[89] Hsia's judgment is made on the basis of the conventions of specific dramatic genres; the creative license Settle exercised *vis-à-vis* the "history and truth," in his opinion, was not unconventional in the writing of a typical heroic play. Hsia's comments also corroborate with Settle's protest against "truthful representations" cited earlier that dramatic transformation has occurred in the depictions of the Chinese characters; they were anglicized and interculturalized to become stereotyped not in the sense of negative, gendered racial depictions which, as Yang argues, were ambiguous at this historical moment, but rather in the sense of heroes and villains "as they should be." In *Conquest*, in addition to the valiant Amavanga and virtuous Quitazo, the Chinese characters also include the impetuous Chinese king, the vengeful Orunda, the wicked Lycungus, and a multitude of loyal Chinese queens and princes. These characters exhibit a variety of human qualities and cannot be generalized as exhibiting a distinctive, shared trait as Chinese.

To summarize, earlier in the chapter I discuss the conceptualization of the Tartars, the character Amavanga and her name, and the royal courtship as examples in Settle's *Conquest* that manifest the interculturalization of disparate cultural elements. Settle's *Conquest* may be considered as a historical example of intercultural performance that intentionally incorporates elements from disparate cultures as an approach to artistic creation.[90] In his study of intercultural performance, Patrice Pavis observes that the use of other cultures often becomes a quest for foreign sensuality and for coded abstraction.[91] When Mary Lee entered the stage dressed in a man's habit to show off her female physique, the audience probably had seen this display of sensuality in many other Restoration plays. *Conquest* did not intend to offer it as uniquely "Chinese." The rants of the Chinese king and Lycungus, their group suicide, and the sudden unveiling of the murdered Chinese queens in various forms of death might have been sensual, but the audience must have seen similar uses of language and theatrical tropes in plays not related to China or the Chinese. On the other hand, despite the contradictions and complexities involved in its making, the conflict between the "softer," civilized Chinese and "rougher" Tartars stands out among the ways in which Settle used and interculturalized the Chinese elements as, in Pavis's wording, a "coded abstraction" that becomes a highly popular shorthand for the dramatization of China. In its transition from an instance of interculturalization to a prominent trope that enters the process of interculturation, this coded abstraction of the Chinese-Tartar conflict persisted in later London theatre productions that dramatized China during the following centuries.

In his dedication of *Conquest* to Lord Castle-Rizing, Settle confessed that: "*... this* Poem *wants that* Perfection *to make it so. For, to deviate from the general Style of my* Brethren, *without imputing its ill success to Malice, I acknowledge it Faulty.*"[92] Later, in a response to the derisive accusation of one of his detractors, Thomas Shadwell, that he had spent three years writing an awful play, Settle defended the amount of time he took to finish the play, but admitted that it is "an ill Design, and therefore no good Play."[93]

Settle's own negative evaluation does not specify what he meant by the play's "ill Design" and its "Faulty" deviation from "the general style" of his fellow playwrights. His quarrels with Dryden and others, the sensational success of his *Morocco*, and his pursuit of royal patronage inform the following conjectures: perhaps Settle regretted that he had attempted to incorporate both the "Love to Virtue" and "Hatred to Vice" plot progressions, thereby dividing and diluting the play's focus; perhaps Settle thought that he could have designed an even more visually spectacular "Object" of "Song, Dance, and Shew" that would have further grabbed the audience's attention; and perhaps his political allegory on behalf of the

Duke of Monmouth was detected by Charles II, his special audience, and was not appreciated. Although deemed by Settle himself to be faulty and unsuccessful, the production of *Conquest* likely did entertain and shock its audience, with Mary Lee in the breeches role, the masked dance, the fighting scenes, the poisoning, the horrifically sensational speeches, and the final group suicides.

In 1692, seventeen years after *Conquest*, an extravagant opera version of Shakespeare's *A Midsummer Night's Dream*, called *The Fairy Queen*, was staged at Dorset Garden, with music by Henry Purcell and a book credited to Settle.[94] At the end of the opera, for magic and wonder, "*a transparent Prospect of a Chinese garden*" is revealed after the stage is suddenly illuminated. The garden is depicted with "*the Architecture, the Trees, the Plants, the Fruit, the Birds, the Beasts, quite different from what we have in this part of the World.*"[95] A Chinese ensemble of men and women enter the stage to sing and dance, joined by six monkeys. Then "*Six pedestals of China-work rise from under the Stage; they support six large Vases of Porcelain, in which are six China-Orange-trees.*"[96]

This second dramatization of China by Settle may be regarded as another manifestation of his sustained artistic preference for visual spectacular shows. On the other hand, the kind of China depicted in the opera is very different from that in *Conquest*. Far from an empire beset by foreign invasion and inner turmoil, China in *Fairy Queen* is a wonderland with exotic flora and fauna and Chinese joyfully singing and dancing. The highlight of the show is a display of Chinese orange trees kept inside Chinese porcelain vases that are supported by Chinese pedestals, demonstrating the attraction of and interest in Chinese produce and material goods.

In 1704, Nicholas Rowe's comedy *The Biter* was staged at Lincoln's Inn Fields.[97] The main character is Sir Timothy Tallapoy, "an *East-India* Merchant, very Rich," and "a great Affecter of the *Chinese* Customs."[98] In Act II, accompanied by "ridiculously habited" servants, Tallapoy enters the stage cursing and fussing over a careless servant for breaking "the great Pagode," the "Representation of the great *Callasusu*, who was Nephew to the Great *Fillimafo*, who was descended from the Illustrious *Fokensi*, who was the first Inventor of eating Rice upon Platters." When his daughter refuses to marry a suitor proposed by him, Tallapoy threatens to marry her to the Giant *Tansu*, a woman eater who "inhabits in the prodigious Mountains of *Tartary.*"[99]

Living up to his character depiction, as a merchant working for the East India Company Tallapoy "affects" his deep knowledge about the East by tossing out names and associations in a nonsensical manner. The comedy mocks his affectation of true knowledge as well as his obsession with material goods that he procures from the East. His name derives from *talapoin*, meaning Buddhist monks in Southeast Asia. He probably displays his "great pagod," which is very likely a large figure of a Buddhist deity, in a way that is similar to the display of Chinese orange trees in porcelain vases in *Fairy Queen*. His material obsession extends to dressing his servants in "ridiculous"-looking Eastern costumes. The now familiar locale of Tartary enters the comedy as a wild place where the mythical woman-eater lives.

The scenes in *Fairy Queen* and Rowe's *Biter* exemplify and foreshadow a new development in the representation of China on the London stage beyond the Jesuit influences. As Anglo-Chinese contacts increased through trade, England's interest in Chinese goods soared. Porcelains, plates, statuettes, and other products were imported into England, and information about Chinese architecture and design was introduced. The trade relationship informed stage depictions of and reflections on England's obsessive material interest in China. The next chapter examines two London productions that were presented when England's craze over Chinese goods reached its height in the mid-eighteenth century.

NOTES

1. For the romanization of Chinese characters, I adopt the now-standard *pinyin* system. However, for words which have long been known and accepted in English such as Peking and Canton, I retain their old spellings and put their *pinyin* romanizations, Beijing and Guangdong, respectively, in parentheses when these terms first appear in the text. Romanizations of the historical Chinese names are written in the Chinese style, that is, surname before given name. The Chinese characters are written in traditional (*fanti*, 繁體) characters, which were used in Chinese writing before the adoption of the simplified (*jianti*, 簡體) characters in China in the mid-twentieth century and continue to be used in Taiwan and Hong Kong.

2. See, for example, Tingyu Zhang et al., *Ming Shi* [History of the Ming Dynasty], ed. Qiyun Zhang (Taipei: Guo Fang Yan Jiu Yuan, 1962–63), 1:163, 5:3510–3511; Gang Tang and Bingwen Nan, *Ming Shi* [History of the Ming Dynasty] (Shanghai: Shanghai Ren Ming Chu Ban She, 1985–91), 2:1232–1233, 1244–1247; Shouyi Bai, ed., *Zhongguo Tong Shi* [General History of China] (Shanghai: Shanghai Ren Min Chu Ban She, 2004), 16:2000–2005, 2092–2094.

3. Edwin J. Van Kley, "News from China; Seventeenth-Century European Notices of the Manchu Conquest," *Journal of Modern History* 45, no. 4 (1973): 561.

4. Ibid., 561–582.

5. Van Kley, "News from China." Also, see Van Kley, "An Alternative Muse: The Manchu Conquest of China in the Literature of Seventeenth-Century Northern Europe," *European Studies Review* 6 (1976): 21–43; Adrian Hsia, "History as Fiction, Fiction as History: The Manchu Conquest of China in Dutch and English Drama of the 17th Century," in *Chinesia: The European Construction of China in the Literature of the Seventeenth and Eighteenth Centuries* (Tübingen: Max Niemeyer Verlag, 1998), 23–39. In his letter to his sons at Rome dated September 3, 1697, John Dryden wrote that he intended to revise a play by Sir Robert Howard, his brother-in-law, called *The Conquest of China by the Tartars*, which, he said, Howard had written long ago. Howard's script was apparently never printed and Dryden's effort not realized. See Dryden, "Letter XXIII: To His Sons at Rome," in Walter Scott, ed., *The Works of John Dryden*, rev. George Saintsbury, vol. 18 (London: William Paterson & Co., 1893), 132–135.

6. Southern Illinois University Press, *The London Stage 1660–1800: A Calendar of Plays, Entertainments & Afterpieces, Together with Casts, Box-receipts and Contemporary Comment* (Carbondale: Southern Illinois University Press, 1960–68), 1:233 (hereafter cited as *London Stage*); Allardyce Nicoll, *A History of Restoration Drama, 1660–1700*, 3d ed. (Cambridge: Cambridge University Press, 1940), 310. Although Frank C. Brown claims that, based on John Downes's *Roscius Anglicanus*, *Conquest* was performed in 1673–74, more recent scholarship argues that this is unlikely. See Frank C. Brown, *Elkanah Settle: His Life and Works* (Chicago: University of Chicago Press, 1910), 17; Montague Summers, ed., *Roscius Anglicanus*, by John Downes (London: Fortune Press, 1928), 223; Judith Milhous and Robert D. Hume, eds., *Roscius Anglicanus*, by John Downes (London: Society for Theatre Research, 1987), 75.

7. The most comprehensive study of Settle's life and works to date is still Brown's *Elkanah Settle*, published in 1910, more than one hundred years ago. For comments on Settle's caliber as a playwright, see, for example, Robert D. Hume, *The Development of English Drama in the Late Seventeenth Century* (Oxford: Clarendon Press, 1976), 198; Derek Hughes, *English Drama, 1660–1700* (Oxford: Clarendon Press and Oxford University Press, 1996), 85.

8. For the life and works of Settle, see, for example, Brown; the entry on Settle in *A Biographical Dictionary of Actors, Actresses, Musicians, Dancers, Managers & Other Stage Personnel in London, 1660–1800*, eds. Philip H. Highfill, Jr., Kalman A. Burnim, and Edward A. Langhans (Carbondale: Southern Illinois University Press, 1973–1993); Abigail Williams, "Settle, Elkanah (1648–1724)," in *Oxford Dictionary of National Biography* (Oxford University Press, 2004–), doi:10.1093/ref:odnb/25128.

9. According to Settle: "The Entertainment you [the duchess] gave it [the script] in loose sheets, when it first saw light, encourages me to this presumption, now in its riper growth, to devote it wholly to your Self..." See Settle, "The Epistle Dedicatory," in *Cambyses King of Persia: A Tragedy* (London: William Cademan, 1671).

10. See *London Stage*, 1:206; Nicoll, 310; Settle, *The Empress of Morocco. A Tragedy. With Sculptures* (London: William Cademan, 1673). The engravings of the Dorset Garden theatre where the play was performed as well as key scenes from the play in the published script provide invaluable visual clues to the Restoration theatre house and stage.

11. See Settle, "Epilogue. Spoken by Mrs. Lee [Mary Lee]," in *The Conquest of China by the Tartars. A Tragedy, Acted at the Duke's Theatre* (London: W. Cademan, 1676).

12. The dates refer to the earliest traceable performance dates, see *London Stage*, 1:177–180. The script, with the preface, was published in 1672.

13. John Dryden, "Of Heroique Playes, An Essay" (preface to *The Conquest of Granada, Part I*), in *The Works of John Dryden*, ed. Edward Niles Hooker and H. T. Swedenberg, Jr. (Berkeley: University of California Press, 1956–), 11:10.

14. Ibid., 11:14.

15. See, for example, Zhongshu Qian, "China in the English Literature of the Seventeenth Century" in *The Vision of China in the English Literature of the Seventeenth and Eighteenth Centuries*, ed. Adrian Hsia (Hong Kong: Chinese University Press, 1998), 29–68; Van Kley, "An Alternative Muse"; Hsia, "History as Fiction, Fiction as History."

16. Settle, Elkanah, *The Preface to Ibrahim: Reprinted from the Edition of 1677* (Oxford: Basil Blackwell, Published for the Luttrell Society, 1947), 6.

17. *London Stage*, 1:179, 206; Summers, *Roscius Anglicanus*, 190–191; Milhous and Hume, *Roscius Anglicanus*, 59–60. Their studies do not agree with Brown's research that Settle's three earlier plays were all written and produced at much earlier dates. See Brown, 9–17.

18. Martini's name has various spellings in English: Martino Martini, Martinio Martini, Martin Martini, and Martin Martinius.

19. See cover page of Martino Martini, *Bellum Tartaricum, or The Conquest of the Great and Most Renowned Empire of China, by the Invasion of the Tartars, Who in These Last Seven Years, Have Wholly Subdued That Vast Empire* (London: John Crook, 1654).

20. For a study on the differences between the two English editions, see, for example, David E. Mungello, *Curious Land: Jesuit Accommodation and the Origins of Sinology* (Honolulu: University of Hawaii Press, 1989), 106–107 (hereafter cited as *Curious Land*).

21. See cover page of F. Alvarez (Alvaro) Semedo, *The History of that Great and Renowned Monarchy of China* (London: E. Tyler for Iohn [John] Crook, 1655); "Alvazo Semodo," Rare Books from the Jesuitica Collection at Boston College, http://ricci.bc.edu/people/alvaro-semedo.

22. See Juan de Palafox y Mendoza, "An Advertisement to the Reader," in *The History of the Conquest of China by the Tartars* (London: W. Godbid and M. Pitt, 1671).

23. For a bibliography of European writings on the conquest, see Henri Cordier, *Bibliotheca Sinica: dictionnaire bibliographique des ouvrages relatifs à l'empire chinois* (Staten Island, NY: Maurizio Martino, 1996), 1:623–631.

24. As described in the introduction, the Jesuits adopted an accepting attitude toward Chinese culture. They sought to convert the Chinese to Christianity while respecting indigenous Chinese practices such as ancestor worship. This accommodative approach provoked attack from other Catholic orders as well as Christians in Europe. See Mungello, *Curious Land*; chap. 2 in *The Great Encounter of China and the West, 1500–1800* (Lanham, MD: Rowman and Littlefield, 2013).

25. For Martini's journey, see, for example, "Martino Martini," Rare Books from the Jesuitica Collection at Boston College, http://ricci.bc.edu/people/martino-martini.

26. See Palafox y Mendoza, "An advertisement to the Reader."

27. For further discussions of these two works by Martini and Palafox y Mendoza, see, for example, Min-sun Chen, *Mythistory in Sino-Western Contacts: Jesuit Missionaries and the Pillars of Chinese Catholic Religion* (Thunder Bay, ON: Lakehead University Printing Services, 2003), 143–172; Van Kley, "News from China"; Mungello, chap. 4 in *Curious Land*.

28. See Settle, *Conquest of China by the Tartars*. Hereafter the act, scene, and page numbers refer to the 1676 edition.

29. See, for example, Dryden, "Of Heroique Playes, An Essay," 11:8–9, 13–14.

30. See, for example, J. L. Austin, *How to Do Things with Words* (Oxford: Oxford University Press, 1976), 109.

31. The number in parentheses, as well as the following references, refers to the page number in the 1655 edition of Martini's *Bellum Tartaricum* appended to Semedo's *History*.

32. See, for example, Bai, 13:345–355; Tang and Nan, 1:175–177.

33. See Semedo, "Chapter 21. Of the Warre Which the Tartars Made Upon China," in *History*, 100–105.

34. For a brief account about Heylyn, see, for example, Anthony Milton, "Heylyn, Peter (1599–1662)," in *Oxford Dictionary of National Biography* (Oxford University Press, 2004–), doi:10.1093/ref:odnb/13171.
35. See Peter Heylyn, *Cosmographie in Four Bookes. Containing the Chorographie and Historie of the Whole World, and All the Principall Kingdomes, Provinces, Seas, and Isles Thereof* (London: Henry Seile, 1652), 3:185, 186. Similar descriptions are seen his earlier publication, *Mikrokosmos: A Little Description of the Great World. Augmented and Reuised* (Oxford: Iohn Lichfield and William Turner, 1625), 658–660.
36. See, for example, the entry of "Scythia" in *Oxford Dictionary of the Classical World, Oxford Reference Online*, ed. John Roberts (Oxford University Press, 2007), http://www.oxfordreference.com/view/10.1093/acref/9780192801463.001. 0001/acref-9780192801463-e-1993. Gocha R. Tsetskhladze, "Scythia," in the *Oxford Encyclopedia of Ancient Greece and Rome* (Oxford University Press, 2010), http://www.oxfordreference.com/view/10.1093/acref/9780195170726.001. 0001/acref-9780195170726-e-1141.
37. For critical study and analysis of the term Tartars in various European writings, see, for example, Chi-ming Yang, *Performing China: Virtue, Commerce, and Orientalism in Eighteenth-Century England, 1660–1760* (Baltimore: The Johns Hopkins University Press, 2011), 34–36.
38. Yang suggests that Zungteus's address could be read as directed toward either Quitazo or Amavanga, see Yang, 50.
39. Dryden, "Heads of an Answer to Rymer," in *Works*, 17:186.
40. Ibid.
41. This and other accounts by Martini suggest that he was describing Qin Liangyü (Ch'in Liang-yü, 秦良玉), a valiant female general who with her husband and brothers quelled bandits in times of civil disturbances and assisted with the Ming court's resistance against the Manchu invasion. See, for example, Arthur W. Hummel, ed., *Eminent Chinese of the Ch'ing Period (1644–1912)* (Taipei: Ch'eng Wen Publishing Company, 1970), 168–169; Zhang et al., 4:3041–3042; Qin Liangyu Shi Yanjiu Bianji Weiyuan Hui [Research and Editorial Board of Histories of Qin Liangyu], *Qin Liangyu Shiliao Jicheng* [Collection of Historical Records on Qin Liangyu] (Chengdu: Sichuan Daxue Chuban She, 1987).
42. The Tartar king's name is spelled Theienmingus or Thienmingus in Martini (259, 264), while in Settle's play his name is spelled Theinmingus.
43. Martini wrote that after Theienmingus died, the throne was passed on to his son Thienzungus. After Thienzungus died, his son Zungteus succeeded him (264, 266). This example shows that Martini probably mistook the Manchu rulers' reign titles (*nianhao*, 年號) as their names. Theienmingus (presumably the Latin spelling of Tianming, 天命) is the reign title of Nuerhachi (奴爾哈赤), and Thienzungus (i.e., Tiancong, 天聰) and Zungteus (i.e., Chongde, 崇德) are the first and second reign titles of his son Huangtaigi (皇太極). While Martini described Theienmingus (Nerhachi) and Zungteus (Huangtaigi) as grandfather and grandson, Settle's simplification of their relationship to father and son fortuitously concurred with what the Chinese sources describe about their relationship. See, for example, Bai, 17:77–128, 18:1–74; Tang and Nan, 2:1038–1043. Also, according to Chinese sources it was Theienmingus (Nuerhachi), not Zungteus (Huangtaigi) as Martini claimed, who at a young age had contact with Chinese culture and was alleged to have been adopted by or served under a

Chinese general. See, for example, Shaozhen Teng, *Nuerhachi Pingzhuan* [A Critical Biography of Nuerhachi] (Shenyang: Liaoning Renmin Chuban She, 1985), 32–40; Dongfang Wang, *Mingqing Shi Kaoyi* [Queries into the Ming and Qing Histories] (Beijing: Beijing Yanshan Chuban She, 2010), 496–506.

44. Hsia, "History as Fiction, Fiction as History," 36; Yang, 38–43.

45. As Settle read Martini, he very likely would have come across the passage stating that Zungteus (Huangtaigi) died shortly before the Manchus entered Peking (276). Between the two accounts about Zungteus in Martini, Settle apparently chose the first one about his sojourn in China and overlooked the second about his death, to make him the hero of the play. Instead, Settle had Theinmingus suddenly die of "a Gangrene of a Poison'd Arrows Head" (V.i.; 55), which compels Zungteus to take on command left by his father and complete the conquest.

46. Yang, 41–42.

47. The word *maskal* is not recognized by Oxford English Dictionary (OED). Judith Milhous suggests it is probably a made-up word or a typographical error in the quarto, for "masked." Judith Milhous, letter to the author, March 10, 2002.

48. See, for example, Martini, 269–271, 275–276; Palafox y Mendoza, "An advertisement to the Reader," 5–7, 52–54.

49. As Qian notes, Settle's invention of the character Alcinda fortuitously coincides with the Chinese legend, which is not reported in either Martini or Palafox y Mendoza, that Wu sought help from the Manchus in order to rescue his mistress Chen Yuanyuan (陳圓圓) abducted by the Li camp. see Qian, 57.

50. Bridget Orr, *Empire on the English Stage, 1660–1714* (Cambridge: Cambridge University Press, 2001), 108–109; Semedo, "Chap. 23. How the Kings of China Are Married," 120.

51. See, for example, Terry Castle, "Masquerades," in *The International Encyclopedia of Dance*, (Oxford University Press, 1998), http://www.oxfordreference.com/view/10.1093/acref/9780195173697.001.0001/acref-9780195173697-e-1125; Gilbert Burnet, *Bishop Burnet's History of His Own Time. Vol. I: From the Restoration of King Charles II to the Settle of King William and Queen Mary at the Revolution* (London: Thomas Ward, 1724), 262.

52. In order to clarify my reference, I need to explain an ambiguity in the scene divisions in the seventeenth-century text of Settle's *Conquest* I cite. On page 26 of the published script it is written "SCENE the Third" before the entrance of Lycungus and Orunda, which probably means the third so-called French scene at this same location. Preceding their entrance, there is one scene of Zungteus and the Tartars and one scene of Amavanga and Vangona. There is no indication of scene change in these three sets of entrances and exits of characters. I therefore consider that the second scene of Act Three begins, after a change of scenery, with the king of China disclosed sitting on a throne on page 28.

53. In his article, "The Pass That Will Not Pass," Nolte asks, "Did the National Socialists or Hitler perhaps commit an 'Asiatic' deed merely because they and those like them considered themselves and their kind to be potential victims of an 'Asiatic' deed? Was 'Gulag Archipelago' not prior to Auschwitz?" For Nolte's article and a discussion on the heated *Historikerstreit*, see, for example, Roderick Stackelberg and Sally A. Winkle, *The Nazi Germany Sourcebook: An Anthology of Texts* (London: Routledge, 2002), 413–424. I am indebted to Jonathan Kalb for bringing this heated debate to my attention and its relevance to Settle's depiction of Lycungus's indiscriminate killing.

54. In *Conquest* Settle directly refers to Zhang (whom he calls "Chanquincungus") twice, once as Zungteus's inspiration to rise and claim the Chinese throne (I.i.; 6), and again as the murderer of Amavanga's brother (I.i.; 7). Martini says that the Chinese woman commander is from the province of Suchuen (i.e., Sichuan) where she defended the attacks of rebels and where Zhang invaded and proclaimed himself the king (261, 269, 299). Martini's accounts may have inspired Settle to depict Chanquincungus as Amavanga's mortal enemy and to show the inhuman cruelties the king of China and Lycungus plan to execute on their victims.

55. Brian Singleton, "Narratives of Nostalgia: Oriental Evasions about the London Stage," in *Representing the Past: Essays in Performance Historiography*, ed. Charlotte M. Canning and Thomas Postlewait (Iowa City: University of Iowa Press, 2010), 351–377.

56. See John Dryden, Thomas Shadwell, and John Crowne, *Notes and Observations on* The Empress of Morocco; Or, Some Few Errata's to Be Printed Instead of the Sculptures with the Second Edition of That Play (London: 1674) and Elkanah Settle, *Notes and Observations on* The Empress of Morocco Revised; With Some Few Errata's to Be Printed Instead of the Postscript, with the Next Edition *of* The Conquest of Granada (London: William Cademan, 1674).

57. Settle, *Empress of Morocco*, 70.

58. Ibid., 24.

59. Dryden, Shadwell, and Crowne, "The Preface," in *Notes and Observations*.

60. John Dryden, "Of Dramatick Poesie, An Essay," in *Works*, 17:74, 79. See also Dryden, "To the Right Honourable Roger Earl of Orrery," *The Rival Ladies*, in *Works*, 8:100–101.

61. Dryden, Shadwell, and Crowne, "The Preface," in *Notes and Observations*.

62. Ibid., 70. Dryden's authorship in these sections of the joint-attack has been confirmed by, for example, Anne T. Doyle, "Authorship" in *Elkanah Settle's* The Empress of Morocco *and the Controversy Surrounding It: A Critical Edition* (New York: Garland Publishing, 1987), lxiii–xci; Dryden, *Works*, 17:393–396.

63. See Doyle, "The Counter-Attack," ci–cviii; Maximillian E. Novak, "Introduction," in The Empress of Morocco *and Its Critics; Settle, Dryden, Shadwell, Crowne, Duffet* (Los Angeles: William Andrews Clark Memorial Library, UCLA, 1968). Novak states that it is in this quarrel that the rhymed heroic play "met its Waterloo," as Settle showed that Dryden also erred on the side of fancy and they both turned away from using rhyme in their plays after the quarrel. See Novak, "Introduction," iii, xv–xvii.

64. Novak, "Introduction," ii.

65. Settle, "Prologue," in *Love and Revenge: A Tragedy* (London: William Cademan, 1675).

66. Dryden, "Of Heroique Playes, An Essay," 11:13–14.

67. Hume, 199–202, 269–273.

68. For discussions about the actresses on the Restoration stage, see, for example, Elizabeth Howe, *The First English Actresses: Women and Drama 1660–1700* (Cambridge: Cambridge University Press, 1992).

69. Dryden, Shadwell, and Crowne, *Notes and Observations*, 42.

70. Settle, *Notes and Observations*, 62.

71. I am indebted to Judith Milhous's clarification on interpreting Settle's defense. Milhous, letter to the author, March 10, 2002.

72. Nicoll, 121; Hume, 164–166.

73. Dryden, "To His Royal Highness, the Duke," *The Conquest of Granada, Part I*, in *Works*, 11:3, 6–7.
74. Settle, "The Epistle Dedicatory," in *Cambyses*.
75. Settle, "The Epistle Dedicatory," in *Morocco*.
76. Dryden, "To the Most Excellent and Most Illustrious Princes Anne, Dutchess of Monmouth," *The Indian Emperor*, in *Works*, 9:25.
77. Nicoll, 121.
78. Hume, 166.
79. Nancy Klein Maguire, *Regicide and Restoration: English Tragicomedy, 1660–1671* (Cambridge: Cambridge University Press, 1992), 16–21.
80. Charles II is recorded to have seen Dryden's *Indian Queen, Indian Emperor, Conquest of Granada, Part I*, and *Aureng-Zebe*, and Settle's *Morocco* and *Conquest*. See *London Stage*, 1:74, 100, 206, 233, 240–241; Nicoll, 305–308, 310, 316.
81. Hughes, 84–88, 92–95, 97–100, 110.
82. Ibid., 98–100.
83. Jeannie Dalporto, "The Succession Crisis and Elkanah Settle's *The Conquest of China by the Tartars*," *Eighteenth Century* 45, no. 2 (2004): 132–134, 142–143.
84. Ibid., 132, 137, 142–143.
85. See Van Kley, "An Alternative Muse," 22; "News from China," 567.
86. Orr, 106–107.
87. Ibid., 25–27.
88. Yang, 37.
89. Hsia, "History as Fiction, Fiction as History," 39.
90. See, for example, Patrice Pavis, "Introduction: Towards a Theory of Interculturalism in Theatre?" in Patrice Pavis, ed., *The Intercultural Performance Reader* (London: Routledge, 1996), 8–10; Jacqueline Lo and Helen Gilbert, "Toward a Topography of Cross-Cultural Theatre Praxis," *The Drama Review* 46, no. 3 (2002): 32–38.
91. Patrice Pavis, *Theatre at the Crossroads of Cultures*, trans. Loren Kruger (London: Routledge, 1992), 211.
92. See the Dedication of *Conquest*.
93. Settle, *The Preface to Ibrahim*, 6.
94. See *London Stage*, 1:408–409; Milhous and Hume, eds., *Roscius Anglicanus*, 89.
95. Henry Purcell, *The Fairy Queen: An Opera* (London: Jacob Tonson, 1692), 48.
96. Ibid., 51. An earlier reference to the China orange and porcelain appeared in William Wycherley's *The Country Wife*, which very likely premiered in London on January 12, 1675, *London Stage*, 1:227.
97. *London Stage*, 2: 82.
98. See the description of the character under "Dramatis Personae" in Nicholas Rowe, *The Biter: A Comedy* (London: Jacob Tonson, 1705).
99. Ibid., 18–20.

REFERENCES

Anonymous. "Alvazo Semodo." *Beyond Ricci: Rare Books from the Jesuitica Collection at Boston College.* http://ricci.bc.edu/people/alvaro-semedo.
———."Martino Martini." *Beyond Ricci: Rare Books from the Jesuitica Collection at Boston College.* http://ricci.bc.edu/people/martino-martini.

————."Scythia." In *Oxford Dictionary of the Classical World*, edited by John Roberts. Oxford University Press, 2007. http://www.oxfordreference.com/view/10.1093/acref/9780192801463.001.0001/acref-9780192801463-e-1993.

Austin, J. L. *How to Do Things with Words*. Oxford: Oxford University Press, 1976.

Bai, Shouyi, ed. *Zhongguo Tong Shi* [General History of China]. 22 vols. Shanghai: Shanghai Ren Min Chu Ban She, 2004.

Brown, Frank C. *Elkanah Settle: His Life and Works*. Chicago: University of Chicago Press, 1910.

Burnet, Gilbert. *Bishop Burnet's History of His Own Time. Vol. I: From the Restoration of King Charles II to the Settle of King William and Queen Mary at the Revolution*. London: Thomas Ward, 1724.

Castle, Terry. "Masquerades." In *The International Encyclopedia of Dance*. Oxford University Press, 1998. http://www.oxfordreference.com/view/10.1093/acref/9780195173697.001.0001/acref-9780195173697-e-1125.

Chen, Min-sun. *Mythistory in Sino-Western Contacts: Jesuit Missionaries and the Pillars of Chinese Catholic Religion*. Thunder Bay, ON: Lakehead University Printing Services, 2003.

Cordier, Henri. *Bibliotheca Sinica: dictionnaire bibliographique des ouvrages relatifs à l'empire chinois*. 6 vols. Staten Island, NY: Maurizio Martino, 1996.

Dalporto, Jeannie. "The Succession Crisis and Elkanah Settle's *The Conquest of China by the Tartars*." *Eighteenth Century* 45, no. 2 (2004): 131–146.

Doyle, Anne T. *Elkanah Settle's* The Empress of Morocco *and the Controversy Surrounding It: A Critical Edition*. New York: Garland Publishing, 1987.

Dryden, John. *The Works of John Dryden*. Edited by Edward Niles Hooker and H. T. Swedenberg Jr. 20 vols. Berkeley: University of California Press, 1956–.

Dryden, John, Thomas Shadwell, and John Crowne. *Notes and Observations on* The Empress of Morocco; *Or, Some Few Errata's to Be Printed Instead of the Sculptures with the Second Edition of That Play*. London: 1674.

Heylyn, Peter. *Cosmographie in Four Bookes. Containing the Chorographie and Historie of the Whole World, and All the Principall Kingdomes, Provinces, Seas, and Isles Thereof*. 4 vols. London: Henry Seile, 1652.

————. *Mikrokosmos: A Little Description of the Great World. Augmented and Reuised*. Oxford: Iohn Lichfield and William Turner, 1625.

Highfill, Jr., Philip H., Kalman A. Burnim, and Edward A. Langhans, eds. *A Biographical Dictionary of Actors, Actresses, Musicians, Dancers, Managers & Other Stage Personnel in London, 1660–1800*. Carbondale: Southern Illinois University Press, 1973–93.

Howe, Elizabeth. *The First English Actresses Women and Drama, 1660–1700*. Cambridge: Cambridge University Press, 1992.

Hsia, Adrian. *Chinesia: The European Construction of China in the Literature of the Seventeenth and Eighteenth Centuries*. Tübingen: Max Niemeyer Verlag, 1998.

Hughes, Derek. *English Drama, 1660–1700*. Oxford: Clarendon Press and Oxford University Press, 1996.

Hume, Robert D. *The Development of English Drama in the Late Seventeenth Century*. Oxford: Clarendon Press, 1976.

Hummel, Arthur W., ed. *Eminent Chinese of the Ch'ing Period (1644–1912)*. Taipei: Ch'eng Wen Publishing Company, 1970.

Lo, Jacqueline, and Helen Gilbert. "Toward a Topography of Cross-Cultural Theatre Praxis." *The Drama Review* 46, no. 3 (2002): 31–53.

Maguire, Nancy Klein. *Regicide and Restoration: English Tragicomedy, 1660–1671.* Cambridge: Cambridge University Press, 1992.

Martini, Martino. *Bellum Tartaricum, or The Conquest of the Great and Most Renowned Empire of China, by the Invasion of the Tartars, Who in These Last Seven Years, Have Wholly Subdued That Vast Empire.* London: John Crook, 1654.

Milhous, Judith, and Hume Robert D, eds. *Roscius Anglicanus.* By John Downes. London: Society for Theatre Research, 1987.

Milton, Anthony. "Heylyn, Peter (1599–1662)." In *Oxford Dictionary of National Biography.* Oxford University Press, 2004–. doi:10.1093/ref:odnb/13171.

Mungello, David E. *Curious Land: Jesuit Accommodation and the Origins of Sinology.* Honolulu: University of Hawaii Press, 1989.

———. *The Great Encounter of China and the West, 1500–1800.* Lanham, MD: Rowman and Littlefield, 2013.

Nicoll, Allardyce. *A History of Restoration Drama 1660–1700.* 3rd ed. Cambridge: Cambridge University Press, 1940.

Novak, Maximillian E. "Introduction." In The Empress of Morocco *and Its Critics; Settle, Dryden, Shadwell, Crowne, Duffet,* i–xix. Los Angeles: William Andrews Clark Memorial Library, UCLA, 1968.

Orr, Bridget. *Empire on the English Stage, 1660–1714.* Cambridge: Cambridge University Press, 2001.

Palafox y Mendoza, Juan de. *The History of the Conquest of China by the Tartars.* London: W. Godbid and M. Pitt, 1671.

Pavis, Patrice, ed. *The Intercultural Performance Reader.* London: Routledge, 1996.

———. *Theatre at the Crossroads of Culture.* Translated by Loren Kruger. London: Routledge, 1992.

Purcell, Henry. *The Fairy Queen: An Opera.* London: Jacob Tonson, 1692.

Rowe, Nicholas. *The Biter: A Comedy.* London: Jacob Tonson, 1705.

Qian, Zhongshu. "China in the English Literature of the Seventeenth Century." In *The Vision of China in the English Literature of the Seventeenth and Eighteenth Centuries,* edited by Adrian Hsia, 29–68. Hong Kong: Chinese University Press, 1998.

Qin Liangyu Shi Yanjiu Bianji Weiyuan Hui [Research and Editorial Board of Histories of Qin Liangyu]. *Qin Liangyu Shiliao Jicheng* [Collection of Historical Records on Qin Liangyu]. Chengdu: Sichuan Daxue Chuban She, 1987.

Scott, Walter, ed. *The Works of John Dryden.* Revised by George Saintsbury. Vol. 18. London: William Paterson & Co., 1893.

Semedo, F. Alvarez (Alvaro). *The History of that Great and Renowned Monarchy of China.* London: E. Tyler for Iohn [John] Crook, 1655.

Settle, Elkanah. *Cambyses King of Persia: A Tragedy.* London: William Cademan, 1671.

———. *The Conquest of China by the Tartars. A Tragedy, Acted at the Duke's Theatre.* London: W. Cademan, 1676.

———. *The Empress of Morocco. A Tragedy. With Scriptures.* London: William Cademan, 1673.

———. *Love and Revenge: A Tragedy.* London: William Cademan, 1675.

———. *Notes and Observations on* The Empress of Morocco Revised; *With Some Few Errata's to Be Printed Instead of the Postscript, with the Next Edition of* The Conquest of Granada. London: William Cademan, 1674.

————. *The Preface to Ibrahim: Reprint From the Edition of 1677*. Oxford: Basil Blackwell, Published for the Luttrell Society, 1947.

Singleton, Brian. "Narratives of Nostalgia: Oriental Evasions about the London Stage." In *Representing the Past: Essays in Performance Historiography*, edited by Charlotte M. Canning and Thomas Postlewait, 351–377. Iowa City: University of Iowa Press, 2010.

Southern Illinois University Press. *The London Stage, 1660–1800: A Calendar of Plays, Entertainments and Afterpieces, Together With Casts, Box-Receipts and Contemporary Comment*. 5pts. Carbondale: Southern Illinois University Press, 1960–68.

Stackelberg, Roderick, and Sally A. Winkle. *The Nazi Germany Sourcebook: An Anthology of Texts*. London: Routledge, 2002.

Summers, Montague, ed. *Roscius Anglicanus*. By John Downes. London: Fortune Press, 1928.

Tang, Gang, and Bingwen Nan. *Ming Shi* [History of the Ming Dynasty]. 2 vols. Shanghai: Shanghai Ren Min Chu Ban She, 1985–91.

Teng, Shaozhen. *Nuerhachi Pingzhuan* [A Critical Biography of Nuerhachi]. Shenyang: Liaoning Renmin Chuban She, 1985.

Tsetskhladze, Gocha R. "Scythia." In the *Oxford Encyclopedia of Ancient Greece and Rome*. Oxford University Press, 2010. http://www.oxfordreference.com/view/10.1093/acref/9780195170726.001.0001/acref-9780195170726-e-1141.

Wang, Dongfang. *Mingqing Shi Kaoyi* [Queries into the Ming and Qing Histories]. Beijing: Beijing Yanshan Chuban She, 2010.

Williams, Abigail. "Settle, Elkanah (1648–1724)." In *Oxford Dictionary of National Biography*. Oxford University Press, 2004–. doi:10.1093/ref:odnb/25128.

Van Kley, Edwin. "An Alternative Muse: The Manchu Conquest of China in the Literature of Seventeenth-Century Northern Europe." *European Studies Review* 6 (1976): 21–43.

————. "News From China; Seventeenth-Century European Notices of the Manchu Conquest." *Journal of Modern History* 45, no. 4 (1973): 561–582.

Yang, Chi-ming. *Performing China: Virtue, Commerce, and Orientalism in Eighteenth-Century England, 1660–1760*. Baltimore: The Johns Hopkins University Press, 2011.

Zhang, Tingyu, et al. *Ming Shi* [History of the Ming Dynasty]. Edited by Qiyun Zhang. 6 vols. Taipei: Guo Fang Yan Jiu Yuan, 1962–63.

2 "China-Mania"

The Chinese Festival (1755) and The Orphan of China (1759)

> ACCORDING to the present prevailing whim every thing is Chinese, or in the Chinese taste; or, as it is sometimes more modestly expressed, *partly after the Chinese manner.* Chairs, tables, chimney-pieces, frames for looking-glasses, and even our most vulgar utensils are all reduced to this new-fangled standard; and without doors so universally has it spread, that every gate to a cow-yard is in T's and Z's, and every hovel for the cows has bells hanging at the corners.
>
> —Letter to the editor of *The World*, March 1753[1]

When the reader, signed H.S.,[2] wrote the editor of the weekly *World* to complain about "the present prevailing whim" in the middle of the eighteenth century, a craze for the "Chinese taste" was transforming English decorative arts and architecture. Illustrated pattern-books recommended new designs "after the Chinese manner" to be applied on chairs, mirrors ("frames for looking-glasses"), fireplaces, and temples. Gardens were encouraged to incorporate irregular paths ("in T's and Z's") and feature Chinese pagodas (with "bells hanging at the corners") and bridges. English craftsmen embellished cabinets and dressing tables with Chinese-like ornaments. Porcelain factories produced pottery painted with Chinese figures, flowers, and birds.[3] "The new epidemic of China-mania," as Hugh Honour phrased it,[4] reached its height in England in the 1750s.[5] The rage exploded as England joined France and other European countries in their enthusiasm for Chinese goods,[6] while the East India Company successfully established its trade in Asia, bringing home cargoes of goods from China.[7] This midcentury "China-mania" thus brought China into the homes of the British through its various material goods which further inspired imitation and creative designs "after the Chinese manner." China in the mid-eighteenth century was no longer merely a distant, faraway country read about in news reports of events such as the Manchu Conquest discussed in Chapter One; it had also become a concrete and substantial material presence in the everyday life of the British.

This chapter examines *The Chinese Festival* (1755), a spectacular dance entertainment that manifests material Chinaface, and *The Orphan of China* (1759), a tragedy that moralizes the Chinese-Tartar conflict, as two related but contrasting examples of dramatizing China that vividly manifest Britain's keen material interest in China and anti-French antagonism. *Chinese Festival*, a grand-scale dazzling visual spectacular, consists of a sequence of different styles of dances, elaborate scenery and costumes, and a grand and magic finale of transforming the dancers into porcelains. *Orphan of China*, on the other hand, depicts the sacrifice made by virtuous Chinese characters whose patriotic devotion eventually brings about the overthrow of the invading Tartars. Whereas *Chinese Festival* manifests a theatrical "China-mania" (which in this case may be called "china-mania," the lowercase "china" signifying China's best-known export) that literally turns its people (the cast) into its goods (china) in a fantasy of material desire,[8] *Orphan of China* represents a literary "China-mania" of politicized anti-French gestures that heightens moral virtues and passions and dramatizes its exemplary Chinese characters as purposely devoid of romantic implications.

In a Saidian, orientalist reading, *Chinese Festival* provides an early example of theatrical extravaganza depicting Oriental material affluence and abundance, to the extent of indulgence and recklessness, that is typical of later Orientalist visual spectaculars of sumptuous costumes and elaborate scenery (see *Chinese Sorcerer* in Chapter Three and *Chinese Honeymoon* in Chapter Four). *Orphan of China*, like Settle's *Conquest* (see Chapter One), portrays a militarily weaker but culturally stronger China forced to submit to the rougher, invading Tartary. It nevertheless revises and reverses the power correlations between race and gender by de-sexualizing the feminine (or feminized) China as a moral absolute that wins over the rougher Tartary. Mandane, wife of the loyal mandarin Zamti, is an affectionate matron who rejects the romantic advances of the Tartar emperor Timurkan. She demonstrates maternal care and complete devotion to her husband and continues the legacy of Chinese women's heightened agency and courageous acts as seen in Settle's *Conquest*. Mandane acknowledges that she learned every virtue from Zamti, the inspiring moral exemplar and patriarch. When Chinese culture is gendered as feminine, as in the case of the Chinese-Tartar conflict, Zamti stands for that ideal femininity (and complete emasculation), which eventually inspires the Chinese to rise up and overthrow the Tartars. At this historical moment, the "cultural effeminacy," to use Chi-ming Yang's term,[9] of China was a triumphantly positive trait. This feminized but favorable depiction of Chinese culture exemplifies the zenith of cultural "China-mania," the cultural appreciation of China that was informed by further Jesuit missionary work after the generation of Martini (discussed in Chapter One), which brought Europe more information about the country and continued to highly praise its cultural achievements.

These two modes of dramatizing China in London, through materialization and moralization, were informed by and operated through Paris (France): *Chinese Festival* was a direct French import, and *Orphan of China* was a localized/anglicized knock-off that intentionally rebelled against its French models. As the cultural center of eighteenth-century Europe, Paris (France) set the trends of fashion and taste, including admiration of China for its material goods and culture. *Chinese Festival* was conceived by Jean Georges Noverre (1727–1810), father of modern ballet,[10] and presented in Paris in 1754 with sensational success. David Garrick (1717–1779), the most prominent English theatre manager and actor of the eighteenth century,[11] promptly imported the dance, intending to capitalize on this latest Paris sensation the following year. *Orphan of China* was written by Arthur Murphy (1727–1805), a fairly successful English actor and playwright,[12] who reworked *L'Orphelin de la Chine* (1755) by the prominent French literary figure and philosopher Voltaire (pen name of François-Marie Arouet, 1694–1778) to exhibit patriotic rhetoric and heighten patriotic sentiment. Murphy's play wages a cultural war against Voltaire, France, and the admiration of both Voltaire and France for China at a time when Britain and France were in the midst of the Seven Years War (1756–1763). Voltaire's and Murphy's use of the Chinese-Tartar conflict suggests that this racial opposition, informed and interculturated by continuing Jesuit writings, had become a common trope to dramatize China. Similar to Settle, Voltaire and Murphy interculturalized the sources they consulted, including an incomplete translation of a Chinese play, and their plays respectively conformed to the conventions of French neoclassical tragedy and British moral tragedy.

Murphy's rewriting of Voltaire may also represent a lesson he learned first-hand as an actor at Drury Lane when *Chinese Festival* ended in fiasco, causing one of the biggest audience riots in English theatre history and damned as an outrageous French import on the eve of the impending war. In evaluating the *Chinese Festival* fiasco, I interpret a head-on clash within the audience between what I call the middle-class, Chinaface view and, borrowing from art historians, the upper-class, *chinoiserie* view of the dance, which prolonged the riot. The riot may exemplify an early instance of how theatrical works bearing an intercultural dimension could be received very differently by their audiences; while one audience focuses on the national/racial identity of the performers, the other focuses on their cultural/artistic identity. In the riot, I see a historical precedent that may be relatable to protest against blackface and/or yellowface practices and claims of the right to artistic freedom in later times.

Noverre's dance entertainment, Voltaire's play, and Murphy's reworking of Voltaire give rise to examples of interculturalization: the arbitrary inclusion of various peoples in one place, the deist depiction of Confucian philosophy, and the making of authentic-looking Chinese costumes. In these instances, interculturalization occurs on spatial, conceptual, visual, and material levels through juxtaposition, simplification, and merging. The Chinese costumes, especially, were commented on as striking, which affirms the novel visual attraction of the Chinaface aspect of the productions. After the mid-eighteenth century, Britain would continue to engross and enlarge its interest in China's material goods and visual splendor.

THE CHINESE FESTIVAL

On Saturday, November 8, 1755, *The Chinese Festival* premiered at Drury Lane in London. It was advertised as "a new grand Entertainment of Dancing," "Compos'd by Mr. Noverre" and performed by a huge cast of sixty, "[w]ith new Music, Scenes, Machines, Habits, and other Decorations."[13] A year earlier, on July 1, 1754, this dance entertainment choreographed by Noverre, with its French title *Les Fêtes chinoises*, was presented under the Opéra Comique at the Saint-Laurent fair in Paris and thrilled its spectators. Jean Monnet, manager of the Opéra Comique, boasted that *Les Fêtes chinoises* was "seen by all of Paris."[14] Charles Collé, a librettist and diarist,[15] also attested that "all of Paris rushed to see a Chinese ballet,"[16] which presumably means *Les Fêtes chinoises*. Both Monnet and Collé described *Les Fêtes chinoises* as unique (*"singularité," "singulier"*). Its novelty, picturesqueness, and magnificence earned hearty applause.[17]

The sensational success of *Les Fêtes chinoises* in Paris quickly caught Garrick's attention. Within two months, in September 1754, Noverre was already replying to Garrick's invitation to present *Les Fêtes chinoises*, titled *The Chinese Festival* in English, at Drury Lane.[18] According to Thomas Davies and Arthur Murphy, who were engaged at Drury Lane during the preparation and performance of *Chinese Festival*,[19] Garrick was determined to "surprise and captivate all ranks of people" by producing "the entertainment of the town." Instead of a British production that would be familiar to the British audience in style and content, *Chinese Festival*, a spectacle of "multifarious figures" in which "the dresses and customs of the Chinese were exhibited, in almost innumerable shapes and characters," adorned by "scenery and splendid decorations," "would most probably have the attraction of novelty."[20] The English accounts by Davies and Murphy corroborate and help qualify the descriptions in the French reports by Monnet and Collé about the dance entertainment: The praises for its uniqueness, novelty, picturesqueness, and magnificence have to do with its representation of the Chinese ("the dresses and customs of the Chinese"), the variety of performances ("multifarious figures") it offers, and its enormous performance scale ("innumerable" shapes and characters). In his own writings, Noverre considers the dance entertainment along with many of his early comical ballets as "almost plotless, intended exclusively for the amusement of the eye." The whole merit of such works consist in "the novelty of forms, in the variety and brilliance of the figures."[21]

In terms of scale, the English advertisement of the entertainment listed a cast of sixty; French contemporary accounts reported that there were at least forty-eight dancers.[22] In terms of variety, three different kinds of performances were described in the French accounts: dances, quick scene changes by machinery, and a characterized march (*une marche caractérisée*). The dances were presented in a sequence of a pantomime, a wave dance, a ballet (the main dance), and a contradanse (*contredanse*). The opening featured a magical scene change in which an avenue ending in terraces and steps that led up to a palace on a hill was turned into a public square decorated for a festival, with the palace on a hill turned into an amphitheater. This magical opening scene change was followed by a sudden doubling of dancers from sixteen to thirty-two, who then danced the first pantomime dance. In the entertainment's final spectacle, the amphitheater to which the Chinese dancers returned was transformed into a porcelain cabinet. Before the eyes of the spectators, "thirty-two vases arose and concealed the thirty-two Chinese they had just seen before."[23] Last but not least, in the characterized march, six white slaves carried a mandarin in an elaborate palanquin, while two Negroes pulled a wagon on which a young Chinese girl was seated. They were preceded and followed by a crowd of Chinese who played various musical instruments used in their country.

By reframing the entertainment from a palace to an amphitheater to a porcelain cabinet, the magical scene changes portrayed the transformations of a magnificent Chinese locale (palace), first theatricalized into a performance space (amphitheater) suitable for the dances, and eventually objectified into a display case (cabinet) to showcase its much admired and sought-after goods (china/porcelains). The high point of the entertainment bears witness to how China and its people are commodified, or, in other words, how China turns into china, manifesting a theatricalized fantasy that satiates the material desire for the country. This vase trick and the one designed by Settle for *The Fairy Queen* (see Chapter One) exemplify the display of Chinese porcelains as a theatrical spectacle and demonstrate the value of china as a precious curiosity that could serve as the main/grand attraction of a theatre/dance performance.[24]

In the dances performed in the entertainment, emphasis is placed on the scale and variety of formations and poses. After the first dance of pantomime by thirty-two dancers, the next wave dance features forty-eight dancers in a succession of lowerings and risings, imitating the waves of a stormy sea. The ballet by the cast (their number unspecified) exhibits "the variety or the sharpness of the figures,"[25] and in the contradanse, the thirty-two dancers form "an extraordinary amount of new and perfectly designed poses that link together and dissolve with the greatest ease."[26] These descriptions do not provide much that could be considered Chinese about the dances' content and/or presentation style; among "the variety or the sharpness of the figures" in the ballet and the "new and perfectly designed poses" in the contradanse there might be some examples of movements and poses that could be called Chinese. But most obviously, if superficially, the dancers assume roles that are called Chinese, such as mandarins and slaves; presumably, their costumes and make-up styles appear Chinese.

In the characterized march staged between the wave dance and the ballet, the dancers assume not only Chinese roles but also those of white slaves who bear a Chinese mandarin's palanquin and of two Negroes who pull a wagon carrying a Chinese girl. These role assignments and activities immediately call attention to their impossibility in actual occurrence and therefore heighten the artificiality of the march, and by extension the whole dance entertainment. The march's heightening of the entertainment's artificiality can be read as an instance that calls into question the basis for the occurrence of interculturalization, leading to awareness of the instance's artificiality. In the march the Chinese are served by white slaves and Negros; they are interculturalized as they are related to each other by the activity of the march, but on what grounds? One possible explanation may be Noverre's interest in enhancing the variety of the entertainment by including non-Chinese characters, which may justify this instance of interculturalization on the basis of artistic or arbitrary criteria, rather than on any precedent. The march, in other words, makes explicit that the dance entertainment is an artistic/artificial fantasy.

Quite noticeably, the fantasy relies on visual signification—the scenery, porcelains, musical instruments played in the march, and presumably the dancers' costume and make—up to characterize itself as Chinese, in what I call the Chinaface style, which operates on the superficial, appearance level. The final spectacle, in which the dancers are concealed and replaced by the porcelains, may be interpreted as eventually stowing away the Chinaface pretense and revealing the very material object (porcelain), and the contemporary "china-mania" behind it, that inspires Noverre's artistic/artificial fantasy.

More specifically, Monnet—the manager of the Opéra Comique and the one who hired Noverre as ballet master—remembered that in *Les Fêtes chinoises* "the set designs were all made up and based on the drawing of the late M. Boucher, the King's favorite painter."[27] François Boucher (1703–1770), a prominent French painter of the eighteenth century,[28] provided the royal Beauvais manufactory of tapestry with a series of paintings depicting Chinese scenes in 1742.[29] This series was very successful and Boucher's paintings were widely reproduced in prints. *La foire chinoise* (*The Chinese Fair*, Figure 2.1), one of these paintings, portrays a street fair with various onlookers and vendors on both sides of the diagonal street. In the foreground below the stage, a man pulls a rickshaw in which a young lady is seated with a fan in her hand. In *La danse chinoise* (*The Chinese Dance*, Figure 2.2), another painting from the series, four men are dancing in the right foreground, with their hands held up in the air. They surround a fifth man who is wearing a wide, pointed straw hat. Next to the group of dancers, there are men and women, sitting in the foreground and on the steps and standing in the background, playing various musical instruments. The street fair scene, the young lady sitting in the rickshaw, and the playing of musical instruments by men and women in the paintings very likely provided inspiration for Noverre to compose and choreograph *Les Fêtes chinoises*.[30]

Within his lifelong career as a painter, Boucher's production of paintings and other artworks depicting Chinese or Oriental themes was limited to a brief but intense period.[31] As art critics observe, Boucher had many accessible resources: his own collections, shops that sold porcelains and bibelots

Figure 2.1 *La foire chinoise* (*Chinese Fair*) by François Boucher (1703–1770). Musée des Beaux Arts Besançon. Photo Credit: Gianni Dagli Orti / The Art Archive at Art Resource, New York.

Figure 2.2 *La danse chinoise* (*Chinese Dance*) by François Boucher (1703–1770). Musée des Beaux Arts Besançon. Photo Credit: Gianni Dagli Orti / The Art Archive at Art Resource, New York.

Figure 2.3 La foire chinoise (*Chinese Fair*), by François Boucher (1703–1770), detail view of the young lady sitting in the rickshaw. Musée des Beaux Arts Besançon. Photo Credit: Gianni Dagli Orti / The Art Archive at Art Resource, New York.

from Asia, and the illustrations and paintings about China and other Asian countries published before his time.[32] Boucher, in other words, personally participated in "China-mania" as a consumer and collector. In *La foire chinoise* (Figure 2.1), for example, the composition of the man pulling a young lady sitting in the rickshaw (Figure 2.3) resembles very closely an illustration from Arnoldus Montanus's *Gedenkwaerdige Gesantschappen* (Figure 2.4).[33] The painting also includes a camel behind the porcelain dealers in the left foreground and an elephant carrying a tent in the far background (Figure 2.1). The inclusion of a Japanese lady, a camel, and an elephant in a Chinese fair has an impact similar to that of the white slaves and Negros in *Les Fêtes chinoises*, discussed earlier, in that these elements, when placed together, bring awareness to the artificiality of the painting as an artistic fantasy, calling into question the occurrence of interculturalization. In *Les Fêtes chinoises*, Noverre expands upon Boucher's Oriental fantasy, not only interculturalzing Oriental peoples and animals, but also placing them together with white and black characters, which further heightens the degree of fantasy in his dance, thereby serving Noverre's intention to create novelty as an attraction in the entertainment.

Figure 2.4 Japanese woman in a rickshaw, from Arnoldus Montanus, *Ambassades mémorables de la Compagnie des Indes Orientales des Provinces Unies, vers les empereurs du Japon* (1680). General Research Division, The New York Public Library, Astor, Lenox and Tilden Foundations.

Boucher's *La foire chinoise* (Figure 2.1) and *La danse chinoise* (Figure 2.2), as described earlier, were originally painted as design patterns for the French royal Beauvais manufactory of tapestry. His Chinese paintings joined other works of European decorative art—in interior design, pottery, textile, and garden design, to name a few—that exhibit distinct motifs identified as "taken after the Chinese manner." In general these works contain so-called Chinese patterns, figures, plants, and activities. The design concepts of Chinese arts are applied, but not truthfully followed. Art historians describe these works as *chinoiserie*, works that carry "fanciful European interpretations of Chinese styles" and are distinguished by the imaginative creativity of the European artists who integrate Chinese motifs and concepts into their artwork.[34]

Boucher's interculturalization of Oriental peoples and animals exemplifies his imaginative creativity and qualifies his Chinese paintings as *chinoiserie* in that they bear Chinese-inspired motifs but are clearly not Chinese. Noverre's *Les Fêtes chinoises*, in taking inspiration from Boucher, may be regarded as a derivative theatre work of *chinoiserie*. Using a Chinese setting and costumes and a display of the country's signature import, Noverre incorporates

Chinese motifs into his creative and fanciful imagination of a nominally Chinese fair that features other peoples, together with the Chinese, dancing in several European dance styles. On the other hand, Noverre's dance entertainment appears to contain very few other Chinese elements beyond those of visual signification, so that toward what "Chinese manner" *Les Fêtes chinoises* conceptually aims as a dance entertainment is unclear.

The difference I see between Boucher's Chinese paintings and Noverre's dance entertainment may be explained from the perspective of interculturation. In Boucher and Noverre's time, works of *chinoiserie* had already been created and circulated over a substantial period of time in the decorative arts; they had gained recognition as a distinct European artistic form with Chinese elements interculturalized and infused into the hybrid European forms. Decorative works of *chinoiserie*, that is, could claim to have undergone the process of interculturation. As an entertainment that was specifically intended to stand out for its novelty, Noverre's *Les Fêtes chinoises* can be read as an example of French dance that interculturalized, but did not yet interculturate, visual Chinese elements;[35] that is, these visual elements were not recognized as a distinct French/European dance form with infused Chinese elements and therefore could not necessarily claim to have gone through the process of interculturation, as could be said of similar elements in later Oriental visual spectaculars.

The possible and different interpretations of Noverre's dance entertainment—as a novel, superficially interculturalized Chinaface production, or, alternatively, as a derivative theatre work of interculturated *chinoiserie*—are seen in its reception by British audiences of different social classes when it was staged at Drury Lane. Noverre proposed a contract with Garrick in January 1755 and sealed it in February. He took a short trip to London to inspect the theatre in April; purchased the costumes, hired supernumeraries, and proposed to engage a child dancer by May; and left Paris in October to prepare for *The Chinese Festival* (the English version of *Les Fêtes chinoises*), scheduled for early November of 1755.[36] Louis Réne Boquet (1717–1814), renowned for his costume design and a long-term collaborator and faithful follower of Noverre,[37] designed new costumes for the London production, sketched four sets of decorations, and requested to supervise the execution of costuming and décor for the London production. "Le Sieur Boquet," wrote Noverre, "wants to ... have all the costumes that are necessary for my ballets made under his eyes, have your theatre organized in the most modern way, have your loge-boxes painted, light your theatre without chandelier, and, finally, make it the most agreeable in London."[38]

Boquet's wish to have Drury Lane organized "in the most modern way," according to Sybil Rosenfeld, may have introduced the rococo style of decoration to the London stage.[39] His plan to light the theatre without chandeliers, a common but defective lighting source that obscured the view of the stage, might have influenced Garrick's abandonment of the lighting source and method years later.[40] In costumes, scenery, and lighting, Boquet intended to bring many innovations to the London stage and interculturalize its stage practices with those of the French. The advertisement of *Chinese Festival* as with new "Scenes, Machines, Habits, and other Decorations" was very likely genuine, acknowledging Boquet's contribution. His works determined the visual effect of *The Chinese Festival* and, if not for the aborted life of the production, might have had a substantial impact on practices in these aspects of British theatre.

The long process of preparation and the unprecedented expenses spent on *Chinese Festival*, unfortunately, ended in disaster. *Chinese Festival* was expected to have a prosperous run at Drury Lane but it lasted only seven performances. Now it is remembered mostly for the riot it caused, one of the biggest theatre riots in English history.[41] The fiasco happened at a time when England and France were about to engage in the Seven Years War (1756–1763), a war prompted by conflicting claims over their North American colonies. Patriotism and xenophobia generated such resentment toward the French that *Chinese Festival*, a French import, became a ready target.

When the season opened in September, 1755, Drury Lane was gilt, painted, and ornamented with festoons,[42] which was probably a preparation for *Chinese Festival*. When Noverre arrived in London in October, he brought a group of twenty-four French artists and dancers.[43] He choreographed the dance and implemented Boquet's designs of costumes and scenery. Besides Davies' account, cited earlier, which recalled that "the dresses and customs of the Chinese" were exhibited in "almost innumerable shapes and characters,"[44] the anonymous author of "Lettre e'crite [écrite] de Londres" ("Letter Written from London"), an eyewitness account of the *Chinese Festival* riot, described the decorations as superb, the costumes magnificent, and the palanquin and wagons very sumptuous. The author also reported that the wing panels of scenery were painted as balconies full of Chinese spectators watching the festival.[45] Noverre, with his plans realized, had the full support of Garrick.[46]

Yet, as the premiere of *The Chinese Festival* approached, the rise in anti-French resentment was alarming. In newspapers and essays, Garrick was attacked for hiring a huge number of French dancers.[47] On November 6, two days before the premiere, when Garrick ended the third act of *Jane Shore* with the line, "Die w[th] [with] pleasure for my Country's good," a person in the gallery cried "No French dancers!" in response.[48] To avoid possible objections to the dance, Garrick published a statement in at least two newspapers on November 8, 1755, the day of the premiere:

> ... The insinuation that at this Time, an extraordinary Number of French Dancers are engaged, is groundless, there being at Drury-lane at Present as few of that Nation, as any other Theatre now has, or perhaps ever had. Mr. Noverre and his Brothers are Swiss of a Protestant Family in the Canton of Berne, his Wife and her Sisters Germans: there are above sixty Performers concerned in the Entertainment; more than forty of which are English, assisted only by

a few French, (five Men and four Women) to compleat the Ballet, as usual. As the Intention of the Managers on this Occasion, is to give Variety to the Entertainments of the Town; it is not doubted it will meet with the public Approbation.[49]

In the above statement, Garrick tried to emphasize Noverre's Swiss ancestry and Protestant religious practice (rather than French and Catholic), downplayed the number of French dancers that he engaged, and explained his intention of "giv[ing] variety to the Entertainments of the Town" in presenting *Chinese Festival*. Garrick also secured the attendance of King George II, whose presence might discourage possible disturbances. His effort to ward off condemnation, unfortunately, was in vain. During the performances, the dance was hissed at and interrupted; fruit was thrown onto the stage; fights, causing injuries, occurred among different parties in the audience; and benches were pulled up. On November 18, the riot grew so out of control that protesters wrecked the stage decorations. Some protesters even went so far as to break the windows of Garrick's house. Garrick had no choice but to abandon the dance in order to appease his audience.[50]

Harry William Pedicord suggests that the strong protest against *Chinese Festival* erupted from a combination of patriotic enthusiasm and class-consciousness.[51] As England and France were about to engage in war, any French then in England would have caused a stir. *The Dancers Damn'd*, an inflammatory pamphlet describing the riot on the night of November 12, offers an example of the extreme patriotic opposition to *Chinese Festival*. According to the pamphlet, when a woman representing Reason argued that Noverre was a Swiss Protestant, not a Frenchman, an angry reply was hurled at her from the gallery representing the patriots: "Swiss!—what the devil do we know of *Swiss*!—a *Swiss* is a foreigner, and all foreigners are *Frenchmen*; and so damn you all."[52] The confrontation between Reason and the patriots is presumably an exaggerated dramatization of what really happened on the night of the riot. Nevertheless, it exemplifies the fanatical, xenophobic attitude that some of the audience members might have had toward *Chinese Festival*.

The consciousness of class difference and divide appears to be the major reason for the fiasco. In all the eyewitness accounts, there is clearly a distinction between the reaction of the upper and lower social classes to *Chinese Festival*. The nobles sitting in the boxes favored the dance, while the common people in the galleries and the pit strongly protested against it. Tension and confrontation arose between these two classes of the audience. If not for this class conflict, the riot would not have lasted as long as it did or caused so many casualties and so much expense for Garrick.[53] In other words, the different perceptions of the dance awakened the consciousness of class difference, which further prolonged the riot. The outcry of the common people against the dance entertainment, having originated in patriotic enthusiasm, was inflamed further by the upper class's approval of the dance. The upper class, on the other hand, was not bothered by the French dancers in the cast and seemed to have taken an interest in the entertainment solely for its novel presentation of "the Chinese manner." They were, in Davies's words, "the people of fashion."[54] They attended the performance to catch the latest "China-mania" but found themselves annoyed by the disturbance from the galleries and the pit.

The conflicting perceptions of *Chinese Festival* informed by patriotism and the pursuit of fashion may be interpreted as a confrontation between the middle-class, Chinaface view and the upper-class, *chinoiserie* view of the dance entertainment. In support of patriotism's call for clear delimitation of national and racial identity, the middle-class, Chinaface view dwelled on the national/racial French identity of the performers (who were, in fact, mostly English, according to Noverre's and Garrick's accounts) and dismissed the performers' superficial assumption (interculturalization) of another national/racial identity (Chinese). Following the fashionable "China-mania" trend, the upper-class, *chinoiserie* view expressed interest in the dance entertainment and regarded it as an interculturated artwork that was distinctive for the cultural identity of its French creator. This may explain the anger from the middle-class audience toward the upper-class audience's support of the dance entertainment as unpatriotic. Garrick's public statement that Noverre was a Swiss Protestant negatively drew further attention to the national/racial identity of the artist, which could have further incited the middle-class, Chinaface view of this issue, as dramatized in the *Dancers Damn'd* pamphlet, and provoked the xenophobic cry that all foreigners in Chinaface are Frenchmen. Garrick's claim that his aim was to give "variety" to London's entertainment scene may be read two ways: it may suggest his emphasis on the Chinaface novelty of the French import, or it may also suggest his introduction of the established European *chinoiserie* trend, which was new to his uninitiated London audience.

Garrick tried to resolve the confrontation between these two opposing views. His request for the attendance of the king, whose presence Garrick hoped would "procure a quiet reception," was granted. But as the dancers entered the stage, commotion broke out, and when told it was because of hatred toward the French, the king "smiled, and withdrew from a scene of confusion."[55] On the night of November 17, Garrick canceled the dance, but the patrons in the boxes requested that he stage it anyway. Garrick did so despite objections from the pit. At last, Garrick reached a compromise with his audience—he would present the dance three nights a week for the boxes and other entertainments the other three nights for the pit. The bargain, however, fell through for unknown reasons.[56] The next night saw the gravest confrontation and such destruction in his theatre that Garrick had to give up on *Chinese Festival* completely. The middle-class, Chinaface view triumphed, and the artistic/artificial Chinaface of *Chinese Festival* was defaced, subsumed by the conflict.

As the rioters disturbed the dance and wrecked the theatre, Noverre and his family sought Garrick's protection. Noverre stayed in England, probably supervised later dance spectacles at Drury Lane, and observed Garrick's acting.[57] Noverre credits Garrick's acting as having inspired him and enriched his theory and practice of ballet,[58] which he shifted from plotless visual spectaculars consisting of separate acts like *Les Fêtes chinoises/Chinese Festival* to dance performances unified under a clear plot and theme, so-called *ballet d'action*.[59]

THE ORPHAN OF CHINA

On the night of November 18, 1755, when the riot caused by *Chinese Festival* reached its height, Arthur Murphy (1727–1805), then an actor engaged at Drury Lane, was there playing the leading role in *The Earl of Essex*, the play that preceded the dance entertainment.[60] Murphy afterwards focused on playwriting, and *The Orphan of China* (hereafter shortened as *Orphan*) was his first tragedy. He started the draft in 1756 and completed a stage-ready version in 1758.[61] The play, 2 hours and 59 minutes in length,[62] premiered at Drury Lane on April, 21, 1759.[63] According to the theatre's prompter, it "went off with great applause."[64] With a cast led by Garrick and the advertised "intirely new" scenery, costumes, and decorations,[65] the play had nine performances in its first season; it stayed in the repertoire of Drury Lane and was staged repeatedly in the next two decades.[66]

Murphy's *Orphan* is the second example examined in this book, after Settle's *Conquest* (see Chapter One), that depicts the Chinese-Tartar conflict. In this instance, the Tartar invader is vilified and eventually destroyed by the Chinese, who demonstrate loyalty to their country in various acts of virtue. Timurkan, the fierce Tartar emperor, has ruled China for twenty years and is fighting the troops of Corea (Korea), the last bastion of liberty and Chinese resistance. Among the captured Chinese fighters is Hamet, a valiant youth rumored to be the orphaned Chinese prince Zaphimri and condemned to death by Timurkan. As feelings of vengeance and patriotic zeal surge among the Chinese, Zamti, a Chinese mandarin, plans a secret attack and discloses that the youth Etan, whom he has raised as his own son, is actually Zaphimri, entrusted to him by the last Chinese king. The true biological son of Zamti is Hamet, who had been sent away as an infant to conceal the identity of Etan/Zaphimri. Zamti's wife Mandane pleads with Timurkan for Hamet's life out of maternal love. Touched by his adoptive family's sacrifice to preserve the royal lineage, Etan/Zaphimri gives himself up in exchange for their lives, an act which Timurkan treats as further trickery by the Chinese. With help from a Chinese serving under the Tartars, Zaphimri kills Timurkan and reunites with Hamet; Mandane, nevertheless, has committed suicide and Zamti has been tortured to death.

Murphy's depiction of the Chinese-Tartar conflict is influenced by and reacts against that in Voltaire's *L'Orphelin de la Chine* (hereafter shortened as *Orphelin*). Shortly after the premiere the script of Murphy's *Orphan* was published.[67] To the published script Murphy appended a letter titled, "To M. De Voltaire," the renowned French philosopher and writer, that opens:

> Sir,
> A letter to you from an English author will carry with it the appearance of corresponding with the enemy, not only as the two nations are at present involved in a difficult and important war, but also because in many of your late writings you seem determined to live in a state of hostility with the British nation. (89)

In his writings, Voltaire often found fault with the works of English playwrights, especially Shakespeare, for violating the classical unities followed by the French.[68] Murphy defended against this criticism in his essays.[69] On August 20, 1755, Voltaire's *Orphelin* premiered in Paris and became one of his most successful plays.[70] Murphy had read the play (90), either the French original or its English translation,[71] which inspired him to write his own, with its title a direct translation of Voltaire's and the names of the characters mostly from Voltaire. His open letter, while acknowledging the "occasional insertions of sentiment" from Voltaire's "elegant performance" (94), heightens and explicates his departures from Voltaire's plan and "the substitution of a new fable" of his own (89).

While Murphy's play evinces Voltaire's and other French playwrights' influences in its plot, characters, and sentiment, his emphasis on patriotic virtue departs from the French models. With this emphasis, Murphy's play differentiates between English constitutional monarchy and French absolutist monarchy and demonstrates China's participation in and contribution to the discourses of British nationalism, patriotism, and sentimentality.[72] The emphasis on patriotic virtue also brings Murphy's *Orphan* closer to the theme of justice and revenge of the Chinese play, *Zhao Shi Gu Er*, an incomplete translation of which both Voltaire and Murphy claimed as inspiration for their respective adaptations.

Voltaire's *Orphelin* depicts Gengis-Kan, the cruel Tartar emperor, as slaughtering his way into the Chinese royal palace and exterminating the royal house. The dying Chinese king entrusts his last infant prince to Zamti, a learned mandarin. Before Zamti and his wife Idamé manage to send away their own baby to Corea and raise the royal orphan in his place as their son, the Tartars demand surrender of the orphaned prince, or they will wreak further havoc. When Zamti turns in their own infant child, Idamé strongly protests and requests to see Gengis-Kan to plead for the life of her son. Their meeting rekindles Gengis-Kan's love for Idamé, who years ago had rejected him for Zamti. Gengis-Kan threatens to harm the royal orphan, her son, and Zamti if she refuses his advances. Idamé requests a last meeting with Zamti and together they attempt double suicide. Touched by their unwavering loyalty and virtue, Gengis-Kan is humbled and transformed; he pardons them, and resolves to rule China as a law-abiding king, not a ruthless conqueror, and learn reason, justice, and morals under Zamti's instruction.[73]

By contrast, Murphy's Timurkan remains a wrathful Tartar conqueror who is eventually killed by the Chinese. This completely opposite ending, and actions by the characters that lead up to it, show that Murphy has significantly revised Voltaire's depiction of the Chinese-Tartar conflict in terms of the characterization of the Tartars, monarch–subject relationships, the female character's participation in the patriotic cause within a patriarchal system, the kinds of passions exhibited by the characters, and the ways those passions are expressed. In Murphy's dramatization, the Tartars are unappreciative of Chinese civilization, the subjects have power to support or overthrow a monarch, Mandane fully submits herself to the patriarchal rule, and moral, patriotic zeal is heightened, often expressed in tears.

Toward the end of Act IV of *Orphan*, Timurkan discusses with Octar, his trusted general, their difficulty finding out who and where the orphaned Chinese prince Zaphimri is. The resistance from Zamti and Mandane and their unflinching attitude toward death irritate and puzzle Timurkan. Octar suggests that Timurkan may try "an artful tale of love" on Mandane to get the truth out, which Timurkan refuses: "I cannot stoop with love-sick adulation / To thrill in languishing desire"; his "only science" is to drive his chariot, its wheels "smo[a]king with gore," "thro' the ranks of war," above "the puling sickness of love" (VI.; 63). This is not the only suggestion that romantic prospects between Timurkan and Mandane are highly improbable: Earlier, when he suggests ("Woman, hear," he says) that Mandane will be able to save her son Hamet if she renounces "[a]ll hymeneal vows," Mandane screams out, "Thou vile adviser!—what, betrayed my lord, / My honour'd husband—turn a Scythian wife!" (III.; 51).

Timurkan's lone, awkward romantic effort in *Orphan* represents the most obvious example of Murphy's anti-French rewriting of Voltaire: to rid his play of romantic pursuits, which he considered secondary to the main subject of patriotic rescue and would instantly turn the rough conqueror into "*Le Chevalier* Gengiskan," which is "the hackneyed and stale stratagem of many modern writers" (91–92). Murphy asserted that Gengis-Kan's courtship of Idamé would be as absurd as if Racine's Athalie the Queen of Juda from his play *Athalie* were to fall in love with her enemy (91–92). To illuminate Voltaire's own contradiction, Murphy further cited Voltaire's objection to Racine's incorporation of a love plot into *Britannicus* (92). As moral concerns dominated mid-eighteenth-century English theatre,[74] and Murphy quoted Milton to define tragedy as "the gravest, moralest, and most profitable of all poems,"[75] a love affair between enemies would have been contrary to morality.

In *Orphelin*, Voltaire indeed, as Murphy describes, depicts Gengis-Kan as love-stricken even as he massacres the royal family, and the play's focus after Act II shifts to his several confrontations with Idamé and his inner struggles dealing with her resistance. Years before, Idamé had met Gengis-Kan, then named Témugin, an unknown, despised Scythian fugitive who sought protection from the Chinese court. Although she felt love for Témugin, Idamé chose the virtuous Zamti as meriting her "suffrage," a choice that was affected by the prohibition on interracial, bi-national marriage and informed by the pride of the jealous Chinese in "China's arts and laws of ancient dignity," time-honored religion, and past glories (I.i.; 3).[76] When pressed by Gengis-Kan, who now submits to her as an emperor, Idamé confesses that she had loved him, and though his fortunes has changed, she continues to support the Chinese paternal right ("le droit paternel"),[77] marital faith ("la foi de la hymen"), honor ("l'honneur"), justice ("la justice"), and the respect for oath ("le respect des sermen[t]s"), upon which the immortal Chinese empire was founded (IV.iv.; 46). The meetings with Idamé enrage and at the same time move Gengis-Kan, in that he sees Idamé has so transcended her private romantic inclinations that she is even willing to sacrifice her maternal care and her own life out of devotion to her country and her husband. When, at the end of the play, he declares that he will rule China as a king, Gengis-kan is subscribing himself to these ethical bases and the laws of the Chinese empire and making himself a conquered conqueror who accepts and is absorbed into the longevity and continuation of Chinese civilization. The several meetings and confrontations between Gengis-Kan and Idamé, which Murphy perceives as secondary to the theme of the destruction and preservation of a nation, actually lie at the very core of Voltaire's dramatization of the Chinese-Tartar conflict, for at the end of the play, Idamé (China) accomplishes what she secretly wished for in her feelings for Témugin (Tartary): that she would "soften the lion in her shackles, bend the great savage to China's customs, instill its virtues in his ferocious courage, and, in the end, succeed in turning him into a dignified citizen among the Chinese one day" (I.i.; 3).[78]

By rejecting "the hackneyed and stale stratagem" of Voltaire, Murphy's Timurkan, the anglicized Témugin, remains a ferocious Scythian who senses but is unable to comprehend the mental fortitude of the Chinese, which is stronger than the Great Wall and powerful enough to withstand his wrath. Although at one point he considers "yielding to their [the Chinese's] softer manners," their "virtue, laws, and customs," in order to blend in and make "the whole one undistinguish'd people" (II.; 23), recalling Gengis-Kan's final declaration in Voltaire, this idea is quickly dropped. In crediting warring and fighting as his "only science," Timurkan paraphrases what Octar (the Tartar emperor's right-hand man in both Voltaire and Murphy) says in Voltaire (III.iv.; 37) and, like him, lacks any intellectual understanding of or curiosity about the Chinese. At one rare moment of soliloquy, Timurkan asks, "What art thou, Virtue, who can'st thus inspire / This stubborn pride, this dignity of soul ... my heart hath never known?" (63). His inability to understand the Chinese is coupled with his disrespect for Chinese cultural achievements. According to Zamti, under Timurkan's tyranny the art of China has died, its science has vanished, and its gods in their holy shrines have been replaced by the living Lama worshipped by the Tartars (65). Facing an outsider who is unable and unwilling to accept Chinese civilization, the Chinese have no other recourse than to rely on a young prince, Zaphimri, a new character of Murphy's invention, who is able to physically overcome Timurkan.

After defeating Timurkan, Zaphimri expresses doubts about what he has accomplished, or destroyed. Seeing that Mandane has committed suicide and Zamti is about to die, Zaphimri asks, "Are these our triumphs?—these our promis'd joys?" (V.; 85). Upon hearing Zamti's dying request to be buried with Mandane, Zaphimri pleads, "Then take, ye pow'rs, then take your conquests back," because he will not survive, as the new king, without Zamti, whose parental care he needs to raise, guide, and animate his virtues (V.; 86, 87). But Zamti enjoins him to live. With the "moral duties of a private man" grafted into his soul and his understanding of virtue as the basis of happiness, Zaphimri is advised to "live the father of a *willing* people" (V.; 86, 87, emphasis mine).

Murphy's depiction of Zamti's last words of wisdom for Zaphimri recalls the operation of constitutional monarchy. In Voltaire, Gengis-Kan requests that Zamti embody and interpret China's laws (V.vi; 65),[79] so as to be a model for Gengis-Kan to emulate. In Murphy, Zaphimri has already acquired his sense of moral duty and virtue, and what he needs as a monarch is the willing support of his people, or he may someday be toppled like Timurkan. As a conqueror of China, Timurkan thinks that his will is the law, to which Zamti strongly protests that "the soul, / which gave our legislation life and vigour, / Shall still subsist," and "[t]he spirit of the laws can never die" (IV.; 66). By the soul and the spirit, Zamti is referring to the moral duty to attend to the "public weal" (I.; 6) in the making and execution of laws, rather than the monarch's mere will. This point is made explicit in the play's prologue, written by the poet laureate William Whitehead and delivered by Charles Holland, who played Hamet, that "Britain knows no Right Divine in Kings," and that it is "in his People's HEARTS OUR MONARCH reigns."

Both Voltaire's Idamé and Murphy's English counterpart, Mandane, express the same sentiment of innate maternal concern, which overwhelms their sense of patriotic devotion, upon learning that their sons are to be sacrificed. Mandane's claim that the kings and their subject are made of the same common clay and drink the same cup of human woe (II.; 32–33) echoes Idamé's that the monarch and their subject are equal by nature and in misfortune (II.iii.; 18). But what Idamé vaguely describes as the "idle marks" ("frivoles marques") that separate them are qualified by Mandane: "Sacred Kings! / 'Tis human policy sets up their claim" (II.; 33). Mandane's comment may be interpreted as implying that without the human policy acknowledged and supported, kings would not be recognized and elevated above their people.

In writing off Mandane as a romantic female character, Murphy accentuates her maternal sentiment. She emphasizes that her cause is "a mother's cause," that of husband, wife, and child (II.; 33). But after she breaks down in front of the Tartars to plead for Hamet and scorns Timurkan's marriage proposal, Mandane returns to be the faithful ally of her husband's patriotic cause, his eager pupil of his moral instruction. Similar to Idamé, Mandane apologizes to Zamti for her "mild maternal love" which made her reveal the secret they had kept for twenty years; Mandane also proposes death and urges Zamti, who has taught her every virtue, to kill her as a way to end their misery (V.; 74).[80] Mandane's regard for Zamti elevates his status above her; her request that he kill her demonstrates her deference to the patriarchal system, especially the "paternal right," which is among the foundations of the Chinese empire identified by Idamé. Mandane, in other words, intends to show her complete devotion to the patriotic cause in death by the hand of the moral patriarch. Only his reluctance and, moreover, inability to take her life (he was being tortured by the Tartars at the time) prompt her to commit suicide.[81]

Murphy follows Voltaire to depict Zamti as a mandarin in charge of religious affairs. His embodiment of both virtue and sanctity wins him respect, even from the Tartars.[82] As noted by Chi-ming Yang,[83] Murphy's Zamti often sheds tears to convey what Murphy and his contemporaries would call passions. In Act II, for example, Zamti *"Bursts into tears"* in thinking about sacrificing his son Hamet (19); he then convinces himself that he can forsake his son with "tears of joy" (20) for the larger good of the country; but moments later after falsely admitting to Timurkan that Hamet is Zaphimri and anticipating Hamet's death, Zamti breaks down: "Flow, flow my tears, and ease this aching breast" (29).

In *A Treatise on the Passions*, Samuel Foote defined passions as "the different Motions and Agitations of the Soul" that "present themselves to the Senses."[84] Aaron Hill defined ten basic dramatic passions—joy, grief, fear, anger, pity, scorn, hatred, jealousy, wonder, and love—and the appropriate gestures for expressing them.[85] Murphy considered "the Exhibition of Character, and the Excitement of the Passions, justly claiming the Precedence in dramatic Poetry."[86] In addition, he believed that the mind of man cannot dwell for long on one specific passion. Various passions are "perpetually taking their Turns in the Breast."[87] Zamti's exhibition of different passions through shedding tears and gesturing exemplifies the various motions and agitations of his soul and the turns they take inside him. As the moral exemplar and teacher, Zamti affects other Chinese characters, from Mandane to Etan / Zaphimri to Hamet, who all resort to the same emotive expression (shedding tears) to publicly display their various passions of distress, grief, and joy, representing their agitations within. Thus, Murphy replaces the passion of romantic love in Voltaire with other kinds in his characters.[88] His goal and hope, as he expresses in the play's epilogue, is to affect the audience and receive the honor of "a single tear" from every lady in the audience.

Yang argues that in Murphy's *Orphan* the profuse emotions shared between the Chinese parents and children create "a circuit of sympathetic identifications that forms the Chinese resistance to Tartar tyranny."[89] Through tears and the sharing of tears, what Yang might call "the feminized channels of sentiment,"[90] the Chinese become empowered to rise against the Tartars. After reclaiming the throne, Zaphimri plans to erect a monument to Mandane and Zamti, where "each weeping muse / Shall grave the tributary verse;—with tears / Embalm their memories" (V.; 88). Zaphimri clearly intends to institutionalize a place of public mourning which will utilize and continue the display of tears as a tool of commemoration and possibly as a source of empowerment. Overall, the Chinese characters in Murphy are fully devoted to the anti-Tartar cause; they may appear overtly sentimental and even feminized, but they eventually triumph over their mortal enemy and retain political, cultural, and religious independence. This patriotic virtue is highly exalted in the panegyric to Murphy by William Woty, who praised his characters as fraught with "moral inference" and "manly thought," and his play as causing "the tragic virgin" to drop a tear as "Virtue weeps." Woty hailed, "MURPHY! proceed, and teach the subject age / To catch the patriot flame from thine and Freedom's page."[91]

To help clarify their distinct approaches to dramatizing China, Murphy's *Orphan* and Voltaire's *Orphelin* can be further compared to the Chinese play that inspired them in terms of plot, character, and dramatic conflict. Both Voltaire and Murphy stated that they had read and were inspired by *Zhao Shi Gu Er* (*The Orphan of the House of Zhao*, 趙氏孤兒), which is included in *Description géographique, historique, chronologique, politique, et physique de l'empire de la Chine et de la Tartarie chinoise*, an encyclopedic work about China edited by the French Jesuit father Jean-Baptiste du Halde (1674–1743).[92] A compilation of various Jesuit writings on China by du Halde who resided in Paris, *Description* was enthusiastically received when it first came out in the 1730s; it was printed in several editions and translated into English and other European languages.[93] Similar to Martini's *De bello Tartarico historia* of the seventeenth century discussed in Chapter One, *Description* was another seminal Jesuit work that significantly influenced Europe's knowledge and understanding of China in the eighteenth century. To give an example of Chinese drama, du Halde included an incomplete translation by friar Joseph-Henry de Prémare of *Zhao Shi Gu Er* that omitted its arias.[94] As the first translated Chinese play to ever reach Europe, *Zhao Shi Gu Er* attracted much attention and was read with great interest. It inspired many European writers, including Voltaire and Murphy, to create dramatic works based on its story.[95]

Written by Ji Junxiang (i.e., Chi Chün-hsiang, 紀君祥, fl. late thirteenth century), *Zhao Shi Gu Er* depicts genocide caused by the animosity between two ministers, the sacrifices virtuous characters make to preserve the house of the loyal minister, and the eventual revenge taken against the traitorous one. Set in China's Spring and Autumn era (722–481 BCE), in the kingdom of Jin (晉), Tu Angu (屠岸賈), the minister of war, tricks the king into believing that Zhao Dun (趙盾), the minister of state, is a traitor. All the members of the house of Zhao are thus killed except a newborn baby by Zhao's son who is entrusted to and smuggled away by Cheng Ying (程嬰), the family's physician. After hearing of the escape, Tu orders all babies under six months to be slain unless the orphan is found. Cheng hands over his own baby son as the orphan and witnesses the boy's brutal execution. Tu thereafter confides in Cheng and adopts the orphan of Zhao, whom he believes to be

Cheng's son. Twenty years later, Cheng reveals the truth to the orphan, who eventually kills Tu to avenge the destruction of his family.[96]

In their plays, both Voltaire and Murphy retain and dramatize the ideal of sacrificing one's child for the larger good of the country. While Voltaire sets his adaptation at the point when the orphaned baby is about to be killed, Murphy depicts the revenge twenty years later, when the orphan has grown up to become a virtuous and valiant youth capable of avenging the wrongs. Unlike in the Chinese play, in neither Voltaire's nor Murphy's version is the baby killed, which may demonstrate their reluctance to depict the brutality of infanticide on stage in conformance with classical as well as contemporary French and British dramatic conventions.

In his dedication of *Orphelin* to the duc de Richelieu, Voltaire stated that in unity of time and action, development of sentiments, and portrayals of manners, eloquence, reason, and passion, the Chinese play is barbarous when compared with contemporary neoclassical French works. Further, the play is similar to the monstrous farces of Shakespeare and Lope de Vega, or *One Thousand and One Nights*, consisting of a heap of incredible events. Nonetheless, it can be deemed a masterpiece ("chef d'oeuvre") compared with French plays of the fourteenth century in that it "reigns with interest" ("régne de l'intérêt") and possesses "the most luminous clarity" ("la clarté la plus lumineuse") (vij–ix). Voltaire's *Orphelin* complies with the neoclassical practices and observes the three unities of time, place, and action; it takes place over the course of one day, instead of twenty years as in the Chinese original. Voltaire focuses on the sentiments of the characters, especially in the confrontations between Idamé and Gengis-Kan who, in eloquent language, express their struggle between reason and passion.

After reading *Zhao Shi Gu Er*, Murphy imagined that he saw a blemish in how the orphan is saved by the "tame resignation [that is, relinquishment] of another orphan in his place." In his version, he chose to portray the struggles of a parent facing such a trying decision.[97] He was then inspired to conceive a fable in which the fates of the father and the two young men would be interwoven with "probability and perspicuity" so as to induce situations in which some of the "nearest affections of the heart" could be awakened (90). By creating Zaphimri and Hamet (the two young men), Murphy believed his play, unlike Voltaire's *Orphelin*, had avoided resembling Racine's *Andromaque* (93). On the other hand, Murphy was aware that by adding the two new roles, his *Orphan* would appear similar to Corneille's *Héraclius*. Yet he simplified the plot to make it less puzzling than Corneille's (90). Murphy depicts how Zamti arouses patriotic sentiments in Etan and other Chinese by recounting the horrifying scene of the Chinese royal court's demise,[98] which resembles the episode in *Zhao Shi Gu Er* in which Cheng Ying through a series of paintings reveals to the orphan of Zhao the homicide of his house. Murphy also portrays a secret visit by Zaphimri to the imprisoned Hamet, during which they exchange and strengthen their determination to rebel against the Tartars. These episodes accentuate the patriotic sentiment for revenge and justice and also bring Murphy's adaptation closer than Voltaire's to the Chinese play.

In *Zhao Shi Gu Er*, Cheng Ying, the family physician, is the counterpart to Zamti, the moral patriarch in Voltaire and Murphy, and Tu, the minister of war, is comparable to Gengis-Kan/Timurkan, the Tartar emperor. The wife of Zamti, Idamé/Mandane, is Voltaire's and Murphy's creative addition to the story. This character shares with her husband the struggle, grief, and pain of a parent in sacrificing a child.[99] When Voltaire recontextualizes the setting of the story to the Chinese-Tartar conflict, which is a critical reconceptualization of the Chinese play followed by Murphy, the feud between the two houses in the Chinese play is transformed and elevated to an ideological and interracial power struggle that exhibits correlations between race and gender. In both Voltaire and Murphy, China triumphs, though in different degrees, as a culturally stronger, feminine (or feminized) political entity which bears the impact of the Jesuits' admiration and promotion for the country's cultural achievements in the seventeenth century and the first half of the eighteenth. China is also further antiquated, emphasizing its long history and past glories, especially the philosophy of its great sage Confucius as embodied and conveyed by his stage spokesperson Zamti. When compared with the China depicted in Settle's *Conquest* discussed in Chapter One, the Chinas in Voltaire and Murphy are less gender-ambiguous and more orientalist in a Saidian way. Voltaire's great admiration for China engendered a clearly gendered and prejudiced view of the country; Murphy's rewriting reduced the admiration but increased the gendered view.

In the dedication to Richelieu, Voltaire argued that as the Chinese play was composed during the Yuan Dynasty (1206–1367) founded by Gengis-Kan (Genghis Khan),[100] it proved that the conquering Tartars did not change the customs ("moeurs") of the conquered China; they protected all of its arts and adopted all of its laws. It was "a grand example of the natural superiority of reason and genius over a blind and barbarous force" (iv–v).[101] In the dedication, Voltaire further stated that in writing the play, he was inspired by the grand epoch of Gengis-Kan because he wanted to contrast the customs of the Tartars and the Chinese in order to inspire virtue ("vertu") (xj). Voltaire also observed that when the Tartars again conquered China in the last century (i.e., the Manchu Conquest in the seventeenth century), they submitted to the wisdom ("sagesse") of the conquered country. That the two peoples had formed one nation, "governed by the most ancient laws of mankind,"[102] so impressed him that it became the basis for his writing of *Orphelin* (v).

Voltaire's revelations suggest why he chose to adapt *Zhao Shi Gu Er* into a play that dramatizes the Chinese-Tartar conflict and features Gengis-Kan as the main character. The depiction of the two peoples is intended to demonstrate the contrast between reason and barbarity; the sacrifice of their infant child demonstrates Idamé's and Zamti's loyalty to their country, which moves Gengis-Kan and inspires his transformation from blind ignorance to enlightenment; his solicitation of Zamti's instruction shows his acceptance of China's wisdom and that he will protect the laws that had allowed the civilization to continue since ancient times.

While Gengis-Kan is regarded as founder of the Yuan Dynasty, the play is set during the Manchu Conquest, which is indicated by reference to the assistance from Corea (Korea) to help China resist against the Tartars, an instance that was recounted in du Halde.[103] By placing the Mongol ruler in the context of the Manchu conquest, Voltaire continues the use of the interculturalized conceptualization of the Tartars as the collective designation of China's perennial political and cultural other, making no distinction between the separate nomadic peoples (see Chapter One). In this way, Voltaire dramatizes the Chinese-Tartar conflict on a conceptual, not a factual, level. He thus adds a larger, symbolic significance to Gengis-Kan's willing submission to China's customs: that China's reason and wisdom will turn its barbarous Tartar other, exemplified by the famed and fearful Gengis-Kan, into one of its noble citizens. In describing Gengis-Kan as a Scythian and a Tartar interchangeably, Voltaire follows the example of Heylyn, discussed in Chapter One, and enlarges the character to embody the political and cultural other to both China and the West. Gengis-Kan's submission elevates China's achievement, signifying how China can subdue the barbarian threat to both Chinese and Western civilizations. Known to have become a sinophile under the influence of his Jesuit teachers,[104] Voltaire in his dramatization of the Chinese-Tartar conflict conveys his high praise and deep admiration for the country.

Murphy, although possessing a Jesuit education,[105] is less enthusiastic than Voltaire about China's power and achievements in his rewriting of Voltaire's depictions of Gengis-Kan, Zamti, and Idamé. Like Voltaire's Gengis-Kan, Murphy's Timurkan prevents Corea from assisting China; he is called "the fell Scythian murderer" by Zamti (II.; 33) and "bloody Tartar" by Zaphimri (V.; 80). Murphy's depiction of Timurkan as unmoved by and destructive of China's arts and sciences suggests that China's "reason and genius" may not receive any respect from its invaders, thus eliminating a source of allure that Voltaire emphasized about China.

In the play's prologue, Whitehead states that, because stories set in Greece and Rome no longer charm the London audience, Murphy, seeking "fresh virtues," boldly bears "Confucius' morals to Britannia's ears." While stating that Murphy's efforts deserve praise, Whitehead cautions that the audience may find Zamti a dubious character, "[a] patriot zealous in a monarch's cause!" If his "undistingu'd loyalty" prevails, Whitehead suggests, "On China's tenets charge the fond mistake, / And spare his error for his Virtue's sake." Whitehead finds fault with Zamti's zeal and what he sees as Zamti's uncritical loyalty to his lord, which hints at the absolute monarchy in France, and more generally China's moral system. His patriotic criticism, which appears to have overlooked the support for British constitutional monarchy Murphy wrote into Zamti's belief system, suggests that China's virtues, specifically the "fresh" Confucian morals, may be laudable but are also inherently defective.

According to Arnold H. Rowbotham, the intelligentsia of Europe, including Voltaire, learned of the philosophy of Confucius (551–479 BCE), the renowned Chinese philosopher and teacher, from the Jesuits, who simplified Confucianism into "a kind of deism functioning through a form of benevolent despotism."[106] Confucianism, in other words, was interculturalized and promoted by the Jesuits as a close analogue to the European conceptions of deism and despotism. In Confucius and Confucianism, Voltaire saw an ideal deist and a kind of deism, an alternative religion he preferred to the Christian church.[107] This helps explain why Zamti, who stands in for Confucius in both Voltaire and Murphy, is depicted as a loyal mandarin-patriarch in charge of religious affairs; he is indebted to his king, his country, and his God of Heaven and Earth, and he criticizes the Scythian/Tartar worship of the Buddhist Bonze or Lama.[108] As an interculturalized Confucian, Zamti supports the causes of French absolutist monarchy in Voltaire and British constitutional monarchy in Murphy; Zamti's beliefs, that is, are further Gallicized and anglicized (interculturalized), respectively. Last but not least, the name Zamti appears to be Voltaire's coinage; it approximates very closely Xamti (Shangdi, 上帝, "Lord on High"), one of the competing terms used to render the name God in Chinese by Christian missionaries in China.[109] By replacing the Christian cross ("X") in the word Xamti with a Z to create a name for the Confucian patriarch, Voltaire infuses Zamti with the implication of an alternative God-like figure, a deist despot. Murphy's rewriting, while inheriting his name and Voltaire's depictions, humanizes this saintly figure by portraying him as tearful and prone to be overzealous.

Nevertheless, Voltaire accompanied his high praise for China with critical commentary. In the dedication of *Orphelin*, Voltaire argued that, cited earlier, *Zhao Shi Gu Er* shows that the Chinese had composed better dramatic works than the Europeans up to the fourteenth century, when he believed it was written.[110] Thereafter, he believed, the Chinese had remained in the primitive infancy of Art ("l'enfance grossiére de l'Art") and made no further progress, whereas the French, with diligence and the passage of time, had produced works without peer anywhere in the world. As with other Asian peoples, the poetry, other arts, and sciences of the Chinese had not advanced beyond their basic elements. Voltaire reasoned that the Chinese did not understand that the French, and the Europeans, who, despite being continually rebuffed, had labored so hard to visit the Chinese and offer their money and instruction, were their superiors. He concluded that China was not yet advanced enough to imitate Europe (ix–x). China (and by extension Asia), in other words, was like a child prodigy in a state of arrested development that has turned disobedient and ignorant, and, therefore, the country was inferior to the progressive, materialistic, and intellectually superior Europe (France).

In the dedication, Voltaire also commented that China was comparable to ancient Western civilizations such as Egypt, Greece, and Rome (v–vj, ix–x). All these comments suggest that Voltaire's deep admiration for the country rested on his perception of its achievements as ancient and stagnant and adhering to the teachings of its ancient sage, Confucius. It then makes sense that Voltaire would interpret the result of the Manchu Conquest as having brought the Manchu and the Chinese under the governance of "the most ancient laws of mankind." In *Orphelin*, Idamé honored "China's arts and laws of ancient dignity" that prevented her from agreeing to a marriage with Gengis-Kan, who in the end declares that he will abide by these ancient laws. Together with his depiction of Idamé's femininity and virtue, and Idamé's triumph over Gengis-Kan, Voltaire's exaltation of China depends upon an orientalist view of the country as time-trapped (immobile), backward-looking, and feminine, a view that foreshadows later orientalist depictions of the country.

In his *Orphan*, Murphy presents a view of a China that is less ancient than Voltaire's and could be considered both feminine and feminized. Zaphimri, the orphan prince and new king, descends from an ancient line (I.; 7, III.; 38); he was nurtured by Zamti in "humanity and virtue" (III.; 40), with his sense of moral duty presumably derived from Confucius's "radiant stores of moral truth" (I.; 6). Zamti, however, defines the sacred laws taught by "hoary elders" as "founded on the base of public weal" (I.; 6). As discussed earlier, Zamti's last counsel for him is to use his sense of moral duty and virtue to care for his people and win their willing support through the system of constitutional monarchy, which acts as a critical check from his people, of here and now, on his rule as Zaphimri leads China forward. Similarly, the earlier discussion of the Chinese characters' public display of their passions, often through tears, may elicit a reading of China as feminine, as they express their passions through "the feminized channels of sentiment." To further this reading, Zamti, the Confucian moral patriarch, could be considered the most feminized, or emasculated, as he breaks into tears the most.

In addition to Whitehead's dismissive attitude toward China in the prologue as discussed above, other contemporary writings about *Orphan* provide further indication of attitudes toward the play's depiction of China. For example, Oliver Goldsmith (1728?–1774), a prominent British writer of the eighteenth century,[111] stated that at the play's premiere the whole theatre house seemed "highly and justly pleased," not by the "*luxury of woe*" (emphasis Goldsmith), but by "the nervous sentiment, the glowing imagery, the well-conducted scenery."[112] Goldsmith apparently found the depictions of the Chinese characters in woe, abundantly shedding tears, too extravagant and indulgent; instead, he credited the "nervous sentiment," presumably referring to the scene in which Zamti and Mandane clash over the decision to sacrifice their son, which he quoted and praised highly in his review (436–439); the costumes ("the glowing imagery");[113] and the scenery as succeeding in pleasing the audience.

Murphy himself complimented the performers' successful portrayals of the characters; he especially admired Garrick's acting, which, "in the various conflicts of the passions, displayed such inimitable powers, that it may be truly said, he never appeared in any character (if we except *King Lear*) with such a brilliant lustre." He thanked Garrick for preparing "a magnificent set of Chinese scenes, and the most becoming dresses."[114] In his letter to Voltaire, Murphy boasted that if Voltaire had attended the performance, he would have seen "a theatrical splendor conducted with a *bienseance* unknown to the *scene Francoise.*"[115]

While Murphy saw that the performers, especially Garrick, effectively conveyed what Goldsmith criticized as the "luxury of woe," he concurred on the attraction of the scenery and costumes. Goldsmith's review and Murphy's self-evaluation, on the play's writing and stage representation, may be interpreted as instances of the Chinaface and *chinoiserie* views I identify earlier in this chapter to analyze the riotous receptions of *Chinese Festival.* Murphy's *Orphan,* similar to the dance entertainment, could be seen as a Chinaface (visual novelty) and/or a *chinoiserie* (distinctly British) work. In this case, critics acknowledged, with discernibly orientalist attitudes, the instances of interculturalization in the play, and advocated for further interculturation that would diminish the Chinese presence and increase its British (European) quality. If we examine Murphy's *Orphan* using Pavis's analysis of intercultural performance cited in Chapter One, to the contemporary audience as well as modern critics the play offers foreign sensuality as a visual and material attraction, in what I call a Chinaface way, and in a de-sexualized manner.

In *An Account of the New Tragedy of "The Orphan of China"* (1759), the anonymous author claimed that the "magnificent, uniform, and proper" scenery offered so many pleasant novelties that "[a]n eastern traveler would imagine himself at Pekin—and a Cockney in a new world." In addition, among the "new, elegant, and characteristic" dresses for the characters, the one worn by Mary Ann Yates, who played Mandane (Figure 2.5), would "make great improvements in the lady's dress for the year 1759," as most of the female audience seemed envious of her "ornamental habit."[116] These comments from *Account of the New Tragedy* suggest that the audience saw and was drawn to the visual novelty in Murphy's *Orphan*; their admiration for the Chinese scenery and costumes suggest that they saw Murphy's play as a Chinaface novelty, with conspicuous and superficial presence of Chinese elements.

Goldsmith began his review by echoing the sentiments about the contemporary "China-mania" expressed by the anonymous reader of *World* (see epigram of this chapter) and further called it a perversion of taste. The British, Goldsmith commented, like "the Asiatic tyrant of antiquity" wearied of the old pleasures, eagerly sought amusement in the new, and it was no wonder that the public was presented with Murphy's *Orphan,* a poetic work "formed upon Chinese manners" (434). Murphy's play, in other words, was a literary response to the visual interest in novelty and drew upon "Chinese manners" to create a Chinaface play. Through his orientalist analogy comparing the British to ancient Asian despots, Goldsmith showed that he found this interest in novelty backward, decadent, and extravagant. The

Figure 2.5 Mrs. Yates as Mandane in *The Orphan of China*, by Tilly Kettle
(1734/5–1786), exhibited 1765. Tate Gallery, London, Great Britain.
Photo Credit: Tate, London / Art Resource, New York.

visual luxury and the "luxury of woe" identified by Goldsmith show his disapproval of excess, in this case Chinese material and emotional excesses.[117]

Goldsmith further observed that Voltaire, aware of the Chinese fashion and "in favor of all that came from China" himself, "embroidered a Chinese plot with all the colouring of French poetry," and the good qualities of his play were only proportionate to his deviation from "the calm insipidity of his Eastern original" (434). As Murphy deviated still further, his plot became more European, and more perfect. "Mr. Murphy has given us a play, if not truly Chinese, at least entirely poetical" (435).

In these comments, Goldsmith may be read as being aware of the interculturalization that occurred as Voltaire "embroidered" together a Chinese plot and French poetic elements. This provides a conceptually similar analogy to the one used by Hazelton and Benrimo in their writing of *Yellow Jacket* (see Chapter Four), albeit one that reverses the ways in which Chinese and Western elements are combined. His comments also suggest that a further process of interculturation took effect as the plot became more European and less

Chinese. With his orientalist, negative opinion about the "insipidity" of *Zhao Shi Gu Er*, Goldsmith's praise for what he sees as the progressive improvements made by Voltaire and Murphy may be interpreted as a typical *chinoiserie* view in that Voltaire and Murphy had transformed the Chinese play into works characteristically French and British, respectively. When Goldsmith critiqued Murphy's depictions of the characters' pathos, he measured the work again those of other English/European writers, as did Murphy's other contemporaries, such as the anonymous author of *A Letter from Mons. De Voltaire to the Author of "The Orphan of China"* (1759), who attacked Murphy's plotting, and David Baker, who expressed dislike toward the play's pompous style.[118] They, in other words, overlooked the Chinaface aspect of the play and focused on its distinct British/European characteristics.

Among the modern critics, Howard Dunbar suggests that the play's success derived from "its novelty, its patriotic appeal, its affecting situations, its excellent cast, and its scenic effects."[119] Its novelty and scenic effects apparently had to do with its visual, Chinaface representation in costume and scenery. Robert D. Spector, interestingly, states that what was most significant about *Orphan* was Murphy's ability to "make the most effective use of his *chinoiserie*." According to Spector, the play depended greatly on "fashionable [French] taste for *chinoiserie* and new effects in stage production" and the Chinese characters in the play are "English Christians in Oriental dress."[120] In associating *chinoiserie* with taste and French influence, and in identifying Chinese/Oriental dress as one of Murphy's uses of *chinoiserie*, Spector appears to be using this word to describe what I would define as Chinaface.

It appears that the interest in the making of Chinaface was not a lone instance. In the 1750s, discussions emerged on the stage representation of other nations and peoples in British theatre. In *Reflections upon Theatrical Expression in Tragedy* (1755), Roger Pickering asked, "Why are not *all* our Plays *dress'd* in *Character* in Point of *Time* and *Place*?" He believed that even indifferent plays would draw a crowded house with the characters dressed in "the *National Mode*, where the Scene is laid."[121] In *A General View of the Stage* (1759), Thomas Wilkes suggested that an actor pay heed to the "sufficient exactitude" of his dress to "the age, time, and circumstances of his character." By this means the actor might introduce "some striking particularity," which would greatly help give the "illusive representation the stronger resemblance of reality." For guidance Wilkes strongly recommended that actors consult *A Collection of the Dresses Different Nations, Antient* [sic] *and Modern*, which is a rich anthology of illustrated figures reproduced from various books, drawings, and paintings and published in a French/English bilingual format.[122]

Unlike Settle, who argued in the previous century that stage costuming should follow the conventional practices of English theatre to avoid impropriety (see Chapter One), Pickering and Wilkes argued for the opposite, in what I see as for the reason of Chinaface. They asserted that the novelty of such dress would draw in the audience to see the "striking particularity" of the characters in the "national mode" of dresses of their time and place and, further, that the dress would bring a sense of reality to "illusive representation." For designing Chinese costumes, guidance could be found in *A Collection of the Dresses* which included illustrations of Chinese dresses; the main source of these images, as acknowledged by the author, was du Halde's *Description*.[123]

Delivering the epilogue of Murphy's *Orphan*, Yates, who played Mandane, told the audience that after wearing a sighing face for five long acts, she could now ramble as she pleased to see the city of London and beyond. Catching sight of the female audience in the theatre, she said: "Ladies, excuse my dress'—'tis true Chinese." Yates presumably sought to justify the "striking particularity" of her costume (Figure 2.4), which recalls the dress for a Chinese lady in *A Collection of the Dresses* (Figure 2.5) and its origin in du Halde (in mirror position, Figure 2.6). In the painting Yates appears to be modeling her posture after that of the Chinese lady;[124] likewise, her hair adornments and the cut and design of her costume exhibit motifs drawn from the Chinese lady. Yates's Chinaface look thus strongly resembles its source. It may be argued that her costume and make-up manifest an occurrence of interculturalization on the visual and material levels between the source and British theatrical practices.

Wearing her authoritative Chinaface look, Yates then assumed the persona of an expert in Chinese taste and fashions and engaged in a "dear small talk" with the female audience. She told them that Chinese beauties all have broad foreheads, pig eyes, and crippled feet in tiny shoes, leading "strange" and "formal" lives. Yates also mimicked the Chinese writing style, which she predicted the audience would never comprehend: "From top to bottom in one straight line." With these pieces of information from du Halde, which are comically reworded and enacted for the audience's benefit,[125] Yates depicted a trivialized, idiosyncratic, and exoticized China that was the complete opposite of the war-torn country of "eastern virtues and patriotic passions," with "[s]o many heroes,—and no one in love," in the high tragedy that was just performed. Yates's "small talk" presumably was delivered in a light-hearted, joking manner intended to offset the impassioned tragedy. In doing so, nevertheless, the particularity or novelty of China, that is, the Chinaface quality, extended from dress to human features, aesthetic values, lifestyles, and mannerisms. Yates's dress and talk may exemplify what Pavis describes as the resort to foreign sensuality in works of intercultural performance (see Chapter One). In this case, the sensuality operates on her Chinese look, her costume and make-up style. The sensuality is desexualized, as no heroes in the play are in love, and both Mandane, the role Yates played, and the Chinese beauties she described lead "formal" lives as obedient wives.

While Chinese beauties may know nothing about British vices such as cards or routs, Yates told her female audience, there is one mode of female behavior in which "both climes [China and Britain] agree." Yates's ultimate secret as a China expert was "The creatures love to cheat as well as we." Strange as the Chinese ladies may be, they share some common humanity

Figure 2.6 Du Halde, Habit of a Lady of China in 1700. Dame Chinoise, from *A Collection of the Dresses* (1736). Art & Architecture Collection, Miriam and Ira D. Wallach Division of Art, Prints and Photographs, The New York Public Library, Astor, Lenox and Tilden Foundations.

with the British women; China, in other words, was humanized, while at the same time Britain was satirized.[126] In all, China in Murphy's *Orphan* may exhibit "undistingu'd loyalty," as Whitehead put it, but it was Murphy's intention to dramatize that patriotic zeal and use it to differentiate between Voltaire's and his depictions of the same subject and between French and British practices of monarchy. The play may depict China as femininely virtuous, which, at worst, was perceived by Goldsmith as an overly sentimental dramatization of what he called the "luxury of woe," but Murphy's goal was to replace Voltaire's romantic love with various kinds of human passions. Lastly, China may be presented as trivial, exotic, and attractive, as depicted in the epilogue that Yates delivered in her Chinaface look, but Britain is shown to have its own peculiar faults, some of which may be identical to those of its Chinese other, and the British are mocked as complicit in desiring China's material goods and appreciating the latest

Figure 2.7 A Chinese lady, in "The various Habits of the Chinese and Tartars," from du Halde, *The General History of China* (1741). General Research Division, The New York Public Library, Astor, Lenox and Tilden Foundations.

Chinese fashion. Through the subject of China, Britain's distinct style of dramatic literature, political practices, moral concerns, and material interests are revealed, and even satirized.

After describing the prevalent Chinese taste as whimsical and predicting that it would be short-lived, the reader of *World* facetiously recommended that large public buildings be executed after the Chinese models and a Chinese town be built as a tourist attraction.[127] Contrary to the reader's prediction, Britain's interest in China's material goods was not a passing trend; it accelerated at an exponential speed. Chinese buildings and bridges were commissioned by the royalty and built in public parks; a discernible "second vogue for chinoiserie" occurred in Britain in the early nineteenth century.

To accommodate the ever growing China trade, in the late eighteenth century, the British government decided to send its first official embassy to China to negotiate better trade relations than those the East India Company had achieved. Instead of obtaining information through the Jesuit missions and disseminated by France/Paris, Britain would now generate its own first-hand accounts about China. The next chapter examines writings by John Francis Davis and London theatre productions such as

The Chinese Sorcerer that arose out of this strong commercial context in the early nineteenth century. Unlike the actress Yates who playfully pretended to be a China expert, Davis could claim to be, and was regarded as, a true expert who wrote about China and the Chinese theatre he personally experienced in the country. *Chinese Sorcerer* was a visual spectacle that allowed the audience to experience China in imitation of the official embassies. Not unlike Yates's epilogue, the spectacular also satirized Britain's own material greed.

NOTES

1. H.S., "To Mr. Fitz-Adam," *The World* 12 (March 22, 1753): 69.
2. According to Charles H. Gray, the contributors to *The World* include Edward Moore (i.e., editor Adam Fitz-Adam), the Earl of Chesterfield, the Earl of Cork, Richard Owen Cambridge, and other writers. The identity of H.S. is to be identified. See Charles H. Gray, *Theatrical Criticism in London to 1795* (New York: B. Blom, 1964), 116.
3. Dawn Jacobson, chaps. 5 and 6 in *Chinoiserie* (London: Phaidon Press Limited, 1993); Hugh Honour, chaps. 5 and 6 in *Chinoiserie: The Vision of Cathay* (London: J. Murray, 1973).
4. Honour, 125.
5. Honour, 132; Jacobson, 125–126.
6. See Honour; Jacobson; Oliver Impey, *Chinoiserie: The Impact of Oriental Styles on Western Art and Decoration* (New York: Charles Scribner's Sons, 1977); Madeleine Jarry, *Chinoiserie: Chinese Influence on European Decorative Art; 17th and 18th Centuries* (New York: Vendome Press, 1981).
7. Philip Lawson, chap. 4 in *The East India Company: A History* (London: Longman, 1993).
8. Chi-ming Yang argues that China's impact on eighteenth-century British society needs to be accessed by its linguistic double register of China/china that yokes together, among other things, empire and commodity. See Yang, *Performing China: Virtue, Commerce, and Orientalism in Eighteenth-Century England, 1660–1760* (Baltimore: The Johns Hopkins University Press, 2011), 3–4 (hereafter cited as *Performing China*).
9. Yang, *Performing China*, 37.
10. As Deryck Lynham calls him in the title of his book, *The Chevalier Noverre: Father of Modern Ballet, a Biography* (London: Sylvan Press and British Book Centre, 1950). Lynham's work is the most-cited biography of Noverre. For other references, see Charles Edwin Noverre, *The Life and Works of the Chevalier Noverre* (London: Jarrold and Sons, 1882); Lincoln Kirstein, chap. 11 in *The Book of the Dance: A Short History of Classic Theatrical Dancing* (Garden City, NY: Garden City, 1942); Marian Hannah Winter, chap. 6 in *The Pre-Romantic Ballet* (Brooklyn, NY: Dance Horizons, 1975); Spire Pitou, *The Paris Opéra: An Encyclopedia of Operas, Ballets, Composers, and Performers* (Westport, CT: Greenwood Press, 1983–), 2:390–391; Ivor Forbes Guest, bk. 2 in *The Ballet of the Enlightenment: The Establishment of the ballet d'action in France, 1770–1793* (London: Dance Books, 1996).

11. There is a huge body of scholarship on Garrick. Garrick's entry in *A Biographical Dictionary of Actors, Actresses, Musicians, Dancers, Managers & Other Stage Personnel in London, 1660–1800*, eds. Philip H. Highfill, Jr., Kalman A. Burnim, and Edward A. Langhans (Carbondale: Southern Illinois University Press, 1973–1993) gives a comprehensive account of his life and work. For an introduction to the study of Garrick, see Leigh Woods, "Bibliographical Essay," in *Garrick Claims the Stage* (Westport, CT: Greenwood Press, 1984), 159–170.

12. For a short biographical account of Murphy, see Richard B. Schwartz, "Murphy, Arthur (1727–1805)," in *Oxford Dictionary of National Biography* (Oxford University Press, 2004–), doi:10.1093/ref:odnb/19569. Book-length biographies include: Robert D. Spector, *Arthur Murphy* (Boston: Twayne Publishers, 1979); John P. Emery, *Arthur Murphy, an Eminent English Dramatist of the Eighteenth Century* (Philadelphia: University of Pennsylvania Press, 1946); Howard H. Dunbar, *The Dramatic Career of Arthur Murphy* (New York: The Modern Language Association of America and Oxford University Press, 1946); Jessé Foot, *The Life of Arthur Murphy, esq.* (London: J. Faulder, 1811).

13. "Drury-Lane," *Public Advertiser*, November 8, 1755.

14. "Ce Ballet fut vu de tout Paris." Jean Monnet, *Mémoire de Jean Monnet, directeur du Théâtre de la foire*, ed. Henri d'Alméras (Paris: L. Michaud, 1909), 176.

15. See the entry of Charles Collé in Pitou.

16. "... tout Paris a couru à un ballet chinois ... " Charles Collé, *Journal et mémoires de Charles Collé sur les hommes de lettres, les ouvrages dramatiques et les événements les plus mémorables du régne de Louis XV, 1748–1772* (1868; reprint, Genéve: Slatkine Reprints, 1967), 1:428.

17. Monnet, 176: "Le premier (*Les Fêtes chinoises*), Ballet national, étonna par sa singularité, et sa magnificence attira le plus grand concours." Collé, 1:428: "... mais j'avoue que ce ballet chinoise est singulier, et qu'au moins par sa nouveauté et le pittoresque dont il est il a mérité une partie des applaudissements outrés qu'on lui a donnés." Collé's comments are translated by Lynham, see Lynham, 20–21.

18. Noverre's letters to Garrick are preserved in David Garrick, *The Private Correspondence of David Garrick: With Most Celebrated Persons of His Time*, ed. James Boaden (London: H. Colburn and R. Bentley, 1831–32), 2:379–391. Lynham has translated almost all the letters of Noverre to Garrick, see Lynham, chap. 2.

19. Thomas Davies, *Memoirs of the Life of David Garrick, esq., Interspersed with Characters and Anecdotes of His Theatrical Contemporaries. The Whole Forming a History of the Stage, Which Includes a Period of Thirty-Six Years* (London: The author, 1780); Arthur Murphy, *The Life of David Garrick, esq.* (London: J. Wright, 1801).

20. Davies, 1:177–179; Murphy, 1:276–277.

21. "... des *métamorphoses Chinoises*, ... et d'un nombre considérable, peut-être trop grand de ballets comiques presque dénués d'intrigues, destinés uniquement à l'amusement des yeux, et dont tout le mérite consiste dans la nouveauté des formes, dans la variété et dans le brillant des figures." Jean Georges Noverre, "Lettre 14," in *Lettres sur la danse, sur les ballets et les arts* (St. Petersbourg: J. C. Schnoor, 1803–04), 199 (hereafter cited as *Lettres*). I use the 1803–04 edition used by Cyril W. Beaumont and consulted his translation. See Jean George Noverre, *Letters on Dancing and Ballets*, trans. Cyril W. Beaumont (Brooklyn, NY: Dance Horizons, 1966). *Les métaporphoses chinoises*, according to Lynham, is another name for *Les Fêtes chinoises*, Lynham, 165.

22. See *Les spectacles de Paris, ou, suite du calendrier historique et chronologique des théâtres* (Paris: Duchesne, 1755), 138–139 (hereafter cited as *Spectacles de Paris*); Jean-Augustin-Julien Desboulmiers, *Histoire du théâtre de l'opéra comique* (Paris: Lacome, 1769), 2:323–324. These two accounts are almost identical except for a few inconsistencies in spelling and wording. It is very likely that Desboulmiers copied the description from *Spectacles de Paris*. Two English translations are often cited: the account in *Spectacles de Paris* is translated by Frank A. Hedgcock, *A Cosmopolitan Actor: David Garrick and His French Friends* (New York: B. Blom, 1969), 128; Desboulmiers's account is translated by Lynham, 21. I consulted both for my own translation.
23. "... trente-deux vases qui s'élevent, dérobent aux spectateurs les trente-deux Chinois qu'on voyoit auparavant." *Spectacles de Paris*, 139.
24. The origin of the vase trick, whether French or English, is yet to be determined. In *The Commedia dell'arte in Paris, 1644–1697* (Charlottesville: University Press of Virginia, 1990), for example, Virginia Scott describes various stage tricks created by machinery in the late seventeenth century Paris, yet none of them featured a sudden appearance of vases.
25. "... le Ballet commence, & ne laisse rien à désirer, soit pour la variété, soit pour la netteté des figures." *Spectacles de Paris*, 139.
26. "... les mouvemens forment une prodigieuse quantité de figures nouvelles & parfaitement dessinées, qui s'enchainent & se dégagent avec la plus grande facilité." Ibid.
27. "Les décorations étaient toutes de l'invention et du dessin de feu M. *Boucher*, premier Peintre du Roi." Monnet, 176.
28. For a discussion of the life and works of Boucher, see, for example, Georges Brunel, *Boucher* (London: Trefoil Books, 1986); New York Metropolitan Museum of Art, *François Boucher 1703–1770* (New York: Metropolitan Museum of Art, 1986).
29. For a discussion of the Beauvais manufactory and the Chinese tapestry, see Jarry, 15–32.
30. Lynham and Winter have drawn special attention to the relation of these two drawings to *Les Fêtes chinoises*. See Lynham, 21–22; Winter, 113.
31. Brunel, 166; Alastair Laing, "Catalog of Paintings," in *François Boucher 1703–1770* (New York: New York Metropolitan Museum of Art, 1986), 202.
32. Brunel, 166–169; Laing, 206–207; Jacobson, 70–75; Honour, 92–94.
33. Montanus's *Gedenkwaerdige Gesantschappen* is an illustrated account of the Dutch East India Company's embassy to Japan in the late seventeenth century and has been translated into several European languages. The illustration is faithfully reproduced in the French edition of the Dutch original. See Arnoldus Montanus, *Gedenkwaerdige Gesantschappen der Oost-Indische Maatschappy in 't Vereenigde Nederland, aan de Kaisaren van Japan* (Amsterdam: Jacob Meurs, 1669), 168; Arnoldus Montanus, *Ambassades mémorables de la Compagnie des Indes Orientales des Provinces Unies, vers les empereurs du Japon* (Amsterdam: Jacob de Meurs, 1680), 145.
34. See the entry of *chinoiserie* in *Encyclopaedia Britannica Online*, http://www.britannica.com/EBchecked/topic/113025/chinoiserie; Honour; Jacobson; Impey; Jarry.
35. In terms of setting, composition, and inspiration from Boucher, Noverre's *Les Fêtes chinoises* shares some similarities with and is possibly to have been composed under the influence of *L'Opérateur chinois* (The Chinese

Quack Doctor), a ballet-pantomime premiered in 1748. See Jean Baptiste François Deshayes, "L'Opérateur chinois," in *Divertissemens du Théatre des petits appartemens pendant l'hiver de 1748 à 1749, 1.[-2.] partie* (Versailles, 1748–1749). Deshayes is also spelled as Dehesse or De Hesse. The English translation of the title is taken from Winter's interpretation, see Winter, 89–90, 101, 103. It is unclear when Noverre completed his composition of *Les Fêtes chinoises*. *Spectacles du Paris* notes that *Les Fêtes chinoises* was performed in Lyon, Marseilles, and Strasbourg before its 1754 Paris premiere (138). C. E. Noverre states that it was composed in 1749 when Noverre was in Paris (9). According to Lynham, Noverre was in either Marseilles or Lyon before 1750, and he was in Lyon between 1750 and 1752 (18–19). C. E. Noverre's statement therefore might be false. Lynham only gives a very inconclusive suggestion that *Les Fêtes chinoises* was first performed in 1751 or earlier (165).

36. Garrick, 2:379–391; Lynham, chap. 2; Hedgcock, pt. 2, chap. 4.
37. Noverre, "Avant-propos," in *Lettres*, III.
38. "Le Sieur Boquet veut s'engager à aller à Londres pour y faire exécuter ses quatre décorations; et faire faire sous ses yeux tous les habits nécessaires à mes ballets; faire arranger vôtre théâtre dans le genre le plus moderne; et faire peindre vos loges; éclairer vôtre théâtre sans lustre, et le rendre, enfin, celui le plus agréable de Londres; ... " Garrick, 2:389.
39. Sybil M. Rosenfeld, *Georgian Scene Painters and Scene Painting* (Cambridge: Cambridge University Press, 1981), 74.
40. Garrick stopped using chandeliers in the 1765–66 season, ten years after the production of *The Chinese Festival*. Scholars agree that Garrick, after his tour abroad, was following the French practice in abolishing chandeliers, see Gösta M. Bergman, *Lighting in the Theatre* (Stockholm: Almqvist and Wiksell International, and Rowman and Littlefield, 1977), 214–219; Colin Visser, "Scenery and Technical Design," in *The London Theatre World, 1660–1800*, ed. Robert D. Hume (Carbondale: Southern Illinois University Press, 1980), 112; Rosenfeld, 60. Although it seems unlikely, Boquet's proposal might have influenced Garrick long before his trip.
41. Vincent Troubridge, "Theatre Riots in London," in *Studies in English Theatre History in Memory of Gabrielle Enthover, O.B.E., First President of the Society for Theatre Research, 1948–1950* (London: Society for Theatre Research, 1952), 90-92. Many of Garrick's biographers describe details of the riot, for example, Hedgcock; Ian McIntyre, *Garrick* (London: Allen Lane and the Penguin Press, 1999); Carola Oman, *David Garrick* (London: Hodder and Stoughton, 1958); George W. Stone, Jr. and George M. Kahrl, *David Garrick: A Critical Biography* (Carbondale: Southern Illinois University Press, 1979).
42. See the note in the beginning of the 1755–56 season in the Cross-Hopkins Diary, a collection of thirteen diaries kept by the prompters of the Drury Lane Theatre now preserved at the Folger Shakespeare Library, cataloged under "London. Drury Lane Theatre. List of plays performed, 1747–1760, 1762–1764, and 1768–1776."
43. Cross-Hopkins Diary, November 6, 1755.
44. Davies, 1:178.
45. "Les décorations étoient superbes & les habits magnifiques... . Le Palanquin & les Chariots étoient très-riches. Toutes les aîles étoient garnies de balcons remplis de Chinois & de Chinoises, spectateurs de la Fête." "Lettre e'crite [écrite] de Londres," *Journal étranger* 2 (1755): 224. Rosenfeld interprets the last sentence as "figures painted on the wings," Rosenfeld, 74.

46. Davies also says that "nothing might be wanting to render this entertainment as perfect as possible," 1:178. The anonymous author of "Lettre e'crite [écrite] de Londres" states that "[l]e célèbre *Garrick*, Directeur du Théâtre, n'avoit rien épargné de ce qui étoit nécessaire pour contribuer à la réussite du sieur *Noverre.*" *Journal étranger* 2 (1755): 224.

47. Murphy, *Life of David Garrick*, 1:278.

48. Cross-Hopkins Diary, November 6, 1755.

49. *Public Advertiser*, November 8, 1755, 1. See also the announcement in the *Daily Advertiser* (November 8, 1755, 1), with very slight wording and punctuation differences.

50. Cross-Hopkins Diary, November 8 to 18, 1755; "Lettre e'crit [écrite] de Londres"; Davies, 1:179–183; *Daily Advertiser*, November 20, 1755.

51. Harry William Pedicord, *The Theatrical Public in the Time of Garrick* (New York: King's Crown Press, 1954), 53–54. In addition to the two reasons suggests by Pedicord, Hsin-yun Ou offers fierce competition among the London theatre houses as another reason. See, Hsin-yun Ou, *"The Chinese Festival* and the Eighteenth-Century London Audience," *Wenshan Review of Literature and Culture* 2, no. 1 (2008): 32.

52. *The Dancers Damn'd; or, the Devil to Pay at the Old House* (London: R. Griffiths, 1755), 10.

53. Pedicord, 53–54.

54. Davies, 1:181.

55. Murphy, *Life of David Garrick*, 1:279.

56. Cross-Hopkins Diary, November 17, 1755.

57. Lynham, 39–49.

58. Noverre, "Letter 9," in *Lettres*, 104–108.

59. For further discussion on *ballet d'action*, see, for example, Guest.

60. Southern Illinois University Press, *The London Stage 1660–1800: A Calendar of Plays, Entertainments & Afterpieces, Together with Casts, Box-receipts and Contemporary Comment*, pt. 4, 1747–1776 (Carbondale: Southern Illinois University Press, 1962), 502, 509 (hereafter cited as *London Stage*); *Public Advertiser*, November 18, 1755; Emery, 27.

61. Dunbar, 51–52; Foot, 15, 143.

62. John Brownsmith, *The Dramatic Time-Piece* ... (London: J. Almon, T. Davies and J. Hingston, 1767), 29.

63. Between 1756 and 1759, Murphy and Garrick went through a difficult and wrangling negotiation about staging *Orphan*. For the different perspectives about their dispute, see, for example, Davies, 1:217–222; Murphy, *The Life of David Garrick*, 1:330–341; Foot, 143–155; Garrick, 1:71–73, 81–82, 87–92, 96–99; Dunbar, 51–64.

64. Cross-Hopkins Diary, April 21, 1759.

65. *Public Advertiser*, April 21, 1759. Four years after its fiasco, the undestroyed costumes and scenery of *Chinese Festival* were reported to have been put in use for the play. See Tate Wilkinson, "Original Anecdotes Respecting the Stage, and the Actors of the Old School, with Remarks on Mr. Murphy's 'Life of Garrick,'" *Monthly Mirror* 13 (January 1802): 48; Foot, 151.

66. See the daily entries in *London Stage*, pt. 4., vols. 2 and 3.

67. In his dedication to John, Earl of Bute, Murphy gave the date as April 30, 1759. The script was very likely published in May 1759. See Arthur Murphy, dedication

to *The Orphan of China, a Tragedy, as It Is Perform'd at the Theatre-Royal, in Drury-Lane*, 1st ed. (London: P. Vaillant, 1759), v. Hereafter all the references to page numbers from the play script, which include dedication, prologue, epilogue, text of the play and Murphy's letter to Voltaire, are cited from this edition.

68. Marvin Carlson, *Voltaire and the Theatre of the Eighteenth Century* (Westport, CT: Greenwood Press, 1998), 25–26.

69. Murphy, *Gray's-Inn Journal* (London: P. Vaillant, 1756), vol. 1, no. 41; vol. 2, no. 61.

70. Carlson, 98.

71. In 1756, the year when Murphy started to draft the play, Voltaire's *L'Orphelin de la Chine* was published in its French original in London, as well as three editions of the same anonymous English translation of the play, two in London, and one in Dublin.

72. See, for example, Hsin-yun Ou, "Gender, Consumption, and Ideological Ambiguity in David Garrick's Production of *The Orphan of China* (1759)," *Theatre Journal* 60, no. 3 (2008): 385–386; Yang, *Performing China*, 148–152.

73. Voltaire, *L'Orphelin de la Chine, Tragédie* (Paris: Michele Lambert, 1755). Hereafter all the references to acts, scenes, and page numbers of the play, including dedication, are cited from this edition. For its English translation, I have mainly consulted the first edition of the anonymous 1756 London publication, *The Orphan of China. A Tragedy. Translated from the French of M. de Votaire*, 1st ed. (London: R. Baldwin, 1756), to assist my reading and analysis.

74. George W. Stone, Jr., *The London Stage, 1747–1776: A Critical Introduction* (Carbondale: Southern Illinois University Press, 1968), xx–xxiii.

75. Murphy, dedication to John, Earl of Bute, *The Orphan of China*, iii–iv.

76. "De nos Peuples jaloux tu [Asséli, Idamé's confidante] connais la fierté, / De nos Arts, nos Loix l'auguste antiquité, / Une Religion de tout temps épurée, / De cent siècles de gloire une suite avérée / Tout nous interdisait nos preventions / Une indigne alliance avec les Nations."

77. It is interesting to note that before Idamé identifies the paternal right as one of the foundations of the Chinese empire, she describes the power ("pouvoir") of Chinese parents (paren[t]s) who serve as the living images of God and deserve their children's respect and obedience. This may have influenced the 1756 English translator's decision to translate "le droit paternel" as parental right, not paternal right. See *Orphan of China. A Tragedy. Translated from the French of M. de Votaire*, 44.

78. "D'adoucir ce lion dans mes fers arrêté, / De plier à nos moeurs cette grandeur sauvage, / D'instruire à nos vertus son féroce courage, / Et de le render enfin, graces à ces liens, / Digne un jour d'être admis parmi nos citoyens."

79. "Soyez ici des Loix l'interprête suprême; / Rendez leur Ministère aussi saint que vous-même."

80. See the similar passages in Voltaire, III.iii.; 34; V.v.; 62–63.

81. My reading of Mandane differs from Ou, who argues that Murphy's rewriting of Voltaire "succeeded in rendering Mandane as a more sympathetic, self-determinate heroine." See Ou, "David Garrick's Production of *The Orphan of China*": 383–384.

82. See comparable passages in, for example, Voltaire, I.ii.; 6; Murphy, I; 4–5.

83. Yang, *Performing China*, 153.

84. Samuel Foote, *A Treatise on the Passions, So Far As They Regard the Stage* ... (1747; reprint, New York: B. Blom, 1971), 10. For a general study of the passions in acting, see Joseph R. Roach, *The Player's Passion: Studies in the Science of Acting* (1985; reprint, Ann Arbor: University of Michigan Press, 1993).

85. Aaron Hill, *The Art of Acting*, in *The Works of the Late Aaron Hill, esq.* ... (London: Printed for the benefit of the family, 1753), 4:337–397.

86. Murphy, *Gray's-Inn Journal* (London: P. Vaillant, 1756), vol. 1, no. 41, 230. A similar statement appeared in vol. 2, no. 94, 241.

87. Ibid., vol. 2, no. 59, 36.

88. Chi-ming Yang suggests that in Murphy "the Chinese passion for principles," i.e., virtue, takes the place of romantic love in Voltaire. See Chi-ming Yang, "Virtue's Vogues: Eastern Authenticity and the Commodification of Chinese-ness on the 18th-Century Stage," *Comparative Literature Studies* 39, no. 4 (2002): 334.

89. Yang, *Performing China*, 152.

90. Ibid., 154.

91. William Woty [J. Copywell, pseud.], "To the Author of The Orphan of China," in *The Shrubs of Parnassus* (London: Printed for the author, sold by J. Newbery, 1760), 56–57.

92. Murphy, *The Orphan of China*, 89–90; Voltaire, iv–v[i]. Murphy called the play *The Orphan of the House of Chau*, and Voltaire *L'Orphelin de Tchao*.

93. For the different editions and translations of du Halde's *Description*, see Henri Cordier, *Bibliotheca Sinica: dictionnaire bibliographique des ouvrages relatifs à l'empire chinois* (Staten Island, NY: Maurizio Martino, 1996), 1:45–54.

94. See Jean-Baptiste du Halde, "Avertissement," *Tchao Chi Cou Ell (Zhao Shi Gu Er)*, in *Description géographique, historique, chronologique, politique, et physique de l'empire de la Chine et de la Tartarie chinoise* ... (La Haye: Henri Scheurleer, 1736), 3:419–421. Identified as "le P. [Père] de Prémare" in "Avertissement," de Prémare's full name is given in du Halde, 1:lx.

95. See, for example, Shouyi Chen, "The Chinese Orphan: A Yuan Play; Its Influence on European Drama of the Eighteenth Century," in *The Vision of China in the English Literature of the Seventeenth and Eighteenth Centuries*, ed. Adrian Hsia (Hong Kong: Chinese University Press, 1998), 359–382; Liu Wu-Chi, "The Original Orphan of China," *Comparative Literature* 5, no. 3 (1953): 193–212; Adrian Hsia, "The Transplanted Chinese Orphan in England, France, Germany, Italy and His Repatriation to Hong Kong," in *Chinesia: The European Construction of China in the Literature of the Seventeenth and Eighteenth Centuries* (Tübingen: Max Niemeyer Verlag, 1998), 75–98. *Zhao Shi Gu Er* has continued to draw attention and inspiration; the most recent example is James Fenton's adaptation, called *The Orphan of Zhao*, presented by the Royal Shakespeare Company in 2012–2013.

96. Ji Junxiang, *Zhao Shi Gu Er Da Bao Chou Za Ju* [Drama of the Revenge of the Orphan of the House of Zhao], vol. 9, bk. 2, of *Yuan Qu Xuan* [Selection of Dramas from the Yuan Dynasty], ed. Zang Maoxun (Shanghai: Zhonghua Shu Ju, 1936).

97. In fact, in the Chinese original Cheng's struggle and pain in witnessing his son being slain are vividly expressed in the arias which, unfortunately, were not translated. In the translation, his relinquishment of his own child consequently appears tame.

98. In Voltaire, Zamti describes the scene to Idamé (I.ii).
99. In 1741, eighteen years before Murphy wrote his play, the English play-wright William Hatchett had also invented a mother figure in his adaptation of *Zhao Shi Gu Er*. See William Hatchett, *The Chinese Orphan: An Historical Tragedy* (London: Charles Corbett, 1741), Act III, Scene i. Hatchett was a minor playwright and his *The Chinese Orphan*, though published, was not produced. His play resembles the original Chinese play more than the works of Voltaire and Murphy do and appears to have had no impact on either Voltaire or Murphy. For discussions of this work, see, for example, Chen and Hsia.
100. While Genghis Khan established a Mongolian empire in 1206, it was his descendant Kublai Khan who named the empire Yuan in 1271, the year when the Yuan Dynasty officially began. For Chinese accounts on the rise of Genghis Khan and his Mongol empire, see, for example, Shouyi Bai, ed., *Zhongguo Tong Shi* [General History of China], vol. 13 (Shanghai: Shanghai Ren Min Chu Ban She, 2004), 345–363. Genghis Khan (成吉思汗, "ferocious king") is his Mongol title; his personal name in Chinese is Tiemuzhen (鐵木真).
101. "Voilà un grand exemple de la supériorité naturelle que donnent la raison et le génie sur la force aveugle et barbare." According to Chinese accounts, during their earlier years of ruling China, the Mongol rulers abolished many of the established Chinese political, social, and cultural practices ("customs"). Notably, they suppressed the scholar-elite class, which turned to playwriting as a way to express its despair and frustration about the new regime. See, for example, Bai, 434–439; William Dolby, "Yuan Drama," in *Chinese Theater: From Its Origins to the Present Day*, edited by Colin Mackerras (Honolulu: University of Hawaii Press), 34–35.
102. "gouverneé par les plus anciennes Loix de monde."
103. Du Halde, 1:460–461.
104. See, for example, Arnold H. Rowbotham, "Voltaire, Sinophile," *Publications of the Modern Language Association of America* 47, no. 4 (1932): 1050–1065.
105. Murphy attended the English College at St. Omer, near Boulogne-sur-Mer, France, run by the Jesuits. See, for example, Foot, 8–9; Emery, 1–4.
106. Arnold H. Rowbotham, "The Impact of Confucianism on Seventeenth Century Europe," *The Far Eastern Quarterly* 4, no. 3 (1945): 224–225. For further discussion on Confucianism and deism, see, for example, Walter W. Davis, "China, the Confucian Ideal, and the European Age of Enlightenment," *Journal of the History of Ideas* 44, no. 4 (1983): 523–548.
107. Rowbotham, "Voltaire, Sinophile," 1056–1060.
108. See, for example, Voltaire, I.vi.; 11–12; Murphy, *Orphan of China*, I.; 7, II.; 15, IV.; 65.
109. This term and others provoked the so-called Chinese Rites Controversy before and during Voltaire's time. For a modern collection of essays on the controversy, see, for example, David E. Mungello, ed., *The Chinese Rites Controversy: Its History and Meaning* (Nettetal: Steyler Verlag, 1994). For a contemporary example of Xamti being discussed as one of the competing terms to render the name of God, see, for example, Michel Villermaules, ed., *Anecdotes sur l'etat de la religion dans la Chine*, vol. 1 (Paris: Aux depens de la Societé, 1733), 246–251.

110. According to modern scholarship, the play was written in the thirteenth century. See, for example, Liu, 193–194.
111. For a brief account about Oliver Goldsmith, see, for example, John A. Dussinger, "Goldsmith, Oliver (1728?–1774)," in *Oxford Dictionary of National Biography* (Oxford University Press, 2004–), doi:10.1093/ref:odnb/10924.
112. Goldsmith, "Art IX. *The Orphan of China*. A Tragedy," *The Critical Review; or, Annals of Literature* 7 (1759): 435. The review appeared anonymously, and Goldsmith's authorship was confirmed in the late eighteenth century; see *Collected Works*, ed. Arthur Friedman (Oxford: Clarendon Press, 1966), 1:145–146. The review is reproduced and annotated in Friedman, 170–179; the following references to page numbers of the review are cited from *Critical Review*.
113. Spector interprets the glowing imagery as referring to Murphy's talents in writing the poetic speeches, see Spector, 138.
114. Murphy, *Life of David Garrick*, 1:338–339.
115. Murphy, *Orphan of China*, 96.
116. *An Account of the New Tragedy of "The Orphan of China"* ... (London: J. Coote, 1759), 11–12.
117. Yang argues that Murphy's *Orphan* visualizes two forms of luxury that are crucial to the discussion of virtue in the mid-eighteenth century: commercial consumption and an excess of sentiment. See Yang, *Performing China*, 149.
118. Goldsmith, 435; the entry of *The Orphan of China* in David E. Baker, *The Companion to the Play-House* ... , vol 1 (London: T. Becket and P. A. Dehondt, etc., 1764); *A Letter From Mons. De Voltaire to the Author of the Orphan of China* (London: I. Pottinger, 1759). The pamphlet was published soon after Murphy published the text of his play in 1759. *Monthly Review* described the pamphlet as written by "some envious and malicious Grubean of *our* country (and not M. de Voltaire, whose name he has the modesty to assume)." "Art. 16. *A Letter from M. de Voltaire, to the Author of the Orphan of China*," *Monthly Review* (June 1759): 566.
119. Dunbar, 75.
120. Spector, 134, 136–137, 138.
121. Roger Pickering, *Reflections upon Theatrical Expression in Tragedy. With a Proper Introduction, and Appendix* (London: W. Johnston, 1755), 74, 75.
122. Thomas Wilkes, *A General View of the Stage* (London: J. Coote and W. Whetstone, 1759), 144. Two volumes of *A Collection of the Dresses* were published in 1757, with another two in 1772. See *A Collection of the Dresses of Different Nations, Antient* [sic] *and Modern* ... (London: Thomas Jefferys, 1757–72).
123. *A Collection of the Dresses*, 1:27, 29.
124. Ou suggests that Yates's posture in the painting shows "her ability to use majestic gestures in the expression of deep passions" to play the character Mandane. See Ou, "David Garrick's Production of *The Orphan of China*": 394.
125. See Jean-Baptiste du Halde, *The General History of China* (London: John Watts, 1736), 2:137–140, 434.
126. Yang provides an interesting reading of the epilogue in relation to the contagious effects of consuming fashion. See Yang, *Performing China*, 173–178.
127. H.S., "To Mr. Fitz-Adam," 70–71.

REFERENCES

Anonymous. *An Account of the New Tragedy of the Orphan of China, and Its Representation: Interspersed With Remarks on the Orphelin de la Chine, by Voltaire. To Which Are Subjoined, by Way of Illustration, the Fundamental Laws of China.* London: J. Coote, 1759.

———. "Art. 16. A Letter From M. De Voltaire, to the Author of the Orphan of China." *Monthly Review* (1759): 566.

———."*chinoiserie.*" *Encyclopaedia Britannica.* http://www.britannica.com/EBchecked/topic/113025/chinoiserie.

———. *A Collection of the Dresses of Different Nations, Antient [sic] and Modern. Particularly Old English Dresses; After the Designs of Holbein, Vandyke, Hollar, and Others, With an Account of the Authorities, From Which the Figures Are Taken, and Some Short Historical Remarks on the Subject. To Which Are Added the Habits of the Principal Characters on the English Stage.* 4 vols. London: Thomas Jefferys, 1757–72.

———. *The Dancers Damn'd; or, the Devil to Pay at the Old House.* London: R. Griffiths, 1755.

———. *A Letter From Mons. De Voltaire to the Author of the Orphan of China.* London: I. Pottinger, 1759.

———. "Lettre e'crite [écrite] de Londres." *Journal étranger* 2 (1755).

———.*Les spectacles de Paris, ou, suite du calendrier historique et chronologique des théâtres.* Paris: Duchesne, 1755.

Bai, Shouyi, ed. *Zhongguo Tong Shi* [General History of China]. Vol. 13. Shanghai: Shanghai Ren Min Chu Ban She, 2004.

Baker, David E. *The Companion to the Play-House; or, An Historical Account of All the Dramatic Writers (and Their Works) That Have Appeared in Great Britain and Ireland, From the Commencement of Our Theatrical Exhibitions, Down to the Present Year 1764. Composed in the Form of a Dictionary, for the More Readily Turning to Any Particular Author, or Performance.* 2 vols. London: T. Becket and P. A. Dehondt; C. Henderson, and T. Davies, 1764.

Bergman, Gösta M. *Lighting in the Theatre.* Stockholm: Almqvist and Wiksell International, and Rowman and Littlefield, 1977.

Brownsmith, John. *The Dramatic Time-Piece: or Perpetual Monitor: Being a Calculation of the Length of Time Every Act Takes in the Performing, in All the Acting Plays, at the Theatres Royal of Drury Lane, Covent-Garden, and Hay-Market ... As Also the Time of Night When Half-Price Will Be Taken, etc.* London: J. Almon, T. Davies and J. Hingston, 1767.

Brunel, Georges. *Boucher.* London: Trefoil Books, 1986.

Carlson, Marvin. *Voltaire and the Theatre of the Eighteenth Century.* Westport, CT: Greenwood Press, 1998.

Chen, Shouyi. "The Chinese Orphan: A Yuan Play; Its Influence on European Drama of the Eighteenth Century." In *The Vision of China in the English Literature of the Seventeenth and Eighteenth Centuries,* edited by Adrian Hsia, 359–382. Hong Kong: Chinese University Press, 1998.

Collé, Charles. *Journal et mémoires de Charles Collé sur les hommes de letters, les ouvrages dramatiques et les événements les plus mémorables du règne de Louis XV, 1748–1772.* 1868. Reprint, 3 vols., Genéve: Slatkine Reprints, 1967.

Cordier, Henri. *Bibliotheca Sinica: dictionnaire bibliographique des ouvrages relatifs à l'empire chinois.* 6 vols. Staten Island, NY: Maurizio Martino, 1996.

Cross-Hopkins Diary. Folger Shakespeare Library.
Daily Advertiser. November 8, 1755.
────. November 20, 1755.
Davies, Thomas. *Memoirs of the Life of David Garrick, esq., Interspersed With Characters and Anecdotes of His Theatrical Contemporaries. The Whole Forming a History of the State, Which Includes a Period of Thirty-Six Years.* 2 vols. London: The author, 1780.
Davis, Walter W. "China, the Confucian Ideal, and the European Age of Enlightenment." *Journal of the History of Ideas* 44, no. 4 (1983): 523–548.
Desboulmiers, Jean-Augustin-Julien. *Histoire du théâtre de l'opéra comique.* 2 vols. Paris: Lacombe, 1769.
Deshayes, Jean Baptiste François. "L'Opérateur chinois." In *Divertissemens du Théâtre des petits appartemens pendant l'hiver de 1748 à 1749, 1.[–2.] partie.* Versailles: 1748–1749.
Dolby, William. "Yuan Drama." In *Chinese Theater: From Its Origins to the Present Day,* edited by Colin Mackerras, 32–59. Honolulu: University of Hawaii Press.
Du Halde, Jean-Baptiste. *Description géographique, historique, chronologique, politique, et physique de l'empire de la Chine et de la Tartarie chinoise enrichie des cartes générales et particulieres de ces pays, de la carte générale et des cartes particulieres du Thibet, et de la Corée; et ornée d'un grand nombre de figures et de vignettes gravées en tailledouce.* 4 vols. La Haye: Henri Scheurleer, 1736.
────. *The General History of China. Containing a Geographical, Historical, Chronological, Political and Physical Description of the Empire of China, Chinese Tartary, Corea and Thibet.* 4 vols. London: John Watts, 1736.
Dunbar, Howard Hunter. *The Dramatic Career of Arthur Murphy.* New York: The Modern Language Association of America and Oxford University Press, 1946.
Dussinger, John A. "Goldsmith, Oliver (1728–?–1774)." In *Oxford Dictionary of National Biography.* Oxford University Press, 2004–. doi:10.1093/ref:odnb/10924.
Emery, John P. *Arthur Murphy, an Eminent English Dramatist of the Eighteenth Century.* Philadelphia: University of Pennsylvania Press, 1946.
Foot, Jessé. *The Life of Arthur Murphy, esq.* London: J. Faulder, 1811.
Foote, Samuel. *A Treatise on the Passions, So Far As They Regard the Stage With a Critical Enquiry into the Theatrical Merit of Mr. G—k, Mr. Q—n, and Mr. B—y. The First Considered in the Part of Lear, the Two Last Opposed in Othello.* 1747. Reprint, New York: B. Blom, 1971.
Garrick, David. *The Private Correspondence of David Garrick: With Most Celebrated Persons of His Time.* Edited by James Boaden. 2 vols. London: H. Colburn and R. Bentley, 1831–1832.
Goldsmith, Oliver. "Art IX. *The Orphan of China.* A Tragedy." *The Critical Review; or, Annals of Literature* 7 (1759): 434–440.
────. *Collected Works.* Edited by Arthur Friedman. 5 vols. Oxford: Clarendon Press, 1966.
Gray, Charles Harold. *Theatrical Criticism in London to 1795.* New York: B. Blom, 1964.
Guest, Ivor Forbes. *The Ballet of the Enlightenment: The Establishment of the ballet d'action in France, 1770–1793.* London: Dance Books, 1996.
H. S. "To Mr. Fitz-Adam," *The World* 12 (March 22, 1753): 67–72.

Hatchett, William. *The Chinese Orphan: An Historical Tragedy.* London: Charles Corbett, 1741.

Hedgcock, Frank A. *A Cosmopolitan Actor: David Garrick and His French Friends.* New York: B. Blom, 1969.

Highfill, Jr., Philip H, Kalman A. Burnim, and Edward A. Langhans, eds. *A Biographical Dictionary of Actors, Actresses, Musicians, Dancers, Managers & Other Stage Personnel in London, 1660–1800.* Carbondale: Southern Illinois University Press, 1973–93.

Hill, Aaron. *The Works of the Late Aaron Hill, esq.; in Four Volumes: Consisting of Letters on Various Subjects, and of Original Poems, Moral and Facetious. With an Essay on the Art of Acting.* 4 vols. London: Printed for the benefit of the family, 1753.

Honour, Hugh. *Chinoiserie: The Vision of Cathay.* London: J. Murray, 1973.

Hsia, Adrian. *Chinesia: The European Construction of China in the Literature of the Seventeenth and Eighteenth Centuries.* Tübingen: Max Niemeyer Verlag, 1998.

Impey, Oliver. *Chinoiserie: The Impact of Oriental Styles on Western Art and Decoration.* New York: Charles Scribner's Sons, 1977.

Jacobson, Dawn. *Chinoiserie.* London: Phaidon Press Limited, 1993.

Jarry, Madeleine. *Chinoiserie: Chinese Influence on European Decorative Art; 17th and 18th Centuries.* New York: Vendome Press, 1981.

Ji, Junxiang. *Zhao Shi Gu Er Da Bao Chou Za Ju* [Drama of the Revenge of the Orphan of the House of Zhao]. Vol. 9, bk. 5, of *Yuan Qu Xuan* [Selection of Dramas From the Yuan Dynasty], edited by Maoxun Zang. Shanghai: Zhonghua Shu Ju, 1936.

Kirstein, Lincoln. *The Book of the Dance: A Short History of Classic Theatrical Dancing.* Garden City, NY: Garden City, 1942.

Laing, Alastair. "Catalog of Paintings." In *François Boucher, 1703–1770*, 90–324. New York: Metropolitan Museum of Art, 1986.

Lawson, Philip. *The East India Company: A History.* London: Longman, 1993.

Liu, Wu-Chi. "The Original Orphan of China." *Comparative Literature* 5, no. 3 (1953): 193–212.

Lynham, Deryck. *The Chevalier Noverre: Father of Modern Ballet, a Biography.* London: Sylvan Press and British Book Centre, 1950.

McIntyre, Ian. *Garrick.* London: Allen Lane and the Penguin Press, 1999.

Montanus, Arnoldus. *Ambassades mémorables de la Compagnie des Indes Orientales des Provinces Unies, vers les empereurs du Japon.* Amsterdam: Jacob de Meurs, 1680.

———. *Gedenkwaerdige Gesantschappen der Oost-Indische Maatschappy in 't Vereenigde Nederland, aan de Kaisaren van Japan.* Amsterdam: Jacob Meurs, 1669.

Monnet, Jean. *Mémoires de Jean Monnet, directeur du Théâtre de la foire.* Edited by Henri d'Almeras. Paris: L. Michaud, 1909.

Mungello, David E., ed. *The Chinese Rites Controversy: Its History and Meaning.* Nettetal: Steyler Verlag, 1994.

Murphy, Arthur. *The Gray's-Inn Journal.* 2 vols. London: P. Vaillant, 1756.

———. *The Life of David Garrick, esq.* 2 vols. London: J. Wright, 1801.

———. *The Orphan of China, a Tragedy, As It Is Perform'd at the Theatre-Royal, in Drury-Lane.* 1st ed. London: P. Vaillant, 1759.

New York Metropolitan Museum of Art. [Boucher, François]. *François Boucher, 1703–1770.* New York: Metropolitan Museum of Art, 1986.

Noverre, Charles Edwin. *The Life and Works of the Chevalier Noverre.* London: Jarrold and Sons, 1882.

Noverre, Jean Georges. *Letters on Dancing and Ballets.* Translated by Cyril Beaumont. Brooklyn, NY: Dance Horizons, 1966.

———— *Lettres sur la danse, sur les ballets et les arts.* St. Petersbourg: J. C. Schnoor, 1803–1804.

Oman, Carola. *David Garrick.* London: Hodder and Stoughton, 1958.

Ou, Hsin-yun. "*The Chinese Festival* and the Eighteenth-Century London Audience." *Wenshan Review of Literature and Culture* 2, no. 1 (2008): 31—52.

————. "Gender, Consumption, and Ideological Ambiguity in David Garrick's Production of *The Orphan of China* (1759)." *Theatre Journal* 60, no. 3 (2008): 383–407.

Pedicord, Harry William. *The Theatrical Public in the Time of Garrick.* New York: King's Crown Press, 1954.

Pickering, Roger. *Reflections Upon Theatrical Expression in Tragedy. With a Proper Introduction, and Appendix.* London: W. Johnston, 1755.

Pitou, Spire. *The Paris Opéra: An Encyclopedia of Operas, Ballets, Composers, and Performers.* Westport, CT: Greenwood Press, 1983–.

Public Advertiser. November 8, 1755.

————. November 18, 1755.

————. April 21, 1759.

Roach, Joseph R. *The Player's Passion: Studies in the Science of Acting.* 1985. Reprint, Ann Arbor: University of Michigan Press, 1993.

Rosenfeld, Sybil M. *Georgian Scene Painters and Scene Painting.* Cambridge: Cambridge University Press, 1981.

Rowbotham, Arnold H. "The Impact of Confucianism on Seventeenth Century Europe." *The Far Eastern Quarterly* 4, no. 3 (1945): 224–242.

————. "Voltaire, Sinophile." *Publications of the Modern Language Association of America* 47, no. 4 (1932): 1050–1065.

Schwartz, Richard B. "Murphy, Arthur (1727–1805)." In *Oxford Dictionary of National Biography.* Oxford University Press, 2004–. doi:10.1093/ref:odnb/19569.

Scott, Virginia. *The Commedia dell'arte in Paris, 1644–1697.* Charlottesville: University Press of Virginia, 1990.

Southern Illinois University Press, *The London Stage, 1660–1800; A Calendar of Plays, Entertainments and Afterpieces, Together With Casts, Box-Receipts and Contemporary Comment.* Pt. 4, 1747–1776. Carbondale: Southern Illinois University Press, 1962.

Spector, Robert D. *Arthur Murphy.* Boston: Twayne Publishers, 1979.

Stone, Jr., George W. *The London Stage, 1747–1776: A Critical Introduction.* Carbondale: Southern Illinois University Press, 1968.

Stone, Jr., George W., and George M. Kahrl. *David Garrick: A Critical Biography.* Carbondale: Southern Illinois University Press, 1979.

Troubridge, Vincent. "Theatre Riots in London." In *Studies in English Theatre History in Memory of Gabrielle Enthover, O.B.E., First President of the Society for Theatre Research, 1948–1950,* 84–97. London: Society for Theatre Research, 1952.

Villermaules, Michel, ed. *Anecdotes sur l'etat de la religion dans la Chine.* Vol. 1. Paris: Aux depens de la Societé, 1733.

Visser, Colin. "Scenery and Technical Design." In *The London Theatre World, 1660–1800*, edited by Robert D. Hume, 66–118. Carbondale: Southern Illinois University Press, 1980.

Voltaire. *The Orphan of China. A Tragedy. Translated from the French of M. de Votaire*. 1ˢᵗ ed. London: R. Baldwin, 1756.

———. *L'Orphelin de la Chine, Tragédie*. Paris: Michele Lambert, 1755.

Wilkes, Thomas. *A General View of the Stage*. London: J. Coote and W. Whetstone, 1759.

——— "Art. 16. A Letter From M. De Voltaire, to the Author of the Orphan of China." *Monthly Review* (1759): 566.

Wilkinson, Tate. "Original Anecdotes Respecting the Stage, and the Actors of the Old School, With Remarks on Mr. Murphy's 'Life of Garrick.'" *Monthly Mirror* 13 (1802): 43–48.

Winter, Marian Hannah. *The Pre-Romantic Ballet*. Brooklyn, NY: Dance Horizons, 1975.

Woods, Leigh. *Garrick Claims the Stage: Acting As Social Emblem in Eighteenth-Century England*. Westport, CT: Greenwood Press, 1984.

Woty, William [J. Copywell, pseud.]. *The Shrubs of Parnassus. Consisting of a Variety of Poetical Essays, Moral and Comic*. London: n.p., 1760.

Yang, Chi-ming. *Performing China: Virtue, Commerce, and Orientalism in Eighteenth-Century England, 1660–1760*. Baltimore: The Johns Hopkins University Press, 2011.

———. "Virtue's Vogues: Eastern Authenticity and the Commodification of Chinese-ness on the 18ᵗʰ-Century Stage." *Comparative Literature Studies* 39, no. 4 (2002): 326–346.

3 Open Views of China
The Literary Works of John Francis Davis and the Spectacular *Chinese Sorcerer* (1823)

In the fall of 1792, the British government sent George Macartney as its ambassador to China with high hopes that his mission would open new ports, abolish the existing trading system, and secure a treaty of commerce and friendship.[1] The embassy accomplished none of its goals.[2] Before meeting the Chinese emperor Qianlong (乾隆), Macartney was advised to *kowtow*,[3] which is a ceremonial ritual that would have required him to prostrate himself and touch his head to the ground. Macartney refused, proposing instead to pay the emperor the same obeisance as he did to his king of Great Britain, namely, kneeling on one knee and kissing the emperors' hand. The proposed kiss was rejected by the emperor's ministers, but McCartney did kneel on one knee when he met the emperor, who, offended, granted him no further audience.[4] Macartney's appointment was preceded by an earlier attempt in 1787 that did not reach China and was followed by another British embassy sent in 1816, led by William Pitt Amherst, which was not granted an audience with the emperor Jiaqing (嘉慶) due to the British protest against the *kowtow* ceremony.[5] To the Chinese, who treated the British embassies as tributary envoys who were seeking favors from the empire, the ambassadors' refusal to *kowtow* appeared ignorant.[6] As J. L. Cranmer-Byng notes, in the dispute over the ceremonial ritual the real issue was the lack of any common understanding between the Chinese and the British.[7] Macartney and Amherst were both turned back even before they could bring up their governments' proposals for expanded trade. Besides thwarting official diplomatic entreaties, China also imposed trade restrictions. Foreign merchants were allowed to trade only in the port city of Canton (Guangdong) and to conduct business only with the Hong Merchants, a group of designated Chinese tradesmen.[8]

Despite the embassies' failures and the discouraging restrictions, Britain's China trade continued to grow. The volume of trade expanded continuously between 1750 and 1800, with a large jump occurring after the British government cut a significant portion of the duty on tea in 1784.[9] From 1800 to 1834, the volume and value of trade multiplied as the East India Company held onto its monopoly over tea while private traders imported an increasingly wide range of other Chinese products.[10] In addition, the embassies brought home fresh observations and first-hand information about China. Macartney, the embassy's principal secretary George Staunton, and Macartney's private secretary John Barrow each kept a journal of their embassy, while the entourage's painter, draftsman, and botanist made sketches of what they discovered in China.[11] In the analogy of George Thomas Staunton, Macartney's page and Staunton's son, China was "laid open" by the visit of the Macartney embassy,[12] and the journals and sketches vividly document what the British visitors had viewed in the country. Likewise, officers in the Amherst embassy recorded detailed daily events in their journals.[13] These eyewitness accounts were published shortly after the embassies returned to Britain. At home, what David Mayer calls "the second vogue for chinoiserie" between 1805 and 1822, largely sparked by the Prince Regent's use of Chinese décor for his own residence and a festival at St. James Park in 1814, inspired the trend of exhibiting Chinese styles of scenery in British pantomime.[14] Owing to commercial activities, the embassies, and the royal taste for Chinese design, China was present in the life and entertainments of the British in the early nineteenth century as they drank tea, read about the embassies' visits to China, and saw Chinese styles of buildings in public and theatre.

This chapter examines an unprecedented dual and parallel development of British literary and theatrical output about China, which, informed by the embassies' visits and the Anglo-Chinese trade, offers up-to-date "open views" of the country in these two fields: in one, the fuller but uneven translations of Chinese drama by John Francis Davis (1795–1890) and his interculturalized but primitivized depictions of Chinese theatre; and in the other, *The Chinese Sorcerer* (1823), an Easter holiday spectacle arranged by Thomas Dibdin (1771–1841) that stages a Chinaface travelogue depicting an impossible, exoticized, and unknowable wonderland, yet contains hidden social satire. While Davis's long-term residence in the country and language skills enabled him to translate two Chinese plays and provide accounts of Chinese theatre as he saw and experienced it, the fairy-tale-like *Chinese Sorcerer* took its audience on a journey to an imaginary China, visiting its signature locales and architecture. Davis clearly intended to provide fuller translations and make Chinese theatre comparable to Western traditions, and *Chinese Sorcerer* offered a visual experience that simulated the embassies' recent trips to the country.

Davis was familiar with earlier Jesuit writings about China, including the incomplete translation of *Zhao Shi Gu Er* (see Chapter Two). The two Chinese dramas he translated are in sharp contrast with each other, one being a comedy of family strife in the Chinese merchant class and the other a tragedy in which the weak Chinese court accedes to the demands of its aggressive northern nomadic enemy. These dramatic depictions of China and the Chinese that Davis translated provide alternative views that differ from those offered by the earlier Jesuits. Furthermore, Davis's second translation demonstrates his changing usage of the interculturated conceptions of the Tartars and the Chinese-Tartar conflict; its apparent incompleteness manifests the challenges inherent in translating Chinese drama and the epistemological barriers to Western recognition of the ontological uniqueness of Chinese theatre as an art form.

As a spectacle, the most prominent feature of *Chinese Sorcerer* was its numerous sets of Chinese scenery, which created a stage travelogue of wondrous visual experiences. In support of its scenic Chinaface novelty, *Chinese Sorcerer* depicts a fairy-tale-like story in which the valor, integrity, and fortunes of three long-lost sons of the Chinese emperor are put to test in various locations as they encounter many diverse characters. Despite its popular success, *Chinese Sorcerer* drew mixed critical reviews that observed a staggering gap between its spectacular stage representation and mediocre script. One drew the analogy of an elaborate oyster shell ("casket") without a pearl enclosed in it, which may be read as a criticism of Britain's excessive material interest in China. While the critics apparently did not detect it, in one of the play's storylines, Dibdin appears to satirize that material obsession, which he seems to view as a consequence of the China trade and the embassy visits, and also to express reservations about the relationship he sees between China's material influence and presence and the rapid changes in London's cityscape.

In Davis's accounts about Chinese theatre, he made great efforts to identify comparable theatre conventions, in terms of dramatic structure and staging, that could be found in both Chinese and British (Western) traditions. In doing so, nonetheless, Davis perpetuated a Voltairean, orientalist view of Chinese theatre as ancient and primitive, a view that would persist and later become a source of inspiration for alternative approaches to theatre-making in modern Euro-American theatre (see *Yellow Jacket* in Chapter Four). In his writing of *Chinese Sorcerer*, Dibdin interculturalized his perceptions about China with fairy-tale and British theatre conventions and depicted the country as an exoticized and trivialized wonderland of funny-looking, gibberish-speaking people with peculiar customs and mannerisms. This may represent a further expansion of the comic depiction of China seen in the epilogue of *Orphan of China* (see Chapter Two). The combination of the overall fantasyland framing with social satire presented in Chinaface would appear again in later plays, constituting the basis of a long-lasting, intercultured British theatre tradition (see *Chinese Honeymoon* in Chapter Four and *Aladdin* pantomimes in Epilogue).

The dual developments of literary and theatrical output represented by the works of Davis and *Chinese Sorcerer* remained parallel to each other and appear not to have intersected; Davis's works seem to have had no impact on contemporary British theatre's depictions and representations of China. There are two possible and related explanations for the lack of intersection between these parallel developments. The first concerns the British attitude toward visual spectacles, which regarded them as a fundamentally visual, not textual, genre of theatre; textual literacy was therefore not deemed critical or even necessary in their scripts. The second concerns shifting perceptions of China driven by embassies and commercial contacts. The increase in these contacts reinforced the close association of China with its material goods, which may have lessened Britain's interest in the country's cultural and literary output. The dual developments make it apparent that, informed by the "open views" of the country and acceleration in trading activities, China in the early nineteenth century appealed to Britain as a material and visual spectacle and had lost much of its allure as a land admired for its high cultural achievements, as had been depicted in the Jesuit writings of the previous centuries.

JOHN FRANCIS DAVIS

John Francis Davis was born on July 16, 1795, and died on November 13, 1890. During his long life, Davis's career and writings in relation to China can be divided into four periods: 1813–1835, when he worked for the East India Company in Canton (Guangzhou), China; 1835–1844, when he returned to England and became known as a Chinese expert; 1844–1848, when he served as governor of Hong Kong (Figure 3.1); and 1848–1890, when he again returned to England and continued to publish about China.[15] It was during his formative years with the East India Company that Davis wrote extensively on Chinese language and literature, including drama and theatre, advocating linguistic and literary approaches to understanding the country and its people.

In 1811 and 1812 Davis studied at the company's college in Hertfordshire, from which he graduated with honors.[16] In 1813, at the age of eighteen, Davis arrived in Canton to work as a junior writer (clerk) at the company's "factory," which was a seasonal trading and lodging station. According to the factory's records, in 1814, Davis was relieved of all other duties in order to focus on studying Chinese. His progress was remarkable: By December 1814, Davis had translated a Chinese document and the following January he finished translating a Chinese novelette.[17] As Davis worked his way up and became president of the Canton factory in 1832, his translations also proliferated. Between 1815 and 1834, he translated a novel, three novelettes, two dramas, and a substantial selection of poems, moral maxims, proverbs, and vocabulary.[18] In addition, he contributed essays about the Chinese language and translations of Chinese official edicts and newspaper articles to the meetings and journals of the Royal Asiatic Society, which was actively seeking works exploring the then "almost untrodden ground" of Chinese literature.[19]

Davis's prolific writing output was intended to provide the British with what he considered much-needed updated information about China. He wondered why the magnitude ("large dealings") of commercial activities Britain had carried on with China for more than half a century had only induced the Britons to produce an imperfect translation of a Chinese novel

Figure 3.1 Portrait of Sir John Davis, Governor of Hong Kong (1844–1848),
mid-nineteenth century, anonymous, watercolor on paper. Hong Kong
Museum of Art Collection. Photo supplied by the Hong Kong Museum
of Art.

before the Macartney embassy.[20] He credited the embassy for "clearing
away much of the obscurity" through personal observations and for inspiring curiosity and desire to know the country better. Clearly seeing commercial interests and trading relations as the driving forces behind literary
output, Davis reasoned that in the beginning, information would have to
come from those agents who superintended Britain's mercantile affairs in

China.[21] As a mercantile agent stationed in China and studying its language, Davis was entitled and obliged to take on the task and demonstrated he was fully capable of doing so.

In choosing Chinese language and literature as his subjects, Davis was consciously producing works distinct from those by Jesuit missionaries. While crediting the Jesuits for their pioneering role as providers of information about China, Davis restated the opinion of his countryman George Thomas Staunton (1781–1859), an accomplished Chinese scholar,[22] that the Jesuit writings were distorted by their religious purpose, thus conveying a favorable attitude toward the government of the country and its people.[23] "It remained for the English," Davis noted, "to give the first correct account" of China, which they discovered "to be neither perfectly wise, nor perfectly virtuous."[24] Davis also concurred with Staunton that the Jesuits focused too heavily on translating classical Chinese texts and that "the best and most authentic information" about a country is actually to be found "in the works of the natives, and in the vernacular language."[25] By translating novels and dramas, Davis aimed to gain "an intimate knowledge of China" and enlighten Britons on the nature of Chinese dramatic composition as well as the actual, contemporary state of drama and general literature.[26]

In 1817, Davis published his translation of *Lao Sheng Er* (老生兒), titled *Laou-Seng-Urh, or, "An Heir in His Old Age,"* prefaced with an essay, "A Brief View of the Chinese Drama, and of Their Theatrical Exhibitions." Twelve years later, in 1829, Davis offered a translation of *Han Gong Qiu* (漢宮秋), titled *Hān Koong Tsew,* or *the Sorrows of Hān,* with a short preface. The ideas Davis expresses in "A Brief View" and the preface to *Sorrows of Hān* are further explicated in two essays.[27] These works of Davis were the English translations of Chinese plays since that of *Zhao Shi Gu Er* (趙氏孤兒), discussed in Chapter Two, and extensive accounts on Chinese theatre after the sporadic descriptions provided by foreign embassies. Having access to the same play collection that includes *Zhao Shi Gu Er, Yuan Qu Xuan* (*Selection of Dramas from the Yuan Dynasty*), Davis chose to translate *Lao Sheng Er* and *Han Gong Qiu,* two very different Chinese plays. Making his long-term residence in Canton and relocating seasonally to Macao when the trading season ended, Davis was able to observe Chinese performers, acting, staging, and performance occasions and locations of the local Cantonese theatre (*yueju*). Through his direct exposure to this regional genre, Davis developed a broad overview of Chinese theatre and was able to provide comprehensive information about the art form. Owing to his translation work and breadth of knowledge, Davis can be considered the first British or Western scholar of Chinese theatre.

Davis's translations were inspired by the incompleteness of the translation of *Zhao Shi Gu Er*; the critical commentaries this earlier translation received also informed Davis's comparative analyses of Chinese drama and observations of Chinese theatre. The main objectives of Davis's undertaking were to provide fuller translations, to offer perspectives on China that he believed were missing from the Jesuit writings, and to identify points of comparison between Chinese theatre and Western traditions.

The translation of *Zhao Shi Gu Er* was evaluated by three writers whose opinions influenced Davis: Jean-Baptiste du Halde, editor of the translation; Voltaire, whose *L'Orphelin de la Chine* was inspired by the translation; and Richard Hurd, a contemporary of David Garrick and Arthur Murphy (see Chapter Two). In the advertisement prefacing the translation of *Zhao Shi Gu Er*, du Halde stated that since the play had been composed in the distant past when dramatic poetry was rather unformed and crude ("très-informe & très-grossiere"), it shouldn't be expected to follow contemporary French dramatic rules such as the unities of time, place, and action; the rules were also unknown to the Chinese, who had always lived separately from the rest of the world. While the translator, the Jesuit friar de Prémare, commented that the Chinese do not distinguish between tragedy and comedy, du Halde called the play a tragedy because it appears quite tragic ("elle a parû assez tragique"). In the printed scripts, du Halde observed that the name of the character is rarely identified; this is because as soon as the performer enters the stage he always declares who he is and the role he plays to the audience. Last but not least, du Halde noted that Chinese tragedies are interwoven with songs, which are interrupted by short phrases of ordinary delivery. The French are shocked ("choquez") that an actor would start to sing in the middle of a dialogue, du Halde said, but they need to be mindful that for the Chinese, singing is to "express some great stirring of the heart" ("exprimer quelque grand mouvement de l'ame"), such as joy, pain, anger, and despair. However, du Halde cautioned that there are plays in which the songs are difficult for Europeans to understand because they are filled with allusions to things ("allusions à des choses") that Europeans do not know and figures of speech ("figures dans le langage") that they have trouble perceiving. As the Chinese have their poetry, Westerners have their own, du Halde reasoned.[28]

Du Halde's depiction of *Zhao Shi Gu Er* as an unrefined work written at an early stage in the development of dramatic poetry is reiterated and further developed by Voltaire who, as discussed in Chapter Two, stated that the play is quite barbarous ("toute barbare") when compared with contemporary neo-classical French works and comparable to the monstrous farces ("farces monstrueuses") of Shakespeare and Lope de Vega consisting of a heap of incredible events ("un entassement d'événemens incroyables"). However, the play can be deemed a masterpiece when placed among French plays written in the fourteenth century. Voltaire claimed that the Chinese cultivated the theatre art (or dramatic poetry) more than three thousand years prior, which was a bit later than the Greeks and four hundred years earlier than the Romans. He therefore credited these three peoples as the only ancients who knew "the true spirit of society" ("le véritable esprit de la societé) as they collectively enjoyed "the pure pleasures of the mind" ("les plaisirs purs de l'esprit").[29] Voltaire, while praising Chinese theatre and ranking it together with the ancient Greek and Roman theatres, considered it time-trapped in an early stage of development.

In "A Discourse on Poetical Imitation," Richard Hurd (1720–1808), a British bishop and literary figure,[30] took du Halde's descriptions as the best accounts about the state of Chinese poetry and used *Zhao Shi Gu Er* to prove "the efficacy of *general principles*" in dramatic composition. Using the classical Greek model, Hurd observed that the essential rules of dramatic poetry are the unity and integrity of action and tight construction to bring the incidents of the story close together, with the action beginning as near the catastrophe as possible. Hurd argued that *Zhao Shi Gu Er* has a single action—the destruction of the enemy of the house of Zhao—and it proceeds with almost as much dramatic rapidity as Aristotle demands. As Chinese theatre developed independently from Western theatre traditions, the play demonstrates the "efficacy" or applicability of the Greek dramatic rules.[31] Hurd, in other words, interculturalized, and in this case universalized, these rules as the most essential basis for dramatic composition. He further offered a few comparable instances ("lesser marks of *coincidence*") between Chinese and Greek dramatic writings, such as the motive of revenge, the chorus-like lyrical songs, and a faithful guardian character.[32]

If Voltaire proposed to place Chinese and Greek theatre traditions on the same footing and status, Hurd furnished this suggestion with critical analysis and specific examples to show that they were indeed similar both in conception and actual writing. In making use of du Halde's accounts, Voltaire developed an orientalist view of Chinese theatre, while Hurd ventured to interculturalize Western (Greek) dramatic conventions and assert their universality and applicability to evaluate Chinese theatre. Almost a century after these writers, Davis used his language skills, his direct exposure to Chinese theatre activities, and the works of his British and European contemporaries to supply more information about the art form, de-orientalize some of the previous notions, and further interculturalize and universalize the Western dramatic conventions.

Davis opened his essay, "A Brief View" by stating that, contrary to what is stated in some Jesuit writings, most ancient Chinese records consist of poetry and the Chinese have a general predilection for epic and lyric poetry. Further, quoting a metaphor from a Chinese account, he states that the "tree" of Chinese poetry yielded "rich supplies of flowers and fruit" as early as the Tang Dynasty (618–907) (v–viii).[33] Davis statement implies that it would be incorrect to claim that *Zhao Shi Gu Er*, a work from the Yuan Dynasty (1279–1368),[34] had been written when Chinese poetry was in an early, imperfect state, as du Halde maintained and others reinterpreted. Regarding Voltaire's comment that *Zhao Shi Gu Er* lacks the beauties of sentiment, eloquence, and passion, Davis attributed this perception to de Prémare's incomplete translation, which left out "most of the poetry," specifically the arias, which are "the very best parts of the play" (xxxiii). Davis also cited

Hurd's analysis of the play in relation to Greek theatre and suggested that had the translation included more of the lyrics, Hurd would probably have found their resemblance to the Greek choral odes more complete (xxxiv).

Davis's first translation of the Chinese drama *Lao Sheng Er, Laou-Seng-Urh, or, "An Heir in His Old Age"* (1817), far surpasses de Prémare's translation of *Zhao Shi Gu Er* in completeness. Davis translated both the dialogues and the singing parts, with the aim to "render *both* [emphasis Davis] into English in such a manner as would best convey the spirit of the original, without departing far from its literal meaning" (xlviii).[35] He translated the script almost in full, leaving out only a few passages, for reasons of indecency or tediousness (xlii, xlix).[36] For doubtful passages, Davis stated that "the opinion of two or more natives was asked" (xlix),[37] and he used footnotes and endnotes to give further explanations. In all, Davis's translation is thorough and careful, and I would argue that it marks a historic achievement in rendering Chinese drama into a foreign language.[38]

Davis described *Lao Sheng Er* as a comedy, "a plain 'unvarnished tale,' in which Chinese manners and Chinese feelings are faithfully delineated and expressed, in a natural manner, and in appropriate language" (xxxiv–xxxv); the characters are "made up entirely of the members of a family in the middling class of society" (xxxvi). Davis concurred with du Halde that the Chinese make no distinction between tragedy and comedy, and he used the subject matter, character, and dialogue as criteria of delimitation.[39] The subject of *Lao Sheng Er* (securing a male heir to carry on family lineage), its depiction of disputes and trickery over an inheritance, its merchant-class characters, and its dialogue, spoken in common colloquial language, qualified it to be called a comedy. Translating the play fulfilled Davis's attempt to gain "an intimate knowledge" about China through an "unvarnished" tale about common people who are "neither perfectly wise, nor perfectly virtuous," depicted in the vernacular language.

Written by Wu Hanchen (武漢臣, fl. thirteenth century), *Lao Sheng Er* depicts Liu Congshan (劉從善), a wealthy old merchant without a male heir, who is caught in a family quarrel with his wife, his son-in-law, and his nephew over his bequest. Liu's wife favors the son-in-law and mistreats the nephew, who, in a fit of rage, leaves the house empty-handed. Liu's son-in-law has misgivings about his share because Liu's concubine is expecting a baby. In a scheme contrived by the son-in-law's wife (Liu's daughter), Liu's concubine is reported missing, which causes Liu much distress. He regards his lack of a male heir as a punishment for his avarice and decides to distribute alms to beggars in a nearby temple. Liu's nephew appears among the beggars, but Liu's wife and son-in-law ridicule the nephew and drive him away. Before the nephew is rushed off, Liu slips him money and suggests that he visit their ancestors' tombs. On Tomb-Sweeping Day, Liu's nephew procures modest offerings and performs rites to the ancestors of the Liu family, while Liu's son-in-law brings luxurious offerings to his own family's tombs before coming to visit those of the Liu family. Using this incident as an example, Liu leads his wife to realize that their nephew has a closer tie to them than their son-in-law does. Enlightened and enraged, Liu's wife evicts the son-in-law and wholeheartedly receives the nephew. Three years later, Liu's daughter and son-in-law come to visit Liu on his birthday and unexpectedly bring along Liu's concubine and her three-year-old son, who have been receiving protection and care from Liu's daughter. Delighted and thankful, Liu divides his fortune into three equal shares among his daughter, his nephew, and the three-year-old son.[40]

To help the reader better understand the "Chinese manners and Chinese feelings" depicted in the play, and therefore its dramatic conflict, Davis in "A Brief View" explained the prominence of filial piety and the importance of the male heir in Chinese society. "Filial piety is, among the Chinese, the first of virtues"; "the greatest misfortune in life is the want of a son to honour and console his aged parents, and to visit annually their tombs when dead." In addition, a Chinese man may take concubines in order to "afford every means of procuring a son"; the concubines have no rights of their own, and their children are considered the children of the legitimate wife (xxxv).[41] Davis thus recognizes that the play portrays the distinct cultural, social, and legal customs of the Chinese and that the dramatic reversal in the story depends on the occasion of Tomb-Sweeping Day, a prominent Chinese holiday on which descendants show filial piety to their ancestors.

Davis's second translation, *Hān Koong Tsew, or the Sorrows of Hān*, is the complete opposite of his first, in terms of both subject matter and completeness. The decision to translate this work indicates Davis's intention to provide an example of a Chinese high tragedy as a contrast to his first translation of a comedy of the common people. His interpretations of the interracial conflict depicted in the tragedy also evince his developing usage of the interculturated conceptions of the Tartars and the Chinese-Tartar conflict. Davis's second translation is also a sharp contrast to his first for its obvious incompleteness, which plainly manifests his failure to achieve his goal of providing fuller translations of Chinese drama. Davis was very aware of the translation's shortcomings; his puzzling explanations demonstrate the challenges and epistemological barriers he encountered in translating Chinese drama and in recognizing Chinese theatre as an ontologically different art form.

Davis described the play *Han Gong Qiu*, taken from the same play collection that includes *Zhao Shi Gu Er* and *Lao Sheng Er*, as "strictly historical," featuring historical figures and set at a time when the weakening of the Chinese government "emboldened the Tartars in their aggressions"; it exposes "the evil consequences of luxury, effeminacy, and supineness in the [Chinese] sovereign."[42] In Davis's interpretation, the play depicts a Chinese-Tartar conflict in which effeminate China is at the mercy of aggressive Tartary. As Davis knew Voltaire's *Orphelin* (discussed in Chapter Two), it is possible that he chose to translate *Han Gong Qiu* as a comparable and yet contrasting Chinese example that dramatized the interracial conflict. In this instance, Davis saw China as in decline, with its patriarchal sovereign totally powerless and its men emasculated, and failing to assert its cultural and political integrity when faced with foreign threats.

Written by Ma Zhiyuan (i.e., Ma Chih-yüan, 馬致遠, 1250?–1324?), *Han Gong Qiu* depicts the weakened state of the Chinese court, which leads to the tragic death of Wang Zhaojun (王昭君), an extraordinary beauty. The play is set in the Han Dynasty (206 BCE–220 CE) when China maintained peace with its northern nomadic enemy Xiongnu (匈奴) by supplying them with princesses for marriage to Xiongnu rulers. Having requested such a princess, the Xiongnu Chief Huhanye (呼韓邪單于, ?–31 BCE), awaits a response from the court of Emperor Yuan (漢元帝, ruled 49–33 BCE).[43] Though she has resided in the royal inner court for ten years, the beauty Wang has never been visited by the emperor because her portrait had been disfigured by Mao Yanshou (毛延壽), a greedy and evil minister, whom Wang refused to bribe. One night, Wang's playing of the *pipa*[44] attracts the attention of the emperor, who is astonished by her loveliness. After learning of Mao's misdemeanor, the emperor decrees that he be executed immediately, but Mao escapes north to the Xiongnu realm. He fabricates a story, telling the chief that Wang had offered herself to him but was thwarted by the Chinese emperor. The chief dispatches an envoy to demand Wang, backed by the threat of invasion. Although unwilling, Wang and the distressed emperor consent to the Xiongnu demand in order to save the country from massacre. However, upon reaching the river that marks the Xiongnu frontier, Wang throws herself into rather than cross it. The chief arrests Mao and returns him to China as a gesture of peace, yet the Chinese emperor is left in deep sorrow over Wang's suicide.[45]

By translating the Chinese term *fanwang* (番王, "king of the barbarians") as "K'han of the Tartars" to describe the character Chief Huhanye,[46] Davis demonstrates his adherence to earlier writers' conception of the Tartars as China's perennial enemy.[47] Similarly, he also calls the chief a "formidable Scythian,"[48] thus following earlier writers to represent the character as a political and cultural other to both China and the West. On the other hand, the "K'han" in Davis's version of Huhanye's title recalls its usage in the titles of Mongol rulers (such as Genghis Khan, discussed in Chapter One and Two) and supports Davis's implication of a direct lineage from the nomadic Xiongnu in the Han Dynasty to the Mongols, who established the much later Yuan Dynasty (1206–1367).[49] Nevertheless, while maintaining the presumption of a common Tartar heritage, Davis distinguished between the Mongols, whom he called the "Western Tartars," and the Manchows (Manchus), named the "Eastern Tartars" by Davis, charting their separate conflicts and ascendance to power.[50] Davis's usages, cited above, suggest that while he maintained the intercultured conception of the Tartars used by earlier writers, he also began to specify the different ethnic groups as distinct peoples, initiating the process of dismantling the firm hold the term Tartars had heretofore held in Western discourse as the designation for China's northern adversaries.

Ma's depiction of China's defenselessness against its invading enemy in *Sorrows of Hān* recalls the trope of the Chinese-Tartar conflict seen in the plays discussed in the previous chapters. In the play, China is saved by Wang's self-sacrifice, and the villain's eventual punishment is prompted by her tragic death. After hearing the Xiongnu chief's demands and threats, the Chinese emperor asks, in Davis's translation: "In vain do we maintain and send forth armies: vain are the crowds of civil and military officers about our palace! Which of them will drive back for us these foreign troops?" His prime minister replies that the roots of the threat derive from the emperor's fondness for Wang and negligence of state affairs. The minister advises that as the army is weak and lacks a valiant general, victory in battle cannot be assured; he thus pleads with the emperor to capitulate. "They take advantage of the compliant softness of her temper," the emperor observes. He then ridicules the emasculation of the Chinese leadership: "It would seem that, for the future, instead of men for ministers, we need only to have fair women to keep our empire in peace!"[51] Wang's subsequent self-sacrifice on behalf of her country and demonstration of her loyalty through suicide dramatically heighten both the overall sense of tragedy and the play's emphasis on the impotency of the Chinese male rulers.

This portrayal of interracial conflict and resolution could easily elicit an orientalist, gendered reading of a weaker, feminized China unable to fend off its stronger, virile barbarian enemy. Davis's characterization of the play as a cautionary tale of "the evil consequences of luxury, effeminacy, and supineness in the [Chinese] sovereign" is highly suggestive of such a reading, accentuated with a sense of decadence and passivity. As Davis perceived China as a country with a high-minded ruling class and masses who were "straitened for the bare means of subsistence," its moral "civil institutions" and "the degraded state of the female sex" would have made the subject of love unfavorable.[52] Concerning the parting scene (Act III), in which the emperor expresses his unwillingness, sadness, and sense of loss over the prospect of parting with Wang, Davis expressed surprise, stating that "the language of the imperial lover is passionate to a degree that one is not prepared to expect."[53] After he eventually lets go of Wang, the emperor mocks himself: "And am I the great Monarch of the line of Hān?" In a footnote to this line, Davis quoted a remark spoken by the Roman general Mark Antony (c. 82–30 BCE) in a similar state of dejection: "Lie there, thou *shadow of an Emperor!* [emphasis Davis]"[54] By citing Antony, who ruled at roughly the same time in the first century BCE as the emperor Yuan, Davis identifies China with the political degeneracy, romantic indulgence, and neglect of state affairs associated with ancient Rome.[55] Further, Davis's reference to Antony suggests a parallel identification of Wang with Cleopatra, thereby invoking the trope of the *femme fatale* in orientalist discourse, which underlies the sexual subtext in his characterization of the play's moral lesson. Davis's decision to translate this instance of the so-called Chinese-Tartar conflict may therefore be his attempt to counter the prevalent perceptions, informed by Jesuit writings, of China as strong and powerful by offering an example that depicts the powerlessness and vulnerability of a Chinese political patriarch and draws a comparison to the Roman empire's decline.

Davis's translation of *Han Gong Qiu* is notably incomplete. He translated only two out of the twelve arias in the parting scene, and even fewer for the other scenes. Having left out the sections that constituted, in his own words cited above, "most of the poetry" and "the very best parts of the play," Davis was very aware that his translation of *Han Gong Qiu* was deficient. Puzzlingly, he cited de Prémare's incomplete translation of *Zhao Shi Gu Er*, which he himself had criticized, to defend his own incomplete translation by stating that the illusions and figures of speech in the arias would be difficult for non-Chinese to understand. Further, the arias are frequently "mere repetitions or amplifications of the prose parts"; they are intended "more for the ear than for the eye," and "rather adapted to the stage than to the closet."[56] Assuming that Davis understood very well the detrimental impact on his translation of leaving out the arias, his stated reasons for not translating the arias may be taken as clues to probe his understanding of the linguistic and conceptual foundations of Chinese theatre. Despite his Chinese language skills, the arias in *Han Gong Qiu* may have been too challenging for him. It appears that Davis observed, but was unable to comprehend, the crucial and fundamental role the arias play in Chinese theatre. Davis's puzzling explanations of his incomplete translation of the play may therefore represent his ultimately unsuccessful attempts to overcome an epistemological barrier and recognize Chinese theatre as an ontologically different art form. In these attempts, Davis instead made great efforts to show how Chinese theatre is interculturally similar to Western traditions.

The two plays Davis translated employ allusions and figures of speech on two very different levels. In tune with the comedic story's portrayal of the merchant class, the language in *Lao Sheng Er* consists of "plain" and "unvarnished" prose for both the lyrics and voluminous dialogues. In contrast, the language in *Han Gong Qiu* is characterized by page after page of refined, poetic lyrics to suit the tragic theme and the noble characters, punctuated by occasional succinct monologues in colloquial speech. Ma Zhiyuan, author of *Han Gong Qiu*, was a poet well known for his lucid, beautiful, and thought-provoking verses. The lyrical arias, especially those in the parting scene describing the Chinese emperor's distress and grief of losing Wang, are some of Ma's finest work and have been praised as rare gems of Chinese poetry.[57] It is likely that Davis's knowledge of classical and literary Chinese was greatly taxed by the need to translate these lyrics within a practical amount of time. In 1829, the same year in which his translation of *Han Gong Qiu* was published, Davis also published his translation of a Chinese novel. Davis stated that the four hundred lines of poetry scattered throughout the novel required nearly as much work to properly translate as all the rest of the text. He then cited George Thomas Staunton's comment that Chinese plays are less rewarding for the translator than Chinese novels,[58] presumably because of the allusions and figures of speech in poetry. It is thus very likely that between the two translations, Davis chose to focus on the novel instead of the play. Further, he acknowledged that his incomplete translation of *Han Gong Qiu* "may perhaps be swayed by partiality towards the subject of his own labours."[59] Davis's "partiality" may indicate his realization that, although commonly treated as popular literature, some Chinese plays, especially those written by scholar-elites such as Ma, require extensive study and effort to understand and translate.

In another justification of his incomplete translation of *Han Gong Qiu*, Davis claimed that, cited earlier, the arias were frequently "*mere* repetitions or amplifications" (emphasis mine) of the prose parts. This claim shows Davis gave priority to prose, believing the arias to be secondary; it also contradicts Davis's earlier assertion that the arias were "the very best parts of the play." Furthermore, Davis, who had seen performances of Chinese theatre firsthand, also raised the justification that, as cited earlier, the arias are intended "more for the ear than for the eye," and "rather adapted to the stage than to the closet." This reasoning suggests Davis recognized that while the arias may have appeared to be redundant when texts were read on the page, they acquired greater importance in stage performance, when, in his observation, they were, "accompanied with loud music."[60] Du Halde had noted that in the Chinese scripts, the arias were printed in a larger font to set them off from the speaking parts,[61] thus providing a visual indication of the precedence of the arias over the prose parts. Davis must have seen this textual format, as he had direct access to at least two hundred volumes of Chinese plays kept in the library of the East India Company.[62] Based on this textual format and the primacy of singing in performance, it may be argued that the arias' function of expressing and explicating the various sentiments of the characters *is* the main objective of many Chinese plays, as in the case of *Han Gong Qiu*, while the prose speeches are intended to further explicate the inner dramatic conflict. By not translating most of the arias in the play, Davis's translation fails to convey the deep sorrow and regret the Chinese emperor experiences, which give the play its title. Davis, despite having read Chinese plays and viewed performances, appeared unable to recognize the arias as the very basis of the writing and staging of Chinese theatre and as informing its ontological difference from Western traditions.

Davis's blind spot may have resulted from his intent to show that Chinese theatre possesses a set of intercultural or universal qualities that define theatre across various cultures, which is reflected in many of his comments. For example, he argued that *Lao Sheng Er* and *Han Gong Qiu* observe the principle of unity of action and, to a lesser degree, unities of time and place and that, as in many plays from the Yuan Dynasty, the introductory act in which the characters introduce themselves to the audience resembles the prologue in Greek theatre.[63] Davis observed that in the Chinese scripts, certain words were used to indicate the general characteristics of specific characters, a practice he compared to the naming of stock characters in

English pantomimes such as Harlequin.[64] In performance, Davis noted the lack of scenery and that Chinese performers conveyed place and action through speech, props, and symbolic movements, accentuated by music. He noted that while this staging approach may seem crude, reminiscent of the staging of the "play within a play" in *A Midsummer Night's Dream*, similar practices were used in the earlier days of English theatre, and that even the best scenic work still relies much on the audience's imagination.[65] Davis further observed that the Chinese did not much respect theatre performers, who were treated as servants or slaves and forbidden to marry into higher social ranks. In his eyes, the status of the Chinese players, who, led by a master or manager, traveled from place to place to perform, was equal to that of those performers defined in English law as vagabonds.[66] Last but not least, Davis saw a parallel between theatrical performances at Chinese temples and the medieval mystery and morality plays performed in European churches, while plays staged at Chinese taverns for entertainment had their English counterparts in Elizabethan inns. As for the temporary makeshift stage erected in front of temples or in open spaces for theatre performances, Davis found it similar to the booths at Bartholomew Fair, though far less substantial.[67]

From textual composition to character types, from performing styles to the social position of the performers, and from performance occasions to locations to staging practices, Davis sought and found parallels between Chinese theatre and many Western traditions and practices, most notably Greek and Elizabethan theatres. He even ventured to argue that Chinese theatre was closer to Western traditions than to Indian theatre.[68] Davis, in other words, appeared eager to interculturalize Chinese and Western theatre practices, and his eagerness may have led to some questionable comparisons. His comments on actresses are a case in point. In an early account, Davis acknowledged their existence in Chinese theatre and that women were banned from the stage quite recently, during the era of Emperor Kien Long (Qianlong). Later he made a general statement, without qualification, that "[t]he female parts [in Chinese theatre] are never performed by women, but generally by boys." He followed this statement with the observation that there were no actresses in Greek and Roman theatres, and that not until the Restoration era did the English see women on the stage.[69] In this instance Davis appears to have stretched a point too far in order to show that the absence of women was an intercultural phenomenon. Actresses actually have been on the Chinese stage ever since its inception, and acting was practiced as a family business, a reality that was implicit in the laws Davis cited that prohibited players from marrying out of their own social class.[70]

Whether the dramatic characteristics or theatre practices identified by Davis can properly be characterized as universal or intercultural is subject to debate. Nevertheless, it is notable that Davis's comparisons focused on the similarities between contemporary Chinese and historical Western theatres. His comparisons imply that in terms of development and progression,

Chinese theatre lagged behind its Western counterparts; Davis, in other words, values but antiquates Chinese theatre in ways that are comparable to the Jesuits and Voltaire in their depictions of China's cultural achievements. As will be discussed in the case of *Yellow Jacket* in Chapter Four, Western theatre practitioners in the early twentieth century also saw parallels between these theatres, and, notably, their creative exploration of Chinese theatre focused on its formal, distinct staging methods, which they perceived as primitive.

In Davis's time, the perception that Chinese theatre was unrefined and resorted to visual attractions can be seen in accounts written by members of the embassies who experienced Chinese theatre firsthand. For example, Macartney was entertained at court with an indoor morning program of theatre entertainments consisting of "great variety, both tragical and comical" and several pieces acted in succession "without any apparent connection with one another." The highlight of the program was "the grand pantomime" depicting what Macartney comprehended as "the marriage of the Ocean and Earth" in which the two separate marine and land processions exhibited their "various riches and productions" of animals and plants. They eventually joined together and made room for the whale who, taking his station exactly opposite to the Emperor's box, "spouted out of his mouth into the pit several tons of water, which quickly disappeared through the perforations of the floor," and received "the highest applause." Later in the evening's outdoor program, the entertainments included "wrestling and dancing, and tumbling, and posture-making" and ended with fireworks, which "in some particulars exceeded anything of the kind I had ever seen." Macartney concluded that, "However meanly we must think of the taste and delicacy of the Court of China" based on the evening program, "together with the wretched dramas of the morning," there was "something grand and imposing in the general effect that resulted from the whole spectacle."[71]

The programs described by Macartney represent very fine examples of court entertainment, which reached its peak of grandeur and sophistication during the reign of the Qianlong emperor. Known for his interest in theatre, Qianlong kept more than a thousand performers at court, appointed court dramatists to revise and elaborate upon popular plays, and requested dazzling theatrical performances to enhance celebratory occasions.[72] The entertainments provided for foreign embassies were clearly designed to impress them with various kinds of spectacles, such as the aquatic scene and fireworks noted by Macartney. Moreover, the contents of these performances were very likely planned to commemorate the occasions of foreign embassies. What Macartney perceived as "the marriage of the Ocean and the Earth" was very likely a stage representation of tributary envoys bringing precious gifts to the emperor, corresponding with the visit of the British embassy.[73] Interestingly, Macartney assumed that the British would look down on the Chinese court's taste for spectacle even after he had been greatly entertained by hours of diverse stunts and spectaculars.

Macartney's assumption suggests that the Chinese theatrical performances lacked elements of refinement and elegance the British had expected would be present. John Barrow, Macartney's private secretary, speculated that the court entertainments had degenerated since the Tartar conquest. "Dancing, riding, wrestling, and posture-making, are more congenial to the rude and unpolished Tartar than the airs and dialogue of a regular drama, which is better suited to the genius and spirit of the ceremonious and effeminate Chinese." In his orientalist perception of the Tartar (Manchu) rulers, Barrow made this claim based on his experiences of having being entertained with regular dramas in his journeys in the country but only by "the juggling tricks" at court.[74] Barrow, in other words, regarded the court entertainments as low and trifling amusements, which reflected the taste of the presumably "rude and unpolished" Tartars.

Barrow appeared to have a general dislike of Chinese theatre, as he judged the regular dramas he saw as little better and stating that the theatre of the waning days of the Roman empire was as "rude and barbarous" as Chinese theatre. After describing a popular Chinese play depicting a woman who is condemned to be flayed alive after murdering her husband as perhaps the most obscene, indelicate, and disgusting piece of theatre, Barrow remarked that a Chinese might make a similar comment on English theatre when seeing "the exhibition of Harlequin Skeleton," and the numerous ghosts, hobgoblins, and bleeding statues which aid the spectacle.[75] For Barrow, Chinese theatre operates strictly on a visual level, providing amusement and shock, and lacking any literary depth. He might not be surprised to learn (or perhaps he knew?) that China was indeed depicted with plenty of dancing, riding, and juggling in contemporary London popular entertainments, featuring Harlequin and his company, that would greet a Chinese audience. Such entertainments as *The Chinese Sorcerer* were, nevertheless, a festive and jocular kind of spectacle that allowed their audiences to vicariously experience what the embassies had seen in China.

THE CHINESE SORCERER

In 1823, for the Easter holiday the Drury Lane theatre in London advertised and presented a "superb Chinese Spectacle" called *The Chinese Sorcerer; or, the Emperor and His Three Sons* (Figure 3.2). Claiming to feature "entirely new Music, Scenery, Dresses, splendid Armour, and corresponding Decorations of a most extensive Description," *Chinese Sorcerer* opened on Easter Monday, March 31, and ran for twenty-three performances.[76] Throughout its run of more than a month, *Chinese Sorcerer* was repeatedly acclaimed in the playbills as "the most successful of the kind" produced at Drury Lane for many years in terms of scenery, costume, and music, and was greeted with a "brilliant reception" by the audience that sustained its continuous appearance on stage.

Figure 3.2 Playbill for Theatre Royal, Drury Lane, March 31, 1823. Department of Theatre & Performance, Victoria and Albert Museum, London. © V&A Images / Victoria and Albert Museum, London.

Chinese Sorcerer exemplifies quite a few London theatre productions presented at various theatre houses from the 1810s until the early 1830s that dramatized China as popular entertainments and heightened visual spectacles.[77] It depicts a fairy-tale-like story that moves from one spectacular Chinese setting to another, intermixed with dancing and singing. Its most prominent feature, detailed as an attraction in the playbill, was the numerous sets of Chinese scenery it offered in an arrangement that promised a wondrous visual experience. If China, in the words of George Thomas Staunton cited at the beginning of the chapter, was "laid open" by the visit of the Macartney embassy, *Chinese Sorcerer* and its peer productions offered stage simulations that invited their audiences to enjoy unprecedented views of China and vicariously experience the country as the embassy did. It is this stage travelogue experience in which China was at once location, commodity, and people that differentiates the Chinese spectacularity of *Chinese Sorcerer* from that of *Chinese Festival* and *Orphan of China* of the previous century (see Chapter Two).[78] *Chinese Sorcerer* creates a scenic, visual Chinaface novelty that emphasizes views of China and the Chinese, which inform the construction of its fairy-tale-like story and the sense of wonder it conveys.

Written and arranged by Thomas John Dibdin (1771–1841), an actor, theatre manager, and prolific writer of popular entertainments in the late eighteenth and early nineteenth centuries,[79] *Chinese Sorcerer* depicts the various trials orchestrated by the sorcerer Fong-Whang, which test the valor, integrity, and fortune of Zam-Ti, Pe-Kin, and Kan-Fu, the three long-lost sons of the Chinese emperor Kein-Long (Qianlong) (Figure 3.3).[80] Zam-Ti, in search of fame and glory, is given a golden galley equipped with soldiers so that he may seek military conquest. Pe-Kin, in love with Bri-Ti,[81] who is held hostage by the Tartars, receives riches from Kein-Long,[82] first to rescue her from captivity and then to satisfy her ever growing desire for larger residences. Kan-Fu, after being thrown into the sea by the Tartars, arrives in a strange land where he is given a sequence of odd orders that prevent him from marrying the object of his desire, Princess O-Me. At the end of the play, Kein-Long deprives Pe-Kin and Bri-Ti of their wealth to teach them a lesson about greed. When Kan-Fu almost ends his life in order to pursue O-Me, whom he had presumed dead, she appears and reveals that she has been the master schemer behind all his trials. Zam-Ti, after a sea voyage, defeats armed furies and rescues his captive mother Quang-Si from an enchanted tower.[83] Fong-Whang then brings all the members of the royal family together in a happy reunion.

Wonder, identified by Jack Zipes in his study of fairy tales as giving rise to "admiration, fear, awe, and reverence," figures prominently throughout *Chinese Sorcerer*.[84] Wonder occurs when, for example, Zam-Ti's fishing boat is turned into a golden galley, when Pe-Kin is given the means to purchase more elaborate dwellings, and when Kan-Fu experiences dramatic turns of fortune, well-fed and richly dressed in one moment and imprisoned and

Figure 3.3 Playbill (top detail) for Theatre Royal, Drury Lane, March 31,
1823. Department of Theatre & Performance, Victoria and Albert
Museum, London. © V&A Images / Victoria and Albert Museum,
London.

ordered to die in the next. Many of these impossible turns of the characters' fortunes are accompanied by wondrous scene changes advertised in the
playbill. The scenery accompanying the transformation of Zam-Ti's fishing
boat, for example, is billed as "Ascent of the Golden Galley." When the Tartars burn down the brothers' huts, the scenery depicts "Conflagration of the
Cottages." Pe-Kin and Bri-Ti move from a "Picturesque Dwelling" with "a
Prospect of the Palace of Shi-Fo" to the "Superb Saloon in the Palace of Shi-
Fo" (Figure 3.4). It is through these visual scenic indications that the wonder
of *Chinese Sorcerer* is realized.

Based on the prominence given to the procession of the scenery, it may
be argued that the main purpose of *Chinese Sorcerer* was to display views
of signature Chinese locales and architectural designs, which constitute
the principal sources of its visual wonder. In addition to the two views of
"the Palace of Shi-Fo" identified above, the Chinese scenery in the play
includes China's frontiers ("Romantic View on the Borders of Chinese
Tartary, by sun-set"), the imperial palace ("Grand Imperial Palace and
Court of Kein-Long" and its vestibule and "Magnificent Hall of Tien"),
the imperial city (a distant view from the brothers' huts and the "Grand
Harbour and Arsenal"), and a marine pavilion (a moonlight view, its

Figure 3.4 Playbill (bottom detail) for Theatre Royal, Drury Lane, March 31, 1823. Department of Theatre & Performance, Victoria and Albert Museum, London. © V&A Images / Victoria and Albert Museum, London.

interior, and its "Supper Garden") (Figure 3.4). The procession of scenery may be compared to a sightseeing tour that, after glimpsing the borders at sunset upon arriving in China, begins at the imperial palace, proceeds to a marine pavilion, the city's harbor, and a grand palace, and has its concluding high point at the audience hall of the imperial palace, decorated for "the Feast of Lanterns" (Figure 3.4). These views of the country created a visual experience that would have been novel, and thus wondrous, to an audience who had not been to China.

Notably, quite a few of the characters are named after Chinese cities and provinces such as Pe-Kin (Peking), Nan-King (Nanjing), and Quang-Si (Guangxi) (Figures 3.3 and 3.4).[85] Dibdin thereby extends the sightseeing tour of China from the scenery to the characters, who appear as personified Chinese locales. Other noteworthy examples of Dibdin's naming include Bo-Hea and Sow-Shong, which are two kinds of Chinese tea; Chop-Stick, the Chinese utensil; Kein-Long (Qianlong), the Chinese Emperor who received the Macartney embassy; and Zam-Ti, which is the name of the loyal Chinese mandarin from Voltaire's *Orphelin* and Murphy's *Orphan* (see Chapter Two). This selection of names suggests that Dibdin identifies China not only with its geographical locations, but also with its commodities (notably the signature import tea), housewares, and personages (both historical and imaginative). Among them, the geographically derived names are the most prominent, suggesting that Dibdin most sought to attract his audience with the enticements of wondrous scenery and vicarious touring.

The story of *Chinese Sorcerer* resembles the fairy tales in Zipes's study depicting competitive brothers who set out to learn different trades such as soldiery and boat building for survival and later use their newfound skills to obtain fortune and marriage.[86] According to Dibdin himself and contemporary reports, the story of *Chinese Sorcerer* was constructed out of three separate French *melo-drames*, and its second act was borrowed from another play staged earlier in 1823.[87] It appears that no Chinese textual sources served as direct inspiration for Dibdin; rather, as discussed above, Dibdin created the visual and aural presences of a Chinese story with scenery and the names of the characters. Through his invention of the three brothers and their trials, Dibdin interculturalized his perceptions of China with fairy-tale and British theatre conventions and also inserted his own social commentary on Anglo-Chinese relations. In Dibdin's rendering, China is an impossible land whose people, though exhibiting morality and integrity, have idiosyncratic aesthetic preferences and follow odd laws that are opposite to Western practices. While one prominent dramatic trope seen in earlier examples, the Chinese-Tartar conflict, is relegated to a secondary plotline that is resolved with money and magic, the Chinese female characters exhibit the peculiar and exoticized qualities that also appeared in the epilogue of Murphy's *Orphan* of the previous century (see Chapter Two). Overall, Dibdin's depictions trivialize China, departing further from earlier works' praise for China's moral standards and cultural achievements. The impossible and wondrous elements in *Chinese Sorcerer* mark it as an interculturalized work incorporating both novel and familiar (intercultured) depictions of the country and its people.

After adventuring at sea with his golden galley and soldiers, Zam-Ti returns home and lands at "a splendid port," depicted on stage as the "Grand Harbour and Arsenal of the Imperial City" (Figure 3.4). Hi-Ho, the sorcerer Fong-Whang's attendant, accompanied by two "comic Joss looking dwarfs," informs Zamti that he has landed on the island of Se-ren-dib (a word that does not make sense to Hi-Ho) where everything is impossible: a lawyer is asked "to decide a case quickly," "a doctor to take his own physic, or an informer to refuse a bribe" (II.iii.; 11).[88] The impossibilities of China are shown to be its funny-looking people, its strange language, and, most importantly, its customs and logic, which, with embedded sarcasm, reverse Western practices and understandings.

Soon Fong-Whang appears and inquires about Zam-Ti's sea voyage. After hearing Zam-Ti express disappointment that while at sea he had neither "met the floating horde of pirates," nor encountered "those sordid trafficking in human flesh," nor "dealt freedom's vengeance on a Tyrant's fleet," Fong-Whang directs him to rescue "an oppress'd despairing woman," his captive mother. With a wave of his wand, the scenery is changed to a "Rude and terrific passage" that leads up to "the tremendous Necromantic Tower" (Figure 3.4). "It depends on thee," Fong-Whang instructs Zam-Ti, "with filial virtue, constancy and valour to rescue her or gloriously perish" (II.iv.; 12–14). In this dialogue, Dibdin inserts topical references to pirates, the slave trade, and presumably Napoleon, which would have been familiar to the contemporary London audience. He also creates a stage moment in which the actor playing Zam-Ti acknowledges that he is British by knowing these occurrences. After nodding at the audience, Zam-Ti returns to his character and is given a task to demonstrate the Chinese virtue of filial piety by rescuing his mother, rather than a damsel in distress, in a fairy-tale-like setting. His task may be read as an instance in which the subject of Chinese filial piety is interculturalized in a European fairy-tale setting. Upon Zam-Ti's successful completion of the task, Fong-Whang lauds him for proving his filiality and wishes that "some beauteous maid" will reward his virtue. Zamti's reply, "My mistress shall be glory" (II.ix.; 35), casts him as filial but unromantic, which recalls the depiction of virtuous Chinese characters in Murphy's *Orphan* (see Chapter Two).

In contrast, Pe-Kin, Zam-Ti's brother, is portrayed as hopelessly love-stricken and dedicated to indulging Bri-Ti's insatiable desire for ever-grander residences. After receiving a jewel from Kein-Long which enables him to rescue Bri-Ti from the Tartars (who are then chased away by Hi-Ho's soldiers), Pe-Kin is elated at the thought of reuniting with his beloved, "whose pretty little foot is no less than nature made it." Pe-Kin further sings a song about a mandarin's daughter with blackened teeth, pea green hair, half-closed eyes, and small feet, who is courted by a young peasant with shaved eyebrows, long whiskers, and pale and rosy cheeks (I.iv.). Similar to the epilogue of Murphy's *Orphan* delivered by Mary Ann Yates (see Chapter Two), Pe-Kin's statement and song call attention to the seemingly peculiar aesthetic tastes of the Chinese, especially the practice of foot binding. Notably, in this case Chinese (foot binding) and Japanese (teeth blackening and eyebrow shaving) practices are interculturalized together, a creative decision which recalls Boucher's insertion of a Japanese lady in a rickshaw in his painting of a Chinese fair (see Figure 2.1). Dibdin therefore also contributed to the process of interculturating two earlier depictions of the Chinese from the previous century and heightened the peculiar aesthetic standards of the "impossible" land of China in a comic and exoticized manner.

Using financial means bestowed by Kein-Long, Pe-Kin and Bri-Ti move from a bare hut that was burnt down by the Tartars to a "very neat and small apartment," with a view of "a superb palace" (II.ii.; 6), indicated by scenery depicting a "Picturesque Dwelling," with "a Prospect of the Palace of Shi-Fo" (Figure 3.4). Bri-Ti is discontented, for her ideal residence includes a waiting chamber, an audience hall, a summer saloon, half a dozen sleeping rooms, hot and cold baths, and a snug cottage. Kein-Long again appears to aid the couple, but warns that "prosperity tries hearts still more

than hard adversity" (II.ii.; 8). After they relocate to the "elegant and magnificent palace" (II.vi.; 21), represented by scenery titled "Superb Saloon in
the Palace of Shi-Fo" (Figure 3.4), Bri-Ti demands that Pe-Kin pull down a
fisherman's cottage that obstructs her view. In its place, she plans to "plant it
out, build it out, and then with a grove and a bridge, and a summer palace,
and a pagoda" (II.vi.; 24). At this point, Kein-Long intervenes and deprives
Pe-Kin and Bri-Ti of their wealth because they have forgotten their humble
beginnings as fisherfolk.

Bri-Ti's desire to have a waiting chamber and an audience hall may be
read as referencing the Macartney embassy, which was received by the Qianlong emperor in these rooms. Her notion of a pleasing view that includes
a bridge and a pagoda recalls Chinese gardening designs, introduced to the
British in the previous century, that often feature these two signature struc-
tures. Moreover, these architectural references can be read as markers of
Chinese material aspirations that have influenced British tastes. If several
of Dibdin's characters are named for Chinese cities and provinces, Bri-Ti
could likewise be read as a personified caricature of Britain who desires and
demands that China (Pe-Kin/Peking) meet her material needs. In his reading
of British pantomime (see Epilogue for further discussion on this genre) in
the same historical period, John O'Brien draws upon Jane Moody's observation and sees its signature fast changes of scenery as a stage analogue to
the pace of accelerated urbanization of London.[89] In expanding O'Brien's
reading approach, Bri-Ti's ever-growing appetite for grander dwelling places
and her intention to pull down a humble cottage to "plant and build it out"
may be read as a social commentary, with an edge of irony, on the swift
changes in London's landscape financed by profits derived from the China
trade and possibly characterized by trendy residences fashioned after the
Chinese styles. When Bri-Ti apologizes to Kein-Long to "only forgive *him*
[Pe-Kin] for *my* faults" (II.vi.; 26), Dibdin could be commenting on this
rapid change in London's cityscape with a reserved attitude toward China's
material influence and presence.

The trials of Kan-Fu, the third brother, are by far the most impossible,
as they are designed by O-Me to test his devotion and sincerity by purpose-
fully surprising and frustrating him. After being thrown into the sea by the
Tartars, Kan-Fu swims to "a beautiful palace built on the sea shore," with
"many windows illuminated toward the sea" (II.i.; 1), which is indicated by
the "Illuminated Marine Pavilion" scenery (Figure 3.4). Hi-Ho informs him
that by law every stranger cast upon the coast must marry the first single
woman he meets, or else be subject to the "pleasant alternative" of having
his head chopped off (II.i.; 2). Among the women Kan-Fu encounters is
O-Me, who sends in a palanquin to carry him into her palace. Kan-Fu then
reappears well-dressed, in "a handsome apartment" (II.v.; 14), indicated by
the "Interior of the Marine Pavilion" scenery (Figure 3.4). However, he is
informed that O-Me has been condemned to die for contemplating marriage, due to her devotion to "the great Fo-giee" in childhood, and that

Kan-Fu is to be imprisoned in a deep dungeon or face public execution (II.v.; 16). Several women come to dissuade Kan-Fu from his commitment to O-Me, but he remains resolute. In the next scene with Kan-Fu, he is brought to "[a] beautiful garden a la chinoise, temples, artificial rocks, fountains" (II.vii.; 27), indicated by the "Supper Garden of O-Me's Pavilion" scenery (Figure 3.4). There Kan-Fu is offered a last banquet before his execution, and he is seduced by a woman who promises that if he consents to marry her, this act will save O-Me. Deceived by this seductress, Kan-Fu becomes enraged when he discovers the promise was a lie. At this point, O-Me appears, "most splendidly drest," and reveals that she has been the master-mind behind all his trials and that Kan-Fu has fulfilled the decree that she could never marry until she found a love who was willing to follow her into death or sacrifice himself to save her. As Kan-Fu marches off with O-Me, her attendants sing celebratory lyrics of Chinese-sounding monosyllabic gibberish such as "Nang tang wang ching chang wang, / Ning pong nang ki no—" (II.vii.; 32–33).

Although in this plotline, China appears odd and unpredictable mostly due to O-Me's invention of whimsical laws and threats, Dibdin's depiction also conveys the sense that the country is governed by certain unchallengeable rules, such as the decree that requires O-Me to test her love before marriage. The plot of trials followed by a surprise reappearance could be compared to that involving Amavanga and Zungteus from Settle's *Conquest* (see Chapter One), but conducted in a comic manner. Especially notable is the choral gibberish, which may signify a drastic shift from earlier depictions of China as a country characterized by its noble civilization and high poetry. In the emerging depiction, it is instead a strange, frivolous land with an incomprehensible language.

By integrating the three separate story lines, Dibdin in the second act of *Chinese Sorcerer* often juxtaposes and complicates the characters and settings from one scene to the next. As the three sons are taken from place to place for their tests, they encounter a series of characters: soldiers, Tartars, imperial guards, O-Me's court ladies, monstrous furies, and the wizard-benefactors (Fong-Whang and Kein-Long) and their attendants. As the scenery changes, these characters appear, clothed in their respective and distinct costumes. O-Me's court ladies who tempt Kan-Fu are disguised as women of different ages and ranks before they eventually reveal their true identities. Their disguises provide further visual interest for the audience. In addition to the choral gibberish sung by O-Me's attendants discussed earlier, Bri-Ti and Pe-Kin sing about love, and the soldiers and imperial guards praise Zam-Ti and Kein-Long in marching songs. In Act I, a grand Chinese ballet is performed at Kein-Long's birthday celebration.[90] In Act Two, while Bri-Ti awaits Pe-Kin's return from the fisherman's cottage, her court ladies dance to amuse her. From the scenery to the costumes, singing, and dancing, *Chinese Sorcerer* offers a variety of visual, aural, and kinetic interests for the audience.

Despite its claim to a "brilliant reception" by its audience advertised in the playbills, during its run *Chinese Sorcerer* received mixed reviews in the press, which, while acknowledging its popularity, emphasized the staggering gap the critics perceived between the play's spectacular stage representation and mediocre script. The review of its premiere in the *Times*, for example, described *Chinese Sorcerer* as "an unusually splendid, and perfectly incomprehensible spectacle." Its story was considered very bad, its acting not brilliant, and its music only average. However, as "there has been a great deal of money laid out upon it," "it will bring some money to the theatre." What stood out in this spectacle was the scenery, which was "entirely new," "all ingenious and splendid in a very high degree," and mostly "in most admirable taste." The critic strongly recommended shortening the story, and the spectacle "was given out for repetition without a dissentient voice."[91] To the *Times* critic, the financial investment in *Chinese Sorcerer* was put to effective use in creating the impressive stage representation, which apparently awed the audience and guaranteed the continuation of its run. Notably, the monetary investment in the Chinese scenery was perceived as novel ("entirely new" and "all ingenious"). Dibdin's sense that the audience would be attracted to a stage travelogue of China paid off, but his script guiding the audience through this wondrous land was criticized as very poor, "perfectly incomprehensible."

Similarly, the review in *London Magazine* commented that *Chinese Sorcerer* was inferior to its rival production at the Covent Garden theatre in every aspect except the scenery; its story "would poze a sphynx."[92] In *Theatrical Magazine*, the review praised its "splendid exhibition of gorgeous dresses, grand and beautiful scenery, and picturesque and varied combinations of theatrical shew." The story, however, was "vastly inferior to the decorations."[93] In the *Examiner*, the review described *Chinese Sorcerer* as "exactly the reverse of the pearl included in the oyster; the casket in the present instance being everything, and the enclosure nothing," for "the story amounts to little," and "the scenery, decoration, and accompaniments are all in all ... highly tasteful and beautiful in their peculiar line."[94] While these reviews all contrast the extravagant stage spectacle and the puzzling, inferior, or insubstantial script, the last comment's analogy of casket and pearl is especially noteworthy. The reviewer was very impressed by the superficial visual novelty of *Chinese Sorcerer*, what I call its Chinaface novelty, but criticized the lack of substance inside the ornate outer appearance. The substance or "pearl," according to the reviewers, should at least consist of a substantial and meaningful story that would complement the sensory spectacle.

What the reviewers perceived as a lack of substance may be read as a criticism of Britain's relations with China, which had allowed Britons to glimpse its magnificent sights and acquire its goods, yet failed to provide them with a coherent understanding of the country. Despite their ambivalent reviews, most reviewers reported that *Chinese Sorcerer* was enthusiastically enjoyed by the audience and predicted that it would have a long run, which it did.

Drury Lane's claim in the playbill of a "brilliant reception" by the audience was validated by its run of more than a month. If most audiences were satisfied with the production of *Chinese Sorcerer* so long as it fulfilled the promise of a magnificent spectacle, the discontent and bafflement expressed by the reviewers reveals that to some, the production was emblematic of a troubling cultural phenomenon characterized by excessive focus on visual and material interest in China.

In the review in *London Magazine* quoted above, the critic stated that he had looked into his old teacups for inspiration in order to decipher the incomprehensible plot. He called the play a "*Bohea*-romance," a "China-dish of weak tea," and suggested "a man must be indeed in his cups before he can muster up a Chinese enthusiasm."[95] Though tongue-in-cheek and belittling, the review invites examination of what lay at the foundation of Britain's interest in China. After having experienced a visually interesting but unintelligible stage journey to China, the reviewer looked into his teacups, the Chinese imports that combined the country's signature material good ("China-dish") with its signature beverage (tea), for comprehension. That the production was likened to weak tea and that consumption of tea could help "muster up" and boost interest in a production that dramatized China suggest the immediate association between the material goods (tea) and the country (China) that produced it. Consuming tea, in other words, could help generate appreciation of stage representations of the country; material consumption induces intellectual recognition. This close association between tea and China, in other words, reveals the extent to which Britain's material interest in the country informed its stage representations. By capitalizing on that material interest, *Chinese Sorcerer* exposed the very material basis of Britain's interest in China. Although *Chinese Sorcerer* succeeded in attracting and pleasing the majority of the audience, its success troubled at least a handful of critics who asked for a "pearl" with more than mere material consumption.

Although the reviewers apparently did not perceive it this way, the story line concerning the relationship between Pe-Kin (China) and Bri-Ti (Britain) analyzed earlier could be read as satirizing Britain's material interest in China. Dibdin very likely saw the connection between material obsession and cultural appreciation, and he wrote comments reflecting on that obsession as a consequence of the China trade and the embassy visits. It may be argued that Dibdin's satire actually worked because for the reviewers, the satirical flavor of *Chinese Sorcerer*, a "Bohea-romance" and a "China-dish of weak tea," had an unwelcome aftertaste. After being greatly dazzled with spectacular thrill and wonder, the reviewers reflected, puzzled, and were left not completely pleased at the spectacle that vividly demonstrated Britain's material interest in China.

After their publication, Davis's translations of *Lao Sheng Er* and *Han Gong Qiu* were met with positive but minimal feedback. Concerning his translation of *Lao Sheng Er*, the critic of *Quarterly Review* expressed appreciation for both the information Davis provided and his comparisons of the play with Western dramas. Reading the translation helped the critic understand how the defects contained in the earlier translation of *Zhao Shi Gu Er* generated imperfect knowledge and subjective assumptions.[96] Although less enthusiastic, the review in *British Critic* found that *Lao Sheng Er* resembled English sentimental comedies and commended Davis's work as providing both information and amusement for those who were interested in China and Chinese theatre.[97] Concerning Davis's translation of *Han Gong Qiu*, the translation committee of the Oriental Translation Fund, which sponsored its publication, praised the work for its "dignified simplicity, and the entire absence of all degrading and revolting images."[98] The above comments express appreciation for the knowledge and information Davis provided about Chinese drama and theatre; perhaps inspired by Davis's intercultural comparisons, they also note the parallels between the Chinese plays and sentimental comedy and dignified tragedy.

Although he considered the plot and incidents of *Han Gong Qiu* superior to those of *Zhao Shi Gu Er*, Davis stated that he was far from entertaining "the presumptuous expectation" that his translation of *Han Gong Qiu* would inspire great dramatic works as the earlier translation of *Zhao Shi Gu Er* had, and that he would be quite satisfied if a reader, upon finishing the play, were to pronounce it "a somewhat curious sample of a very foreign literature."[99] Besides suggesting that it did in fact cross his mind that his translation might well inspire great interest and dramatic adaptations, this comment reveals a contradiction, as Davis also stated that he had chosen to translate *Han Gong Qiu* for "its remarkable accordance with our own cannons of criticism."[100] Overall, Davis seems unsure how his translation would be received, whether as a "curious," outlandish example of a foreign literature, or as a work that exhibited remarkable similarities with Western dramas. For the popular entertainments that depicted China such as *Chinese Sorcerer*, Davis's work appeared not to have made an impact on either their content or stage representation.

In *Chinese Sorcerer*, the sources that informed its depictions of China and the Chinese had a range of origins, from the Jesuit writings to Murphy's *Orphan* to the most recent embassy visits. Didbin's use of these sources exhibits the process of interculturation, in which references to China from different historical moments were retained and presented in a single work. It is possible that Dibdin placed great emphasis on the scenery in part because it represented the most recent information about the country and therefore had the greatest novelty factor. Among the scene painters listed in *Chinese Sorcerer*'s playbill (Figure 3.3 and 3.4) is Clarkson Stanfield (1793–1867), who traveled to China in 1815 and returned home in 1816 with a portfolio of sketches.[101] The participation of an artist who had gained firsthand knowledge of China very likely added to the attraction of the spectacle.[102]

Yet while Stanfield's drawings entered the ongoing process in which British theatre interculturated depictions of China, Davis's literary texts, unlike the earlier Jesuit writings and the translation of *Zhao Shi Gu Er*, remained outside of this process.

There are two possible and related reasons that may explain why Davis's work did not participate in the process of interculturation at this historical moment; the first concerns the British attitude toward visual spectacles, and the second concerns shifting perceptions of China driven by embassies and commercial contacts. The review of *Chinese Sorcerer* in the *Morning Post* stated that if the piece, "a holiday trifle," were evaluated not as "a literary production," but as "a dramatic spectacle" it was one of the most splendid ever produced, "prodigally liberal as the Stage has long been in all that related to spectacle." The splendid scenes represented, with superb effect, "the brilliant monstrosities of China" and exhibited pictures "as magnificent as *outrè*, and furnish the eye with a treat such as it does not often realize."[103] Unlike the other critics, cited earlier, who severely criticized Dibdin's script, the *Morning Post* reviewer advised to take the textual, literary aspect of *Chinese Sorcerer* lightly, as it belonged to a different theatre genre ("dramatic spectacle") and was meant as a feast for the eyes. In this case, the rare treat for the eyes was the eccentric ("*outré*"), monstrous Chinese scenic views that were, in the words of David Porter, "at once alluring and repulsive, charming and grotesque, strange and strangely familiar."[104] China's material goods and visual wonders had become so attractive to the British, informed and updated as they were by Britain's commercial activities in China, that a literary understanding was perhaps not necessary.

The review in the *New Monthly Magazine and Literary Journal* expressed a similar opinion and even wished that *Chinese Sorcerer* was presented "without any words at all" since they were "not quite so essential to the interest as the words of Shakespeare," and the performers were but "assistants to the sceneshifter and the mechanist." To be critical about the production, the review complained that the title contained an unrealistic promise because the Chinese, with whose figures "we are so familiar in our cups," seemed incapable of the romantic, and China, "the Celestial Empire," that "great plain of little feet and less minds, where honour is unknown, and where industry and misery seem to reproduce each other," could not contain "any thing light, airy, generous, or terrific."[105] This review furthers the divide between the literary and the spectacular by diminishing the importance of language in the production, perhaps justifying the gibberish lyrics in *Chinese Sorcerer*. It also echoes the close connection between the material consumption of tea (the "China-dish of weak tea" of *Chinese Sorcerer*) and the audience's intellectual recognition of the Chinese as figures in teacups, a peculiar-looking people from an impossible land with strange laws and "monstrous" aesthetics. Instead of being perceived as a country of admired high cultural achievements, as in the Jesuit writings of the previous centuries, China in the early nineteenth-century British perceptions had been exoticized and trivialized as that "great plain of little feet and less minds." The limited linguistic, textual, and literary understanding of the country appears to have been a critical factor.

In 1839, the Society for the Diffusion of Useful Knowledge in London asked Davis to judge an essay contest on the opium trade with China. The contest attracted only a small number of essays and the quality was generally poor. Commenting on this, Davis wrote to Thomas Coates, secretary of the Society, that "the paucity of competition may perhaps arise in some degree from the circumstance, that of those few persons in this country whose pursuits connect them with China, such as are literary are not commercial, and such as are commercial are not literary."[106] Davis's observation of the divide between literary and commercial interests provides another perspective on the impact that Britain's commercial interest in China had on its understanding of the country. The dramatic increase in trade volumes and Chinese imports appeared to have little influence on British study and appreciation of Chinese literary culture.

In 1847, while serving as governor of Hong Kong, Davis was elected president of the China Branch of the Royal Asiatic Society. In the inaugural address, Davis, echoing Thomas Robert Malthus, his professor at the East India Company's college, characterized "a great deal of Asiatic literature" as "childish," which was in fact "a reflex of that general condition of society and intellect in which it originates." Although he praised the Chinese language as a philological miracle for its ingenious application of ideograms, he criticized its "unpliant nature" and "the difficulty of conveying foreign ideas through it." "Under the head of arts," Davis suggested, "we are already too much beholden to Chinese ingenuity to be altogether without hope of something from the future."[107] In these orientalist, pessimistic, and somewhat baffling comments, Davis negated all his earlier work translating Chinese language and literature. The remarks may be indicative of Davis's frustration at how little his efforts had achieved in introducing Chinese literary works to a broader audience; apparently he had given up on exploring further the "unpliant nature" of the Chinese language.

Described as "the last link between the old and the new school of sinologists,"[108] Davis's informal coupling of his official mercantile duties with his private literary interests was replaced by the rise of professional scholars who would devote their full attention to conducting in-depth, scholarly research on China and Chinese literature. Davis's work was therefore largely overlooked by later scholars of Chinese theatre.[109] However, Davis deserves respect for his efforts to produce the best possible translations of Chinese plays that he could and make them available to a British audience. His endeavors and comments also evince the challenge of understanding and translating literary Chinese, even for a longtime student of the language. Davis demonstrated that an Englishman in the early nineteenth century was able to translate Chinese dramas, comprehend Chinese theatre from its various elements, and draw interesting, albeit questionable, intercultural comparisons.

On the London stage, as will be discussed in the next chapter, China continued to be characterized by its sights, commodities, and peculiar mannerisms and aesthetics, while theatre practitioners explored Chinese theatre for its distinct staging approaches. The literary approach was still missing. A newer and more critical factor that came to influence stage representations of China in the later period was the development of direct intercultural contact between the British and the Chinese, which can be attributed to the waves of war and migration that characterized the period of British colonial intrusion into China. This development would inspire depictions of the country and its people that reflect British superiority, anxiety, fear, and paranoia about the interculturalizing impact of closer contact with Chinese on the British themselves.

NOTES

1. J. L. Cranmer-Byng, "Introduction," in *An Embassy to China: Being the Journal Kept by Lord Macartney During His Embassy to the Emperor Ch'ien-lung 1793–1794*, by George M. Macartney (Hamden, CT: Archon Books, 1963), 30.
2. For a brief account of the Macartney embassy's visit to China, see, for example, Mark C. Elliott, "The Macartney Mission," in *Emperor Qianlong: Son of Heaven, Man of the World* (New York: Longman, 2009), 134–139.
3. Alternative English spellings of *kowtow* (*kow-tow*) include *kotow* (*ko-tow*) and *kotou* (*ko-tou*). The term in the Chinese pinyin spelling is *koutou*, 叩頭, "head knocking."
4. Macartney, *An Embassy to China*, 84–85, 119–120. The Qing ministers' counterproposal, for Macartney to kneel on both knees, was refused by Macartney. See Macartney, 119.
5. Henry Ellis, *Journal of the Proceedings of the Late Embassy to China* ... (London: J. Murray, 1817), 230–237.
6. *Da Qing Gaozong Chun (Qianlong) Huang Di Shi Lu* [Chronological Records of the Qianlong Emperor of the Qing Dynasty] (Taipei: Hua Lian Chu Ban She, 1964), vol. 29; *Da Qing Renzong Rui (Jiaqing) Huang Di Shi Lu* [Chronological Records of the Jiaqing Emperor of the Qing Dynasty] (Taipei: Hua Lian Chu Ban She, 1964), vol. 7.
7. Cranmer-Byng, 34.
8. Hampton Pritchard, chap. 2 in *The Crucial Years of Early Anglo-Chinese Relations, 1750–1800* (Pullman, WA: 1936) (hereafter cited as *Crucial Years*); Weng Eang Cheong, *The Hong Merchants of Canton: Chinese Merchants in Sino-Western Trade* (Richmond: Curzon, 1997).
9. Pritchard, chaps. 3 and 4 in *Crucial Years*.
10. Michael Greenberg, chap. 4 in *British Trade and the Opening of China 1800–42* (Cambridge: Cambridge University Press, 1951).
11. John Barrow, *Travels in China* (London: T. Cadell and W. Davies, 1804); George Staunton, *An Authentic Account of an Embassy from the King of Britain to the Emperor of China* ... (London: G. Nicol, 1797); Cranmer-Byng, 34–35.
12. George Thomas Staunton, "Translator's Preface," in *Ta Tsing Leu Lee; Being the Fundational Laws, and a Selection from the Supplementary Statutes, of the Penal Code of China* (London: T Cadell and W. Davies, 1810), vii–viii.

128 *Open Views of China*

13. See Ellis; Clarke Abel, *Narrative of a Journey in the Interior of China* (London: Longman, Hurst, Rees, Orme, and Brown, 1818).

14. David Mayer, *Harlequin in His Element: The English Pantomime, 1806–1836* (Cambridge, MA: Harvard University Press, 1969), 140.

15. For accounts about Davis's life and career, see, for example, K. D. Reynolds, "Davis, Sir John Francis, First Baronet (1795–1890)," in *Oxford Dictionary of National Biography* (Oxford University Press, 2004–), doi:10.1093/ref:odnb/7287; "Obituary: John Francis Davis," *Times*, November 14, 1890, p. 10; Ernest John Eitel, chap. 14 in *Europe in China: The History of Hongkong from the Beginning to the Year 1882* (London: Luzac and Company, 1895); G. B. Endacott, chap. 7 in *A History of Hong Kong* (London: Oxford University Press, 1973); Frank Welsh, chap. 6 in *A History of Hong Kong* (London: HarperCollins, 1993).

16. Frederick Charles Danvers et al., *Memorials of Old Haileybury College* (Westminster: A. Constable and Company, 1894), 579.

17. Hosea B. Morse, *The Chronicles of the East India Company Trading to China 1635–1834*, vol. 3 (Cambridge: Harvard University Press, 1926), 209–210.

18. In chronological order, Davis's Chinese works in this period, published as individual books, include: *San-Yu-Low; or, The Three Dedicated Rooms* [*San Yu Lou*, 三與樓, novelette] (Canton, China: The East India Company's Press, by P. P. Thoms, 1815); *Laou-Seng-Urh, or, "An Heir in His Old Age." A Chinese Drama* [*Lao Sheng Er*, 老生兒, drama] (London: John Murray, 1817); *Chinese Novels* [three novelettes including *San Yu Lou* and 126 Chinese proverbs] (London: John Murray, 1822); *Hien Wun Shoo ...* [*Xian Wen Shu*, 賢文書, Chinese moral maxims] (London: J. Murray, 1823); *A Vocabulary Containing Chinese Words and Phrases Peculiar to Canton and Macao, and to the Trade of Those Places ...* [vocabulary] (Macao, China: The East India Company's Press, by P. P. Thoms, 1824); *The Fortunate Union, a Romance ...* [*Hao Qiu Zhuan*, 好逑傳, novel] (London: The Oriental Translation Fund, 1829); *Hān Koong Tsew, or the Sorrows of Hān ...* [*Han Gong Qiu*, 漢宮秋, drama] (London: The Oriental Translation Fund, 1829); and *Poeseos Sinensis Commentarii. On the Poetry of the Chinese ...* [Han Wen Shi Jie, 漢文詩解, poetry] (London: J. L Cox, 1829).

19. The Royal Asiatic Society was founded in 1823 for "the advancement of Oriental learning." See Frederick E. Pargiter, "A Brief History of the Royal Asiatic Society of Great Britain and Ireland, 1823 to 1923," in *Centenary Volume of the Royal Asiatic Society of Great Britain and Ireland 1823–1923*, ed. Frederick E. Pargiter (London: The Royal Asiatic Society, 1923), vii. Davis's contributions to the Society are listed on 26–27, 123.

20. Davis, "Observations on the Language and Literature of China," in *Chinese Novels*, 1, 4 (hereafter cited as "Observations"). Although Davis did not identify the name of the Chinese novel, presumably he was referring to Thomas Percy's translation of *Hau Kiou Choaan* (i.e., *Hao Qiu Zhuan*) published in 1761. For discussions on this English translation, see, for example, Shouyi Chen, "Thomas Percy and His Chinese Studies," in *The Vision of China in the English Literature of the Seventeenth and Eighteenth Centuries*, ed. Adrian Hsia (Hong Kong: Chinese University Press, 1998), 301–324; T. C. Fan, "Percy's *Hau Kiou Choaan*," *The Review of English Studies* 22, no. 86 (1946): 117–125. Davis provided a translation of the novel himself (see *The Fortunate Union*).

21. Davis, "Observations," 2, 4.

22. Brought along by his father George Staunton, the official secretary of the Macartney embassy, George Thomas Staunton served as Macartney's page and learned to speak Chinese. He accompanied Amherst and was instrumental in the Amherst embassy's refusal to the Chinese *kowtow* ceremonial ritual. For accounts about Staunton, see, for example, Cranmer-Byng, "Appendix A: Biographical Notes on Some Personalities, English and Chinese," in Macartney, 307–308; Richard Davenport-Hines, "Staunton, Sir George Thomas, Second Baronet (1781–1859)," in *Oxford Dictionary of National Biography* (Oxford University Press, 2004–), doi:10.1093/ref:odnb/26325.

23. George Thomas Staunton, "Translator's Preface," v–vi. For assessments of the Jesuit writings' neutrality (or the lack thereof), see, for example, David E. Mungello, *The Great Encounter of China and the West, 1500–1800* (Lanham, MD: Rowman and Littlefield, 2013); *Curious Land: Jesuit Accommodation and the Origins of Sinology* (Honolulu: University of Hawaii Press, 1989), 13–20; Mary Gertrude Mason, *Western Concepts of China and the Chinese, 1840–1876* (Durham, NC: The Seeman Printery, 1939), 3–12.

24. Davis, "Observations," 5–6.

25. George Thomas Staunton, "Translator's Preface," vi–vii, xii; Davis, "A Brief View of the Chinese Drama, and of Their Theatrical Exhibitions," in *Laou-Seng-Urh*, iii–iv. For further details on the various subjects of the Jesuit writings, see, for example, Mungello, *Curious Land*; Mason, 5–9.

26. Davis, "Observations," 9; "A Brief View," iii–iv.

27. In 1829, Davis published an essay, "Chinese Drama, Poetry, and Romance," as Art. IV in *Quarterly Review* 41 (1829): 85–120. This essay was later revised and republished under the title, "The Drama, Novels, and Romances," in *Chinese Miscellanies: A Collection of Essays and Notes* (London: John Murray, 1865). In *The Chinese: A General Description of the Empire of China and Its Inhabitants* (London: Charles Knight, 1836), Davis included a chapter (vol. 2, chap. 16) that draws upon his earlier writings and discusses Chinese drama, poetry, and novels. There are two versions of *Chinese* published by the same London publisher in 1836, set in two slightly different formats which affect their pagination. In the following, I cite the version kept at the New York Public Library.

28. Du Halde, "Avertissement," *Tchao Chi Cou Ell* (*Zhao Shi Gu Er*), in *Description géographique, historique, chronologique, politique, et physique de l'empire de la Chine et de la Tartarie chinoise* ... (La Haye: Henri Scheurleer, 1736), 3:419–421. For its English translation, I have consulted the 1736 version, *The General History of China* ... (London: John Watts, 1736), to assist my reading and analysis. This English version, and its later 1741 edition, translates all of the French original, except one short paragraph about not using masks in performance (du Halde, 3:420) and the last example (the Chinese have their own poetry) that I cite in this paragraph.

29. Voltaire, *L'Orphelin de la Chine, Tragédie* (Paris: Michele Lambert, 1755), v–vij.

30. For a brief account about Richard Hurd, see, for example, G. M. Ditchfield and Sarah Brewer, "Hurd, Richard (1720–1808)," in *Oxford Dictionary of National Biography* (Oxford University Press, 2004–), doi:10.1093/ref:odnb/14249.

31. Richard Hurd, "A Discourse on Poetical Imitation," in Horace, *Q. Horatii Flacii Epistola ad Augustum. With an English Commentary and Notes*, ed. Richard Hurd (London: W. Thurlbourn, 1751), 163–166. The sections on Chinese drama

were later reprinted in Thomas Percy, ed., *Miscellaneous Pieces Relating to the Chinese* (London: R. and J. Dodsley, 1762), 1:221–232.

32. Hurd, 165–167.

33. John Francis Davis, "A Brief View." Hereafter all the page numbers refer to this edition.

34. Davis dated the dynasty as from 1260 to 1333. See Davis, "A Brief View," xxxii.

35. Instead of following the layout in the Chinese text, which clearly separates the arias from the dialogues, Davis's translation integrated them and used quotation marks to set off the arias. This format choice may suggest that Davis saw the two parts as closely interconnected.

36. Of the thirty-seven arias in the play, Davis left out about seven. Among the voluminous dialogues, Davis left out only a few sections.

37. Davis also stated that he was in China when translating the play and "could avail himself of native references." See Davis, *Chinese*, 2:193.

38. Davis stated that "[t]his specimen of the Chinese stage [*"An Heir in His Old Age"*] had the advantage of being edited, during my absence from England, by the late Sir John Barrow, of the Admiralty." See Davis, "The Rise and Progress of Chinese Literature in England," in *Chinese Miscellanies*, 68. Barrow, the private secretary of Macartney, therefore may have contributed to the rigor and completeness of the translation.

39. Davis, *Chinese*, 2:190–191.

40. Wu Hanchen, *San Jia Cai Tian Si Lao Sheng Er Za Ju* [Drama of Heaven Grants an Heir to an Old Man Who Dispenses His Fortune], vol. 3, bk. 2, of *Yuan Qu Xuan* [Selection of Dramas from the Yuan Dynasty], ed. Zang Maoxun (Shanghai: Zhonghua Shu Ju, 1936).

41. Similar comments are offered in Davis, *Chinese*, 2:193–194.

42. Davis, "Preface," in *Sorrows of Hān*, v.

43. During the Han period, the Chinese court resorted to both warring and marriage alliances in order to ward off or maintain peace with the Xiongnu. It is recorded that Chief Huhanye actively sought peace with China and submitted himself as a tributary lord. He requested to marry a Han woman so that he would become a son-in-law of the Hans, and was presented with Wang by Emperor Yuan. See, for example, Shouyi Bai, ed., *Zhongguo Tong Shi* [General History of China] (Shanghai: Shanghai Ren Min Chu Ban She, 2004), 5:324–326, 384–392, 6:339–347.

44. The *pipa* is a traditional Chinese string instrument that is played by plucking.

45. Ma Zhiyuan, *Po Yiu Meng Gu Yan Han Gong Qiu Za Ju* [Drama of the Cries of a Lonely Goose Disturb a Wishful Dream and Evoke Autumn in the Palace of Han], vol. 1, bk. 1, of *Yuan Qu Xuan* [Selection of Dramas from the Yuan Dynasty], ed. Zang Maoxun (Shanghai: Zhonghua Shu Ju, 1936). As Davis explained, "Han Gong Qiu" literally means "autumn in the palace of Han." In Chinese, the season of autumn connotes sorrow, and thus he translated "Qiu" (autumn) as "sorrows." See Davis, *Sorrows of Hān*, 3.

46. It may seem strange that in his translation Davis called the character Hanchenyu, a name which appears to combine part of the historical figure's name ("han" from Huhanye) with his honorific title, Chanyu (單于, which I translate as Chief). In fact, Davis understood the name and title together as the character's full name, which he spelled "Hoo-han-ye-chen-yu," and he treated the syllables hoo and ye as superfluous adjuncts. While the syllable ye

is also treated as dispensable in the Chinese original, Davis apparently mistook the syllable hoo/hu (呼) for its independent, literal meaning, "call," and thought it was also unnecessary. See Davis, "Preface," in *Fortunate Union*, 1:xx–xxi.

47. Davis was aware that during the Han Dynasty the northern nomadic people were called Heung-noo (i.e., Xiongnu), a term he regarded as having been used in the period to designate the Tartars. See Davis, *Chinese*, 1:175.

48. Davis, "Chinese Drama, Poetry, and Romance," 87.

49. Davis noted that K'han translates as Ko-han (Kehan, 可汗) in Chinese. See Davis, *Sorrows of Hān*, 3. In Chinese writings, Kehan was used to address rulers of so-called barbarian tribes, while in English it is normally used to designate Mongol rulers. Davis described the play as hinging on "the misfortunes of one of the native [Chinese] Emperors against the Mongol Tartars." See Davis, *Chinese*, 2:198. According to Chinese sources, there is no relationship between the Xiongnu and the Mongols, who were centuries apart from each other. See, for example, Bai, 5:130–138, 13:332–345.

50. Davis, *Chinese*, 1:181–187. Davis states that when the last of the Mongols were expelled from China at the end of the Yuan Dyansty, they sought the protection of the Manchus' forebears, and that the Manchus who conquered China in the 17th century descended from intermarriage between these two peoples (187). These statements are not supported by Chinese sources. See, for example, Bai, 13:543–550, 18:1–7.

51. Davis, *Sorrows of Hān*, 11–12.

52. Davis, "Chinese Drama, Poetry, and Romance," 87.

53. Davis, *Chinese*, 2:200. A similar statement is made in Davis, "Chinese Drama, Poetry, and Romance," 87.

54. Davis, *Sorrows of Hān*, 14. The line is from John Dryden's *All for Love*, a reworking of Shakespeare's *Antony and Cleopatra*. See John Dryden, *Plays: All for Love, Oedipus, Troilus and Cressida*, vol. 13 of *The Works of John Dryden*, ed. Edward Niles Hooker and H. T. Swedenberg, Jr. (Berkeley: University of California Press, 1984), 30 (I.i.216).

55. Another parallel Davis finds between China and Rome is despotism. See Davis, "Chinese Drama, Poetry, and Romance," 93.

56. Davis, "Preface," in *Sorrows of Hān*, vii.

57. Geng Zhang and Hancheng Guo, *Zhongguo Xi Qu Tong Shi* [General History of the Chinese Theatre] (1992; reprint, Taipei: Da Hong Tu Shu, 1998), 1:211–224; Xueqi Wang et al., eds., *Yuan Qu Xuan Jiao Zhu* [Yuan Qu Xuan, with Notes and Edits], by Maoxun Zang (Shijiazhuang Shi: Hebei Jiao Yu Chu Ban She, 1994), 1:169–172; Yongyi Zeng, ed., *Zhongguo Gu Dian Xi Ju Xuan Zhu* [Selections of Classical Chinese Theatre, with Notes] (Taipei: Guo Jia Chu Ban She, 1983), 171–172.

58. Davis, "Preface," in *Fortunate Union*, 1:xvii, xxii. George Thomas Staunton's comment was similarly referenced as an authority in Davis, "Observations," 9–10. Staunton's statement was published in George Thomas Staunton, "Preface," in *Narrative of the Chinese Embassy to the Khan of the Tourgouth Tartars* (London: John Murray, 1821), xxiii.

59. Davis, "Preface," in *Sorrows of Hān*, vii.

60. Ibid.

61. Du Halde, "Avertissement," 3:421.

62. Davis, *Chinese*, 2:185.

63. Davis, "A Brief View," xli–xlii, xliii–xliv; "Preface," in *Sorrows of Hān*, vi; *Chinese*, 2:192–193, 196–197. These comparisons by Davis expand upon Hurd's analyses discussed earlier in this chapter. See Hurd, 165–167. Barrow makes a similar point on the Greek prologue analogy. See Barrow, 220.

64. Davis, *Chinese*, 2:197; "Chinese Drama, Poetry, and Romance," 93.

65. Davis, "A Brief View," x–xii; *Chinese*, 2:187–189. Davis appears to be citing the examples of Chinese theatre performance given by Barrow and interpreting them in a more favorable light. See Barrow, 219–220.

66. Davis, "A Brief View," xii–xvii; *Chinese*, 2:185.

67. Davis, "A Brief View," x, xvii–xviii; *Chinese*, 2:185.

68. Davis, "A Brief View," xlv.

69. Ibid., xii–xv; *Chinese*, 2:185 fn.* (which extends to the next page). Davis gave an anecdote that it was rumored that because Emperor Kien Long (Qianlong) unlawfully took an actress to be his concubine, women were afterwards forbidden to appear on the stage (xiii). In 1772, the Qianlong emperor did issue an edict banning women from performing on stage, but it was ineffective. See, for example, Colin Mackerras, *The Rise of the Peking Opera, 1770–1870* (Oxford: Clarendon Press, 1972), 45–47.

70. Davis, "A Brief View," xiv–xv. For discussion on acting as a family business and the existence of actresses in Chinese theatre, in the example of during the Yuan Dynasty when the plays translated by Davis were written, see, for example, Zhang and Guo, 1:321–325.

71. Macartney, 136–140. Parts of Macartney's account, as well as from the Dutch and Russian embassies, were quoted by Davis. See "A Brief View," xviii–xxvii.

72. Zhang and Guo, 2:1201–1209; Zhizhang Wang, *Qing Sheng Ping Shu Zhi Lue* [Accounts of the Sheng Ping Bureau at the Qing Court] (Shanghai: Shanghai Shu Dian, 1991); Chuanhai Niu, *Qianlong Shi Qi Ju Chang Huo Dong Zhi Yan Jiu* [Studies of Theatre Activities During the Qianlong Era] (Taipei: Hua Gang, 1977); Huiying Qiu, *Qianlong Shi Qi Xi Qu Huo Dong Yan Jiu* [Studies of Theatre During the Qianlong Era] (Taipei: Wen Jin, 2000); Wilt L. Idema, "Performances on a Three-tiered Stage Court Theatre During the Qianlong Era," in *Ad Seres et Tungusos …*, ed. Lutz Bieg, Erling von Mende, and Martina Siebert (Wiesbaden: Harrassowitz, 2000), 201–219.

73. According to the extant records of court entertainments held during the late Qing period, one often repeated feature in the repertoire was tributary envoys, either from barbarian lands or from the supernatural world, who present precious gifts to the court for various celebratory occasions. These records suggest that a similar practice might have been used in the early court performances. See Gu Gong Bo Wu Yuan, ed., *Qing Dai Nan Fu Yu Sheng Ping Shu Ju Ben Yu Dang An* [Archives and Play Scripts of the Bureaus of Nan and Sheng Ping in the Qing Dynasty] (Haikou Shi: Hainan Chu Ban She, 2001).

74. Barrow, 218.

75. Ibid., 221–223.

76. Thomas John Dibdin, *The Reminiscences of Thomas Dibdin …* (London: Henry Colburn, 1827), 2:256; "New Theatre Royal, Drury Lane," *Theatrical Observer*, May 5, 1823; "Drury-Lane," *Theatrical Observer*, May 6, 1823.

77. These productions include: *The Mandarin; or, Harlequin in China* (1811, pantomime, Astley's Amphitheatre); *Whang-Fong; or, The Clown of China* (1812, pantomime, Sadler's Wells); *Aladdin; or, The Wonderful Lamp* (1813–22, 1825, Melo-Dramatic

Romance, Covent Garden); *Harlequin and Fortunio; or, Shing-Moo and Thun-Ton* (1815–16, Christmas pantomime, Covent Garden); *Kouli Khan; or, The Terrific Signal* (1818, Melodrama, Surrey); *Xaia of China; or, The Fatal Floodgate* (1820, equestrian Melo-Drama, Astley's Amphitheatre); *Pong Wong; or, The Horoscope* (1826, Extravaganza, Haymarket); *The Sacred Standard and the Chinese Prince; or, The Forest of Palms* (1828, Melo-Drama, Coburg); *Dragon's Gift; or, The Scarf of Flight and the Mirror of Light* (1830, Melo-Drama, Drury Lane).

78. Here my argument is indebted to John O'Brien's discussion of "the pleasures of a kind of travelogue" that pantomimes offer and Elizabeth Hope Chang's statement that for nineteenth-century Britons, China "was at once place, commodity, people, and, at the same time, something more than all of those." See John O'Brien, "Pantomime," in *The Cambridge Companion to British Theatre, 1730–1830,* ed. Jane Moody and Daniel O'Quinn (Cambridge: Cambridge University Press, 2007), 109; Elizabeth Hope Chang, *Britain's Chinese Eye: Literature, Empire, and Aesthetics in Nineteenth-Century Britain* (Stanford: Stanford University Press, 2010), 1.

79. For accounts of the life and career of Dibdin, see, for example, Dibdin, *Reminiscences*; John Pruitt, "Thomas Dibdin (1771–1841)," in *Nineteenth-Century British Dramatists,* vol. 344 of *Dictionary of Literary Biography,* ed. Angela Courtney (Detroit: Gale Cengage Learning, 2009), 91–105.

80. The following synopsis is based on Thomas John Dibdin, *Whang-Fong* [as *The Chinese Sorcerer; or, The Emperor and His Three Sons*], Nineteenth Century English Drama: Plays Submitted to the Lord Chamberlain (1823; reprint, New Canaan, CT.: Readex, 1985–). In the manuscript, the third son is called Kanfoo and the emperor Long Kein. In the playbills they are Kan-Fu and Kein-Long.

81. In the manuscript Bri-Ti is listed as Zam-Ti's sister. At the end of the play she is revealed to be the orphaned daughter of the Chinese emperor's brother. The playbill (Figure 3.3) listed her as "Orphan Daughter of a poor Fisherman."

82. The actual Kein-Long (Qianlong) emperor who received the Macartney embassy was himself a Manchu and, in the perception of Barrow (Macartney's private secretary) cited earlier, a Tartar ruler. In Dibdin's dramatization here, he is depicted as a Chinese emperor opposed to the Tartars.

83. The character was not provided a name in the manuscript; she was, however, listed as Quang-Si on the playbill (Figure 3.4).

84. Jack Zipes, ed., *The Great Fairy Tale Tradition* (New York: W. W. Norton, 2001), 848–849.

85. Kan-Fu is very possibly a creative transformation of the name of the province Kan-Soo or Kan-Sou (Gansu). Spelled Kan-Fu in the playbill, in the manuscript the name of the character is spelled Kanfoo. Likewise, the name Po-Ning could be the reverse spelling of the city Ningpo (Ningbo). If my interpretation is correct, these names can be added to the list of characters that are named after Chinese cities or provinces.

86. Zipes, 335–346.

87. Dibdin, *Reminiscences* 2:256; "Drury-Lane," *Theatrical Observer,* March 24, 1823; "Theatres. Drury Lane." *Times,* April 1, 1823, p. 3.

88. Dibdin, *Whang-Fong.* Here and after the scenes, lines, and pages are referred to this manuscript, which is unpaged in Act I.

89. O'Brien, 113.

90. The manuscript does not specify at what point in Act One the ballet occurs, but according to the review in the *Observer*, it was performed for Kein-Long's birthday. See "Drury Lane: 'Chinese Sorcerer,'" *Observer*, April 7, 1823, p. 3.

91. "Theatres. Drury Lane," *Times*, April 1, 1823, p. 3.

92. "The Drama," *London Magazine*, May 1823, p. 560.

93. "New Drury Lane Theatre," *Theatrical Magazine*, April 1823, p. 190.

94. "Theatrical Examiner," *Examiner*, April 6, 1823, p. 232.

95. "The Drama," *London Magazine*, May 1823, pp. 560–561.

96. "Art. VI," *Quarterly Review* 16 (Oct. 1816 and Jan. 1817): 396–407.

97. "Art. XIII," *British Critic* (May 1817): 526–535.

98. The Oriental Translation Fund, "Second Report of the Oriental Translation Committee, Presented to the Subscribers to the Oriental Translation Fund on the 30th of May, 1829," in *Report of the Proceedings of the Second General Meeting of the Subscribers to the Oriental Translation Fund ...*, by the Oriental Translation Fund (London: J. L. Cox, 1829), 15.

99. Davis, "Preface," in *Sorrows of Hàn*, vii.

100. Ibid., vi.

101. Pieter T. van der Merwe, "Clarkson Stanfield (1793–1867)," in *The Spectacular Career of Clarkson Stanfield 1793–1867 ...* (Newcastle upon Tyne: Tyne and Wear County Council Museums, 1979), 14. For Stanfield's scene painting career, see also Sybil M. Rosenfeld, *Georgian Scene Painters and Scene Painting* (Cambridge: Cambridge University Press, 1981), 104–109.

102. Another name whose work was often advertised in other Chinese visual spectacles of the time was William Alexander (1767–1816), the official draftsman attached to the Macartney embassy, who drew a series of watercolor sketches of Chinese landscapes and people during the journey. His Chinese drawings became a major source of Chinese scenery consulted by English scene painters and advertised in playbills. For a brief discussion of Alexander and some of his works, see Royal Pavilion, Art Gallery and Museums (Brighton), "Introduction," In *William Alexander: An English Artist in Imperial China ...*, (Brighton: Royal Pavilion, Art Gallery and Museums, 1981), 7–17; Mildred Archer, "Works by William Alexander and James Wales," in *The Royal Asiatic Society, Its History and Treasures ...*, ed. Stuart Simmons and Simon Digby (Leiden: E. J. Brill, published for the Society, 1979), 117–119.

103. "Theatres. Drury-Lane," *Morning Post*, April 1, 1823.

104. David Porter, *The Chinese Taste in Eighteenth-Century England* (Cambridge: Cambridge University Press, 2010), 4–10. Porter characterizes Chinese objects and aesthetic ideas as possessing a "monstrous beauty" in his study of the role of what he calls the "Chinese taste" in the making of British modernity in the eighteenth century.

105. "The Drama. Drury-Lane Theatre," *New Monthly Magazine and Literary Journal*, May 1, 1823, pp. 203–204.

106. Letter to Thomas Coates, January 8, 1839, kept in the Society for the Diffusion of Useful Knowledge Archives at University College London.

107. Davis, "Address to the China Branch of the Royal Asiatic Society. On Its Inauguration at Hongkong," in *Chinese Miscellaneous*, 113–115. The address was first published as *Preliminary Address Delivered at the Inaugural Meeting of the Asiatic Society of China, on Monday, 15th February, 1847* (Hong Kong: Office of the China Mail, 1847).

108. Henri Cordier, *Bibliotheca Sinica: dictionnaire bibliographique des ouvrages relatifs à l'empire chinois* (Staten Island, NY: Maurizio Martino, 1996), 3:1792.
109. Among the few modern critical assessments of Davis's work are, for example, Cyril Birch, "On the History of the Translation of Chinese Plays into English," in *Europe Studies China: Papers From an International Conference on the History of European Sinology*, eds. Ming Wilson and John Cayley (London: Han-Shan Tang Books, 1995), 215–227; A. Owen Aldridge, "The First Chinese Drama in English Translation," in *Studies in Chinese-Western Comparative Drama: 4th International Comparative Literature Conference Papers*, ed. Luk Yun-Tong (Hong Kong: Chinese University Press, 1990), 185–191.

REFERENCES

Abel, Clarke. *Narrative of a Journey in the Interior of China, and of a Voyage to and from That Country, in the Years 1816 and 1817; Containing an Account of the Most Interesting Transactions of Lord Amherst's Embassy to the Court of Pekin, and Observations on the Countries Which It Visited.* London: Longman, Hurst, Rees, Orme, and Brown, 1818.

Aldridge, A. Owen. "The First Chinese Drama in English Translation." In *Studies in Chinese-Western Comparative Drama: 4th International Comparative Literature Conference Papers*, edited by Luk Yun-Tong, 185–191. Hong Kong: Chinese University Press, 1990.

Anonymous. "Art. VI." *Quarterly Review* 16 (1816): 396–407.

———. "Art. XIII." *British Critic* (1817): 526–535.

———. "The Drama." *London Magazine*, May 1823, pp. 560–561.

———. "The Drama. Drury-Lane Theatre." *New Monthly Magazine and Literary Journal*, May 1, 1823, pp. 203–204.

———. "Drury-Lane." *Theatrical Observer; and Daily Bill of the Play*, March 24, 1823.

———. "Drury-Lane." *Theatrical Observer; and Daily Bill of the Play*, May 6, 1823.

———. "Drury Lane: 'Chinese Sorcerer,'" *Observer*, April 7, 1823, p. 3.

———. "New Drury Lane Theatre." *Drama; or, Theatrical Magazine*, April 1823, p. 190.

———. "New Theatre Royal, Drury Lane." *Theatrical Observer*, May 5, 1823.

———. "Obituary: John Francis Davis." *Times*, November 14, 1890, p. 10.

———. "Theatres. Drury-Lane." *Morning Post*, April 1, 1823.

———. "Theatres. Drury Lane." *Times*, April 1, 1823, p. 3.

———. "Theatrical Examiner." *Examiner*, April 6, 1823, p. 232.

Archer, Mildred. "Works by William Alexamder and James Wales." In *The Royal Asiatic Society, Its History and Treasures: Published in Commemoration of the Sesquicentenary Year of the Foundation of the Royal Asiatic Society of Great Britain and Ireland*, edited by Stuart Simmonds and Simon Digby, 116–125. Leiden: E. J. Brill, 1979.

Bai, Shouyi, ed. *Zhongguo Tong Shi* [General History of China]. 22 vols. Shanghai: Shanghai Ren Min Chu Ban She, 2004.

Barrow, John. *Travels in China, Containing Descriptions, Observations, and Comparisons, Made and Collected in the Course of a Short Residence at the Imperial Palace of Yuen-Min-Yuen, and on a Subsequent Journey Through the Country From Pekin to Canton. In Which It Is Attempted to Appreciate the Rank That*

This Extraordinary Empire May Be Considered to Hold in the Scale of Civilized Nations. London: T. Cadell and W. Davies, 1804.

Birch, Cyril. "On the History of the Translation of Chinese Plays into English." In *Europe Studies China: Papers From an International Conference on the History of European Sinology*, edited by Ming Wilson and John Cayley, 215–227. London: Han-Shan Tang Books, 1995.

Chang, Elizabeth Hope. *Britain's Chinese Eye: Literature, Empire, and Aesthetics in Nineteenth-Century Britain.* Stanford: Stanford University Press, 2010.

Chen, Shouyi. "Thomas Percy and His Chinese Studies." In *The Vision of China in the English Literature of the Seventeenth and Eighteenth Centuries*, edited by Adrian Hsia, 301–324. Hong Kong: Chinese University Press, 1998.

Cheong, Weng Eang. *The Hong Merchants of Canton: Chinese Merchants in Sino-Western Trade.* Richmond: Curzon, 1997.

Cordier, Henri. *Bibliotheca Sinica: dictionnaire bibliographique des ouvrages relatifs à l'empire chinois.* 6 vols. Staten Island, NY: Maurizio Martino, 1996.

Cranmer-Byng, J. L. "Introduction" and "Appendix A: Biographical Notes on Some Personalities, English and Chinese." In *An Embassy to China: Being the Journal Kept by Lord Macartney During His Embassy to the Emperor Ch'ien-Lung, 1793–1794*, by George Macartney, 1–58, 307–331. Hamden, CT: Archon Books, 1963.

Da Qing Gaozong Chun (Qianlong) Huang Di Shi Lu [Chronological Records of the Qianlong Emperor of the Qing Dynasty]. 30 vols. Taipei: Hua Lian Chu Ban She, 1964.

Da Qing Renzong Rui (Jiaqing) Huang Di Shi Lu [Chronological Records of the Jiaqing Emperor of the Qing Dynasty]. 8 vols. Taipei: Hua Lian Chu Ban She, 1964.

Danvers, Frederick Charles, et al. *Memorials of Old Haileybury College.* Westminster: A. Constable and Company, 1894.

Davenport-Hines, Richard. "Staunton, Sir George Thomas, Second Baronet (1781–1859)." In *Oxford Dictionary of National Biography.* Oxford University Press, 2004–. doi:10.1093/ref:odnb/26325.

Davis, John Francis. "Art. IV: Chinese Drama, Poetry, and Romance." *Quarterly Review* 41 (1829): 85–120.

———. *The Chinese: A General Description of the Empire of China and Its Inhabitants.* 2 vols. London: Charles Knight, 1836.

———. *Chinese Miscellanies: A Collection of Essays and Notes.* London: John Murray, 1865.

———, trans. *Chinese Novels, Translated from the Originals; to Which Are Added Proverbs and Moral Maxims, Collected from Their Classical Books and Other Sources.* London: John Murray, 1822.

———, trans. *The Fortunate Union, a Romance, Translated From the Chinese Original, With Notes and Illustrations. To Which Is Added, a Chinese Tragedy.* 2 vols. London: The Oriental Translation Fund, 1829.

———, trans. *Hān Koong Tsew, or the Sorrows of Hān: a Chinese Tragedy. Translated From the Original, With Notes.* London: The Oriental Translation Fund, 1829.

———. *Hien Wun Shoo. Chinese Moral Maxims, With a Free and Verbal Translation; Affording Examples of the Grammatical Structure of the Language.* London: J. Murray, 1823.

————, trans. *Laou-Seng-Urh, or, "An Heir in His Old Age." A Chinese Drama.* London: John Murray, 1817.

————. *Poeseos Sinensis Commentarii. On the Poetry of the Chinese, (From the Royal Asiatic Transactions). To Which Are Added, Translations and Detached Pieces.* London: J. L. Cox, 1829.

————. *Preliminary Address Delivered at the Inaugural Meeting of the Asiatic Society of China, on Monday, 15th February, 1847.* Hong Kong: Office of the China Mail, 1847.

————, trans. *San-Yu-Low: or, The Three Dedicated Rooms.* Canton, China: The East India Company's Press, by P. P. Thoms, 1815.

————. *A Vocabulary Containing Chinese Words and Phrases Peculiar to Canton and Macao, and to the Trade of Those Places; Together With the Titles and Addresses of All the Officers of Government, Hong Merchants, &c. &c. Alphabetically Arranged, and Intended As an Aid to Correspondence and Conversation in the Native Language.* Macao, China: The East India Company's Press, by P. P. Thoms, 1824.

Dibdin, Thomas John. *The Reminiscences of Thomas Dibdin, of the Theatres Royal, Covent-Garden, Drury-Lane, Haymarket, &c., and Author of The Cabinet, &c... .* 2 vols. London: Henry Colburn, 1827.

————. *Whang Fong* [As *The Chinese Sorceror; or, The Emperor and His Three Sons*]. 1823. Reprint, Nineteenth Century English Drama: Plays Submitted to the Lord Chamberlain. New Canaan, CT: Readex, 1985–.

Ditchfield, G. M., and Sarah Brewer. "Hurd, Richard (1720–1808)." In *Oxford Dictionary of National Biography.* Oxford University Press, 2004–. doi:10.1093/ref:odnb/14249.

Dryden, John. *Plays: All for Love, Oedipus, Troilus and Cressida.* Vol. 13 of *The Works of John Dryden.* Edited by Edward Niles Hooker and H. T. Swedenberg Jr. Berkeley: University of California Press, 1984.

Du Halde, Jean-Baptiste. *Description géographique, historique, chronologique, politique, et physique de l'empire de la Chine et de la Tartarie chinoise enrichie des cartes générales et particulieres de ces pays, de la carte générale et des cartes particulieres du Thibet, et de la Corée; et ornée d'un grand nombre de figures et de vignettes gravées en tailledouce.* 4 vols. La Haye: Henri Scheurleer, 1736.

————. *The General History of China. Containing a Geographical, Historical, Chronological, Political and Physical Description of the Empire of China, Chinese Tartary, Corea and Thibet.* 4 vols. London: John Watts, 1736.

Eitel, Ernest John. *Europe in China: The History of Hongkong from the Beginning to the Year 1882.* London: Luzac and Company, 1895.

Elliott, Mark C. *Emperor Qianlong: Son of Heaven, Man of the World.* New York: Longman, 2009.

Ellis, Henry. *Journal of the Proceedings of the Late Embassy to China; Comprising a Correct Narrative of the Public Transactions of the Embassy, of the Voyage to and From China, and of the Journey From the Mouth of the Pei-Ho to the Return to Canton. Interspersed With Observations Upon the Face of the Country, the Polity, Moral Character, and Manners of the Chinese Nation.* London: J. Murray, 1817.

Endacott, G. B. *A History of Hong Kong.* London: Oxford University Press, 1973.

Fan, T. C. "Percy's *Hau Kiou Choaan.*" *The Review of English Studies* 22, no. 86 (1946): 117–125.

Greenberg, Michael. *British Trade and the Opening of China, 1800–42*. Cambridge: Cambridge University Press, 1951.

Gu Gong Bo Wu Yuan, ed. *Qing Dai Nan Fu Yu Sheng Ping Shu Ju Ben Yu Dang An* [Archives and Play Scripts of the Bureaus of Nan and Sheng Ping in the Qing Dynasty]. Haikou Shi: Hainan Chu Ban She, 2001.

Hurd, Richard. "A Discourse on Poetical Imitation." In Horace, *Q. Horatii Flacii Epistola Ad Augustum. With an English Commentary and Notes*, edited by Richard Hurd, 107–207. London: W. Thurlbourn, 1751.

Idema, Wilt L. "Performances on a Three-tiered Stage Court Theatre During the Qianlong Era." In *Ad Seres Et Tungusos: Festschrift Für Martin Gimm Zu Seinem 65. Geburtstag Am 25. Mai 1995*, edited by Lutz Bieg, Erling von Mende, and Martina Siebert, 201–219. Wiesbaden: Harrassowitz, 2000.

Ma, Zhiyuan. *Po Yiu Meng Gu Yan Han Gong Qiu Za Ju* [Drama of the Cries of a Lonely Goose Disturb a Wishful Dream and Evoke Autumn in the Palace of Han]. Vol. 1, bk. 1, of *Yuan Qu Xuan* [Selection of Dramas From the Yuan Dynasty], edited by Maoxun Zang. Shanghai: Zhonghua Shu Ju, 1936.

Macartney, George. *An Embassy to China Being the Journal Kept by Lord Macartney During His Embassy to the Emperor Ch'ien-Lung, 1793–1794*. Edited by J. L. Cranmer-Byng. Hamden, CT: Archon Books, 1963.

Mackerras, Colin. *The Rise of the Peking Opera, 1770–1870*. Oxford: Clarendon Press, 1972.

Mason, Mary Gertrude. *Western Concepts of China and the Chinese, 1840–1876*. Durham, NC: The Seeman Printery, 1939.

Mayer, David. *Harlequin in His Element: The English Pantomime, 1806–1836*. Cambridge, MA: Harvard University Press, 1969.

Morse, Hosea Ballou. *The Chronicles of the East India Company Trading to China 1635–1834*. 5 vols. Cambridge, MA: Harvard University Press, 1926–29.

Mungello, David E. *Curious Land: Jesuit Accommodation and the Origins of Sinology*. Honolulu: University of Hawaii Press, 1989.

———. *The Great Encounter of China and the West, 1500–1800*. Lanham, MD: Rowman and Littlefield, 2013.

Niu, Chuanhai. *Qianlong Shi Qi Ju Chang Huo Dong Zhi Yan Jiu* [Studies of Theatre Activities During the Qianlong Era]. Taipei: Hua Gang, 1977.

O'Brien, John. "Pantomime." In *The Cambridge Companion to British Theatre, 1730–1830*, edited by Jane Moody and Daniel O'Quinn, 103–114. Cambridge: Cambridge University Press, 2007.

The Oriental Translation Fund. "Second Report of the Oriental Translation Committee, Presented to the Subscribers to the Oriental Translation Fund on the 30th of May, 1829." In *Report of the Proceedings of the Second General Meeting of the Subscribers to the Oriental Translation Fund, With the Prospectus, Report of the Committee, and Regulations*, 14–22. London: J. L. Cox, 1829.

Pargiter, Frederick E. "A Brief History of the Royal Asiatic Society of Great Britain and Ireland, 1823 to 1923." In *Centenary Volume of the Royal Asiatic Society of Great Britain and Ireland, 1823–1923*, edited by Frederick E. Pargiter, vii–xxviii. London: The Royal Asiatic Society, 1923.

Percy, Thomas, ed. *Miscellaneous Pieces Relating to the Chinese*. 2 vols. London: R. and J. Dodsley, 1762.

Porter, David. *The Chinese Taste in Eighteenth-Century England*. Cambridge: Cambridge University Press, 2010.

Pritchard, Hampton. *The Crucial Years of Early Anglo-Chinese Relations, 1750–1800*. Pullman, WA: 1936.

Pruitt, John. "Thomas Dibdin (1771–1841)." In *Nineteenth-Century British Dramatists*. Vol. 344 of *Dictionary of Literary Biography*, edited by Angela Courtney, 91–105. Detroit: Gale, Cengage Learning, 2009.

Qiu, Huiying. *Qianlong Shi Qi Xi Qu Huo Dong Yan Jiu* [Studies of Theatre During the Qianlong Era]. Taipei: Wen Jin, 2000.

Reynolds, K. D. "Davis, Sir John Francis, First Baronet (1795–1890)." In *Oxford Dictionary of National Biography*. Oxford University Press, 2004–. doi:10.1093/ref:odnb/7287.

Royal Pavilion, Art Gallery and Museums. "Introduction." In *William Alexander: An English Artist in Imperial China; the Royal Pavilion, Art Gallery and Museums, Brighton, 8 September to 25 October, 1981, Nottingham University Art Gallery, 23 November to 17 December, 1981*, 7–17. Brighton: Royal Pavilion, Art Gallery and Museums, 1981.

Rosenfeld, Sybil M. *Georgian Scene Painters and Scene Painting*. Cambridge: Cambridge University Press, 1981.

Staunton, George. *An Authentic Account of an Embassy from the King of Britain to the Emperor of China; Including Cursory Observations Made, and Information Obtained, in Travelling through that Ancient Empire, and a Small Part of Chinese Tartary* ... London: G. Nicol, 1797.

Staunton, George Thomas. "Preface." In *Narrative of the Chinese Embassy to the Khan of the Tourgouth Tartars*, iii–xxviii. London: John Murray, 1821.

———. "Translator's Preface." In *Ta Tsing Leu Lee; Being the Fundational Laws, and a Selection from the Supplementary Statutes, of the Penal Code of China*, i–xxxv. London: T Cadell and W. Davies, 1810.

University College London. The Society for the Diffusion of Useful Knowledge Archives.

Van der Merwe, Pieter T. "Clarkson Stanfield (1793–1867)." In *The Spectacular Career of Clarkson Stanfield, 1793–1867: Seaman, Scene-Painter, Royal Academician*, 13–22. Newcastle upon Tyne: Tyne and Wear County Council Museums, 1979.

Voltaire. *L'Orphelin de la Chine, Tragédie*. Paris: Michele Lambert, 1755.

Wang, Xueqi, et al., eds. *Yuan Qu Xuan Jiao Zhu* [Yuan Qu Xuan, With Notes and Edits]. By Maoxun Zang. 4 vols. Shijiazhuang Shi: Hebei Jiao Yu Chu Ban She, 1994.

Wang, Zhizhang. *Qing Sheng Ping Shu Zhi Lue* [Accounts of the Sheng Ping Bureau at the Qing Court]. Shanghai: Shanghai Shu Dian, 1991.

Welsh, Frank. *A History of Hong Kong*. London: HarperCollins, 1993.

Wu, Hanchen. *San Jia Cai Tian Si Lao Sheng Er Za Ju* [Drama of Heaven Grants an Heir to an Old Man Who Dispenses His Fortune]. Vol. 3, bk. 2, of *Yuan Qu Xuan* [Selection of Dramas From the Yuan Dynasty], edited by Maoxun Zang. Shanghai: Zhonghua Shu Ju, 1936.

Zeng, Yongyi, ed. *Zhongguo Gu Dian Xi Ju Xuan Zhu* [Selections of Classical Chinese Theatre, With Notes]. Taipei: Guo Jia Chu Ban She, 1983.

Zhang, Geng, and Hancheng Guo. *Zhongguo Xi Qu Tong Shi* [General History of the Chinese Theatre]. 1992. Reprint, 2 vols., Taipei: Da Hong Tu Shu, 1998.

Zipes, Jack, ed. *The Great Fairy Tale Tradition*. New York: W. W. Norton, 2001.

4 Chinaface Attractions

A Chinese Honeymoon (1901–1904),
The Yellow Jacket (1913), and
Mr. Wu (1913–1914)

After China was "laid open" by the Macartney embassy (see Chapter Three), British visitors brought home extensive reports on the country, which included the observation that China was not as strong or mighty as had been portrayed in the earlier Jesuit writings. The first Opium War (1839–1842), fought over British importation of opium into China, led to the concession of Hong Kong and marked the beginning of a period of colonial intrusions in modern Chinese history. Superior imperial powers, including Western countries and Japan, successively encroached upon China's sovereignty. Between the Opium War and the fall of the Qing dynasty in 1911, China was repeatedly defeated, its inadequate military unable to ward off foreign aggressors, who intruded into China and forced its government to sign a series of so-called "unequal treaties" granting them privileges and colonies and requiring China to pay large indemnities to cover the imperial powers' war losses. Reform movements burgeoned but failed to achieve sufficient modernization. Grassroots xenophobic movements were also aroused, notably the "Righteous and Harmonious Militia" (Yi He Tuan, 義和團), a.k.a. the Chinese Boxers, which sought to drive foreigners out of China. The Qing's fall in 1911 put a temporary halt to the foreign intrusions and brought an end to the monarchy in China.[1]

Writing a decade after the first Opium War and a few years after resigning from his post as governor of Hong Kong, John Francis Davis, whose works are discussed in Chapter Three, commented that the war gave China "a blow unequalled in importance since the Manchow Tartar [Manchu] conquest," and that the British undertaking was "the farthest military enterprise" in world history, surpassing the expeditions of Alexander the Great and Caesar and those of the Spanish conquistadors Hernán Cortés and Francisco Pizarro.[2] Even accounting for Davis's exuberant jingoism, the war indeed marked a historic turning point, exposing China's vulnerability and cementing Western perceptions of its degeneracy and decline. Davis further observed that soon after the war, Chinese emigrants began "swarming from Hongkong across the Pacific" to "the *El Dorado* of California" as well as to Australia. While he was unsure how these developments would affect "the forthcoming revolutions in the channels of national and commercial intercourse," Davis predicted that Hong Kong, a British colony, "is destined to play a part in the drama of the future."[3] Davis's observation reflects how, pushed by worsening conditions at home and pulled by opportunities for economic betterment abroad, Chinese left their homeland in great numbers, which led to the establishment of diasporic Chinese communities, the Chinatowns, in the West. In addition to the laborers of Davis's observation, a much smaller but steady number of Chinese students, inspired by the reform and modernization movements, also left China for educational opportunities at universities in the imperial countries. Davis's prediction for Hong Kong came true as it grew into a vibrant entrepôt for both goods and labor, acclaimed as the British crown's "Pearl of the Orient." One revolutionary outcome of these developments was that Chinese and Westerners became irreversibly "entwined," to borrow Ross G. Forman's usage,[4] as they entered each others' worlds both in China and in the West.

This chapter examines three London productions staged during the last decade of the Qing court and immediately after its fall. Informed by the new historical development of entwined, intercultural contact, these productions dramatized China in three distinct Chinaface fashions: *A Chinese Honeymoon* (1901–1904), an "escapist" musical comedy, depicted an interracial romantic imbroglio in the deliberately artificial, intercultured tradition of Chinaface satire; *The Yellow Jacket* (1913), a fable about a young hero, was presented in authentic-looking Chinaface staging; and *Mr. Wu* (1913–1914), a gruesome melodrama of Anglo-Chinese conflict, featured a devious Chinese villain performed with convincing Chinaface mannerisms. In the scripts, on the stage, and behind the scenes of these productions, Westerners encounter Chinese in many guises, in the process revealing much about not only Westerners' evolving perceptions of China, but also about the purposes, potential, and limits of their attempts to represent China and the Chinese on stage.

In their different Chinaface stage representations, *Chinese Honeymoon* trivializes China as an exotic land, *Yellow Jacket* antiquates Chinese theatre as primitive and childlike, and *Mr. Wu* vilifies the Chinese as perverse, inhuman villains. Moreover, *Chinese Honeymoon* and *Yellow Jacket* continue the interculturation of the earlier gendered, orientalist discourse which casts China as alluring, feminized, and decadent, while *Mr. Wu* exhibits a reversed, menacing, and destructive male version. These depictions of China and the Chinese reflect the conflicted attitudes of Britain and the West toward China, ranging from superiority to anxiety and from fear to paranoia, which relate to the expansion and weakening of British imperial power and the ever-closer and more direct interaction between peoples.

While the three plays exemplify the continuing process in which historical depictions of China and its people were intercultured, they also developed new ways of interculturalizing the country that reflect social commentary, artistic inspiration, and historical development. *Chinese Honeymoon* highlighted and questioned British identity by satirizing British vacationers and their social and cultural practices in an interculturalized, exotic Asian land. Inspired by Chinese theatre, George Cochrane Hazelton and Joseph Henry Benrimo, the playwrights of *Yellow Jacket*, received help from diasporic Chinese and created in their play an alternative, intercultural form of theatre that they hoped would move Western theatre practice beyond a realistic approach. Similarly, Matheson Lang, who played the villain in *Mr. Wu*, also obtained direct assistance from diasporic Chinese, which enabled him to portray the interculturalized Chinese character with believable mannerisms. In contrast to *Chinese Honeymoon*, which used highly fanciful Chinaface scenery and depicted comic, Chinaface Chinese characters, *Yellow Jacket* replicated an actual Chinese stage and re-interpreted Chinese staging practices, while in *Mr. Wu* Lang impressed his audience with his convincing portrayal of a Chinese character. In this respect, *Yellow Jacket* and *Mr. Wu* indicate the critical role diasporic Chinese could play in the making of intercultural performance.

Nevertheless, I argue in this chapter that, as suggested by the contemporary reviews they received, *Yellow Jacket* and *Mr. Wu* only managed to wear a more authentic-looking Chinaface than *Chinese Honeymoon*, as their dramatic content was at least as imaginative and fictitious as the latter play's unmistakable fantasy. Most notable in this regard is the well-intentioned *Yellow Jacket*, as its playwrights demonstrated high regard for Chinese theatre but adopted a formalist approach to taking inspiration from Chinese theatre that seems to have limited their creative achievements. Among the three plays, contemporary audiences most favored the overtly Chinaface *Chinese Honeymoon* for meeting and even exceeding their expectations, criticized *Yellow Jacket* for its lack of substantial content, and found fault with *Mr. Wu* for its contrived ending. The comparatively less popular examples of *Yellow Jacket* and *Mr. Wu* make apparent the critical and fundamental role of dramatic content in attempts to move stage representations of China beyond Chinaface attractions.

A CHINESE HONEYMOON

Originally conceived as a touring production, *A Chinese Honeymoon* was said to have been put together in four weeks' time by its authors, George Dance (1857?–1932), a librettist and touring manager, and Howard Talbot (1865–1928), an American-born composer. After its premiere at Hanley in the Staffordshire Potteries in 1899, *A Chinese Honeymoon* toured extensively in the British provinces and eventually moved to the Strand theatre in London in 1901. Running from October 1901 to May 1904, the play set a record as the first musical in theatre history to top 1,000 consecutive metropolitan performances and became the longest running West End show of the Victorian and Edwardian eras.[5]

Chinese Honeymoon recalls the Kan-Fu story line in *Chinese Sorcerer* (see Chapter Three), being set in an impossible Chinese never-never land where odd laws are implemented that create confusion and complication of romantic relationships. What sets *Chinese Honeymoon* apart from this precedent is the interracial nature of the romantic imbroglio; British people in China are central to the story. While the Chinese continue to be depicted as exoticized and trivialized, the British are mocked for their social and cultural practices and romantic tendencies. Topical references in the play hint at the increasing British imperial presence in China, which is reflected and romanticized in light-hearted, comedic escapades. Together with other so-called "escapist musicals," *Chinese Honeymoon*'s story and characterization depicts Asians as idiosyncratic but attractive, reflecting the sense of superiority as well as anxiety that Britain felt toward the East.[6]

Set in Ylang Ylang, China, *Chinese Honeymoon* tells of the eventful honeymoon of Mr. and Mrs. Pineapple, who become entangled in the Chinese emperor's search for a wife and in a love affair between Tom Hatherton, Mr. Pineapple's nephew, and Princess Soo Soo, the emperor's niece. While staying at a hotel in Ylang Ylang, Mr. and Mrs. Pineapple encounter Tom, who has neglected his commission in the British army to court a Chinese girl who appears to be a humble singer. The girl is actually Soo Soo, who has disguised herself as a pretense in order to see Tom. Mrs. Brown, Mr. Pineapple's old housekeeper, also arrives in Ylang Ylang as an escape from the heartbroken news of Mr. Pineapple's marriage and resides in the same hotel. As Mr. Pineapple flirts with every girl that he sees, including Soo Soo, the enraged Mrs. Pineapple decides to get revenge by flirting herself, with a man who turns out to be the emperor. Unaware that according to Ylang Ylang law, members of the Chinese royal family who are caught kissing must marry immediately on pain of death, the Pineapples are ordered to marry—Mr. Pineapple to Soo Soo, and Mrs. Pineapple to the emperor.

While Mrs. Pineapple temporarily escapes the marriage, Mr. Pineapple marries the tearful Soo Soo and enjoys more flirtations with the court maids. Tom, disguised as a doctor, and Mrs. Pineapple, dressed as a singing girl, sneak into the court and attempt but fail to abduct Mr. Pineapple and Soo Soo. Instead, the emperor demands Mrs. Pineapple's hand in marriage and hires an official mother-in-law, who turns out to be Mrs. Brown, to rule the household. To complicate matters even further, the hotel hostess, Fi Fi, brings in a trance-inducing drug and persuades Soo Soo to enact a Juliet-like suicide, which almost leads to the burning alive of Soo Soo and Mr. Pineapple. At last, a note from the British embassy halts the burning. The entangled love pursuits are resolved—Mrs. Pineapple is reunited with Mr. Pineapple, Soo Soo with Tom, and, in accordance with another Ylang Ylang law, Mrs. Brown with the emperor.[7]

The story of *Chinese Honeymoon* resembles many contemporary British musicals set in Asian countries. Its imaginary Chinese land of Ylang Ylang, for example, quickly calls to mind the fictional Japanese town of Titipu in *The Mikado* (1885), the highly successful comic operetta of Gilbert and Sullivan.[8]

Like the Mikado (the emperor of Japan), the Chinese emperor revels in strange laws and punishments; the emperor's sidekick, the Lord Chancellor, invents new ones as circumstances arise. The double monosyllables in the name of the Chinese emperor's niece, Soo Soo, recalls the funny-sounding name of Yum Yum, given to a beautiful Japanese schoolgirl in *Mikado*.

The interracial courtship depicted in *Chinese Honeymoon*, in which a white male (Tom, a British army officer) falls in love with an Asian female (Soo Soo, a Chinese princess disguised as a singing girl), resembles the plot of *Chinese Honeymoon*'s immediate precedent, *The Geisha* (1896), in which a British sailor (Reginald Fairfax) stationed in Japan flirts with a Japanese geisha (O Mimosa San).[9] One consequence of the romantic escapades in *Chinese Honeymoon*—Mrs. Pineapple being ordered to marry the Chinese emperor—also seems to have taken inspiration from a plot element in *Geisha* in which Reginald's British fiancée, Molly, disguises herself as a geisha and is inadvertently chosen by the local Japanese potentate to be his wife. Furthermore, as critics point out, Mr. Pineapple's forced engagement with Soo Soo and the depiction of Mrs. Pineapple as a jealous wife might have derived from *Fleur de thé* (1868), a French comic opera.[10]

Further evidence that *Chinese Honeymoon* was part of a group of romantic comedies set in Asia is provided by two plays that were staged in London the same year *Chinese Honeymoon* premiered at Hanley. *San Toy* (1899), set in China, features a love affair between a mandarin's daughter and a British captain, while *Florodora* (1899), set in the Philippines, depicts a confusion of courtships between the British and the natives. Moreover, *See See* (1906), an adaptation of a French piece about mistaken courtships and marriages, is also set in China. The name of the heroine, See See, seems likely to have been derived from the name Soo Soo in *Chinese Honeymoon*.[11]

Scholars have variously characterized British musical comedies and dramatic works set in Asia ("the Orient"). In his study, Jeffrey Richards distinguishes musical comedies from the comic operettas of Gilbert and Sullivan, finding that, in a spirit of "dumbing down," they reduce Gilbert's satire and wordplay and Sullivan's allusive and textured music to a simple mélange of "pretty girls, lavish costumes and sets, a formulaic romantic plot, music-hall comedy routines, hummable tunes and scripts with topical allusions, but also a regular injection of patriotism."[12] John M. MacKenzie describes spectacular theatre set in "the Orient," with its Asian locations shifting and expanding from the Middle East to the Far East, that emphasizes sensational set designs and costumes as "Orientalist spectacle."[13] He observes that in these plays and so-called "escapist musicals," the Orient provides "an unrivalled opportunity to portray not only spectacle in setting and costumes, but also peculiar people with funny names, odd laws and customs, and characters who were slippery, grasping, and, even more interestingly, lascivious."[14] In their critical assessment of these British theatrical works, Richards and MacKenzie note the sexualized and idiosyncratic depictions of Asian characters and the visual attractions of spectacular sets and costumes, which I would characterize as examples of Chinaface (see *Chinese Festival* in Chapter Two). These depictions were very likely informed by the expansion of the British Empire and the complex feelings of patriotism and anxiety that were associated with this imperial expansion. By experiencing the Orient as spectacular novelty on stage, the British audience could, in MacKenzie's words, "identify difference and confirm their own supposed uniqueness in appearance, moral value and power." As the Orient had become "a source of anxiety and strain, a place of complex trading relations and periodic warfare," the plays and musical comedies sought to define the position of their British audience by "portraying the foibles of Eastern peoples, ... and their general inadequacy in the face of an easy Western superiority."[15]

In *Chinese Honeymoon*, China is indeed depicted as an outlandish but alluring place with strange people and customs. A significant difference from the earlier examples examined in previous chapters is that the fierce and uncouth Tartars have been replaced by the blundering but ultimately superior British as the foils to the Chinese. Britons' anxiety about their intrusions into Asia is reflected in the absurd but dangerous circumstances in which the characters momentarily find themselves trapped, but British imperial power inevitably steps in to save them from disaster. This triumph, however, is tempered by satirical portrayals of British moral values and the exercise of power.

Also notable in *Chinese Honeymoon* and related "escapist musicals" is the conflation or interculturalization of various Asian countries, a phenomenon also seen in earlier productions. In particular, China is interchangeable with Japan as the locale of a romanticized, unrealistic Asian wonderland. This phenomenon exemplifies, in parallel to the expansion of the British Empire, the expansion and perpetuation of British theatre conventions which retained and intercultured historical stage depictions of China. As the British Empire and its trade contacts expanded and deepened Britain's connection with Asia, rather than incorporating new and differentiated information about China and other Asian countries, the theatre conventions adapted the Chinaface practice of earlier stage works to serve as a backdrop for social satire that poked fun at British foibles in colonial circumstances. The audiences of the day were aware that the portrayal of China in these works was highly fictional and stylized, and that they anticipated the plays would follow the conventions. *Chinese Honeymoon* apparently met and even exceeded the audience's expectations for conformity with what had become a familiar, intercultured tradition of Chinaface satire.

China—via the setting of Ylang Ylang—is portrayed as an idyllic, carefree never-never land. The Chinese are attractively strange, if not completely silly. As expressed in the opening chorus, in Ylang Ylang "the ruby river rolls its billows," "the blossoms hang, and the swallows twitter," and ladies "handle tea and scandal"[16]—that is, tea drinking and gossip parties are daily activities. After they arrive in Ylang Ylang, Mrs. Pineapple and her bridesmaids regard the houses, dresses, and men with pigtails as queer, while Mr. Pineapple is attracted to the native girls who have "pretty little faces," "dainty little feet," and "such fetching little ways" (19).[17] The Chinese emperor is titled "uncle to the moon, and second cousin to all the little stars and comets" (41), which apparently is a comic rendering of the Chinese saying that the Emperor is the Son of Heaven (*tianzi*, 天子). When he learns that Princess Soo Soo has died of poisoning, the emperor does not care because one woman more or less does not matter in China (93). By Ylang Ylang custom, the body of Princess Soo Soo is to be cremated, which in turn will require her husband Mr. Pineapple to be burned alive. However, after receiving a note from the British Embassy demanding the release of Mr. Pineapple and punishment of the instigators of the burning, the emperor, fearing war, immediately surrenders (98). Presumably aware of the embarrassing defeats China had suffered in wars with the British and other imperial powers, the Chinese emperor dares not risk military confrontation.

While the Chinese are shown to be trivial, misogynistic, and cowardly, the British are ridiculed for their social and cultural practices. Mrs. Brown, for example, is characterized as a shrew and a devoted churchgoer. Upon arrival in Ylang Ylang for vacation and recovery from heartbreak, she seeks mutual improvement societies and mothers' meetings to pass the time (12). After she is appointed the official mother-in-law in the Chinese court, she plans a strict schedule around church that includes rising early, praying, reading, and attending sewing classes and mothers' meetings (79–80). To revolt against her tyrannical reign, Tom suggests holding a public meeting, "as every Englishman does when he's got a grievance" (89). He, Mr. Pineapple, and the Chinese emperor then elect a chair, propose and second motions, and deliver speeches and reach resolutions. Their protest, however, quickly dissolves when confronted by Mrs. Brown, who thrashes Mr. Pineapple and the emperor like schoolboys (89–92). In these depictions, British forms of social organization such as church attendance and public meetings are ridiculed, while the authoritative male characters, both Chinese and British, are emasculated and infantilized.

In the depiction of romantic relationships and interracial courtships, the British male characters are portrayed as hopelessly romantic and even lascivious. Tom has come to China to help organize the new native regiments the British Government is raising at its latest possession at Wei-Hai-Wei, but while sightseeing in Ylang Ylang has become infatuated with Soo Soo, and submits his resignation in order to court her.[18] Tom's military position appeals to Soo Soo: "What, are you a Tommy Atkins? ... Oh, I love Tommy Atkinses," she declares (9). As Penny Summerfield observes, between 1900 and 1918 the image of Tommy Atkins, a nickname for a common British soldier, was romanticized and depoliticized in music-hall entertainment.[19] The depiction of Tom as a runaway, romantic Tommy Atkins and Soo Soo's fascination with him may be read as an expression of a favorable attitude toward the imperial operation.

Mr. Pineapple, Tom's uncle, is portrayed as a comic exaggeration of the romantic inclination. As cited earlier, he is attracted to the "pretty little faces," "dainty little feet," and "fetching little ways" of Chinese girls. Despite his old age and newlywed status, he flirts with each and every one he sees. Nonetheless, when he learns that Tom has abandoned his military career to pursue Soo Soo, Mr. Pineapple asserts, "I am going to chastise that Chinese Cleopatra who has lured from the path of rectitude this unfortunate British Marc Anthony" (26), recognizing the Chinese girl as a dangerous *femme fatale* and, hypocritically, the seduced British male as a dissolute rake.

It is not the Chinese women who have turned Mr. Pineapple romantic or lustful; he married Mrs. Pineapple, his former typist, because he was caught kissing her at work, and his behavior is so suspect that Mrs. Pineapple has brought along her two bridesmaids to watch over him. These depictions make fun of Mr. Pineapple's lasciviousness as well as his aggression from a superior male position. Explaining what a typist is and does to Soo Soo, who, being a Chinese, apparently never heard of it before, Tom says that a pretty typist "types her master's letters in the morning, makes him a cup of tea in the afternoon, and goes with him to the theatre in the evening," while a plain typist "only types his letters" (10). Tom's description, rife with sexual innuendo, ridicules the typist profession, a British (Western) career that placed women in a servile position that their bosses could exploit. Although Mrs. Pineapple used her position to secure a marriage, its foundation is mocked as so flimsy that Mrs. Pineapple employs her bridesmaids to guard against her husband's possible misconduct. Through the satirical depiction of the typist career and the marriage of Mr. and Mrs. Pineapple, *Chinese Honeymoon* satirizes male privilege and power relations between the sexes in the context of British workplace. This and other plot elements demonstrate that although set in China, *Chinese Honeymoon*, like the other "escapist musicals," is more concerned with satirizing the British than the Chinese. The Chinaface backdrop serves mainly to place British society into sharp relief, allowing the authors to highlight and question British identity.

As noted earlier, *Chinese Honeymoon* perpetuates the depiction of an exoticized and idiosyncratic China seen in earlier British dramatic works. What is notable about the "escapist musicals" is the increased conflation, or interculturalization, of China with other Asian countries, especially Japan. As discussed in earlier chapters, examples of interculturalization between these two countries can be found as early as the eighteenth century (see Boucher's paintings in Chapter Two), the phenomenon expanded dramatically in the second half of the nineteenth century as Japan's modernization caught the West's attention and was featured in major European and American exhibitions. "Things in the Japanese taste"—evoking a common expression for the eighteenth-century *chinoiserie* fad—came into vogue in Western countries.[20] *Mikado* (1885) and *Geisha* (1896), discussed earlier, represent English theatre's response to this trend. Interestingly, the depictions of Japan in these musicals closely corresponded with stage depictions of China. *Geisha*, for example, sings about the "Happy Japan" where "[f]lower and fan [f]lutter and flitter," "the tiny tea-cups clatter," and Jack Tar, a nickname for a British sailor, flirts with the dear little "Jappy-Jap-Jappy," who hides behind a fan.[21] In other words, *Geisha* depicts Japan as a carefree, tea-drinking never-never land where Japanese females attract British sailors with their "fetching little ways," a portrayal that is nearly identical to that of China and the Chinese in *Chinese Honeymoon*. Furthermore, in *Geisha* a Chinese character owns a Japanese teahouse and manages a group of geishas, implying that the Japanese and the Chinese were compatible and perhaps interchangeable. Although Japan, unlike China, developed into a modern nation-state that could hold its own against Western powers in the late nineteenth century, in British dramatic depictions it was intercultural-ized with China as another trivialized and exoticized Asian wonderland.

While Japan is not directly referred to in *Chinese Honeymoon*, other Asian lands are. The Hindu practice of *suttee* is alluded to in the Ylang Ylang law that requires Mr. Pineapple to be burned alive upon Princess Soo Soo's death.[22] The name Ylang Ylang itself is actually a Tagalog term describing a tree that produces an aromatic oil used as a flavoring. As the nineteenth century progressed, Britain expanded its imperial and trading links to China, Japan, India, and the Philippines, yet in the "escapist musicals," these Asian countries were interculturalized in a trivialized and exoticized manner, which suggests that British theatre practitioners did not develop a nuanced understanding of the separate Asian countries but continued to depict them in purely imaginative and theatrical terms.

In her study of British melodrama, Heidi Holder observes that in the last decades of the nineteenth century, the colonial settings of imperialist dramas relied on "experts" ("authoritative" images and sources) and popular imagery for stage visual representation, while their historical specificity diminished when compared with earlier works. In these plays, the British heroes journeyed to an Oz-like fantasy world to prove themselves and straighten out domestic difficulties.[23] This trope of the late-nineteenth-century imperial melodramas, together with the romanticized Tommy Atkins character cited earlier, helps explain the depiction of Asian countries in the "escapist musicals." What Holder describes as the reliance on "experts" and popular imagery, in my argument, is a component of the mechanism of intercultura-tion that perpetuated references, such as tea drinking and foot binding, from the historical past. This mechanism created a romanticized, fictional world that was a suitable setting for the romantic Tommy Atkinses and Jack Tars to indulge in escapist fantasy. Moreover, the Chinese or Asian characters encountered by these caricatured British figures were themselves highly fictionalized. In fact, the Asian women characters, often farcically cloaked in disguises such as singing girls, could be read as British women who have escaped the mundane world of Britain to follow their unsuspecting, romanti-cized male compatriots to the exotic Orient and assume deliberately unusual and exoticized Chinaface roles so they can engage in flirtatious playacting.[24]

As is apparent from contemporary critical comments, discussed below, this exaggerated theatrical approach was too explicit to have been missed by the audience.

To Holder, the diminishing of historical specificity in late-nineteenth-century imperialist dramas showed that these plays "*enact* an imperialist expansion of British culture by imposing traditional domestic melodramatic plots and characters upon the colonial locale."[25] Following her argument, the "escapist musicals" such as *Chinese Honeymoon* expanded the musical genre to an imperial and international dimension by imposing their trivial plots and conventional Chinaface aesthetics on colonial Asian settings, but the conventions of these plays were retained without incorporating new information about these foreign lands. It is therefore not surprising that the play and its trivialization and exoticization of China or Asia were evaluated by contemporary critics in comparison with other domestic musicals and the musical conventions.

These critics, for example, praised *Chinese Honeymoon* as standing out among its peers for the intelligibility of its story. The review in the *Times*, for example, noted that it possessed "very distinct signs of a plot, which not only begins with the rise of the curtain but is actually followed out to the close of the second and final act." By contrast, other contemporary musicals had grown more and more plotless and were nothing but "a series of music-hall turns, strung together with short passages of pointless dialogue."[26] "Above all," the *Illustrated London News* stated, "its librettist, Mr. Dance, has supplied a good plot, which, however Gilbertian, is ingeniously sustained and consistently amusing."[27] The critics' surprise at the intelligibility of *Honeymoon*'s story points to the low literary quality they perceived in other contemporary musicals, while the second reviewer's characterization of *Honeymoon*'s "good plot" as "Gilbertian" likely referred to the "topsy-turvy" development of events and social satire that Gilbert's writing was known for. A Gilbertian plot would have been enjoyable not for its adherence to linear progression, but for the "amusing" and satirical twists and turns the librettist Dance managed to cobble together into a coherent story.

The staging of *Chinese Honeymoon* was appraised as "mounted picturesquely, its Oriental dresses being especially handsome."[28] In Act I (Figure 4.1), the setting of "the gardens of the hotel in Ylang Ylang" presents a perspective view, featuring pavilions and trees on two sides, a small shrine or palanquin placed near the center of the back and a backdrop painted with Chinese styles of houses and junks, a bridge, and a tall pagoda. Chinese guards hold spears and swords, as well as banners with Chinese-looking gibberish. In Act II (Figure 4.2), the setting of a "room in the emperor's palace" is decorated with engraved, tall, slender columns with coiled dragons on two sides, and a backdrop painted with Chinese houses and a two-tier pagoda. In addition to the lantern hung from above at center stage, various other lanterns are held by supporting cast members, presumably for the act's "feast of lanterns."

Figure 4.1 "Act I–The Gardens of the Hotel at Ylang Ylang." Bassano. "Scenes from 'A Chinese Honeymoon' at the Strand Theatre." *The Sketch*, vol. 35 Oct. 16, 1901, p. 503. Photograph. General Research Division, The New York Public Library, Astor, Lenox and Tilden Foundations.

Figure 4.2 "Act II–Room in the Emperor's Palace." Bassano. "Scenes from 'A Chinese Honeymoon' at the Strand Theatre." *The Sketch*, vol. 35 Oct. 16, 1901, p. 503. Photograph. General Research Division, The New York Public Library, Astor, Lenox and Tilden Foundations.

These two sets of scenery from *Chinese Honeymoon*, not surprisingly, retain and interculturate many signature stage depictions of China from the historical past: Chinese houses and junks, pagodas, arch bridge, pavilions, and lanterns. The presence of these "expert" and popular images, to borrow Holder's characterization, manifests the process of interculturation by which historical approaches were maintained. In consideration of the interculturation phenomenon, the scene design in which cast members held lanterns in Act II (Figure 4.2) suggests what the grand finale of *Chinese Sorcerer* (1823, see Chapter Three), which is also called the "feast of lanterns" (see Figure 3.4) might have looked like. The Chinese-looking gibberish on the props held by the cast in Act I (Figure 4.1) visually indicate the superficial appearance of the Chinese language, but lack actual meaning. They may be taken as symbols that reveal the artificiality of the whole production.

The critics were aware of the whimsy and unreality of the depictions of China and the Chinese in *Chinese Honeymoon*, but nevertheless justified them on the grounds that the play was a musical comedy. "No one goes to a musical comedy in the hope of seeing men and matters portrayed to the life," the critic of the *Times* declared. "*A Chinese Honeymoon* sets out with the object of amusing, and, since it does so, it justifies its existence."[29] The review of the *Sketch* stated that "[t]he learned may suggest that Mr. George Dance displays a violent disregard of Chinese manners, customs, and habits, but nobody cares about this," because the very foundation of the piece is "the staggering [kissing] law" that results in "some whimsical situations."[30] To the critics, *Chinese Honeymoon*'s identity as a musical comedy granted it license to discard lifelike portrayals and to fabricate wholly imaginative, "whimsical" occurrences.

In addition, the review of *Stage* reminded the reader that Dance's libretto for *Chinese Honeymoon* was far from original. It asked, "[H]ave not pantomime librettists familiarised holiday audiences for years past with the manners and customs of Pekin through the medium of our old friend Aladdin?"[31] The critic viewed *Chinese Honeymoon* as continuing the pantomime tradition in its choice of a Chinese subject (see Epilogue for a discussion of *Aladdin* pantomimes). In other words, *Chinese Honeymoon* was simply the latest of many examples of plays which interculturated and formed conventionalized depictions of China. The comment also suggests that British audiences would have been familiar with these intercultur-ated depictions of the country and had developed expectations that China and Chinese subjects would be presented fancifully on stage. The review in *Era*, for example, stated that "[t]he action of *A Chinese Honeymoon* is as whimsical and extraordinary as things Chinese are expected to be. ..."[32] "[T]hings Chinese" presumably referred to the escapist, deliberately funny and conventionalized Chinaface mannerisms and the artificial Chinese-looking representations that appeared on stage. *Chinese Honeymoon* appar-ently satisfied its audience's expectations of "things Chinese" very well that it made a historic long run.

THE YELLOW JACKET

On March 27, 1913, the Duke of York's theatre presented *The Yellow Jacket*, subtitled "A Chinese Play given in the Chinese Manner," which had a run of 154 performances that ended in August.[33] In contrast to *Chinese Honeymoon*, which made use of British theatre's interculturated depictions of China with which London audiences were familiar, *Yellow Jacket* was advertised as a novel artistic creation, imported from the United States, that used "the Chinese manner" in its staging. Co-written by two Americans, George Cochrane Hazelton (1868–1921) and Joseph Henry Benrimo (1871–1942, professionally known as J. Harry Benrimo or simply Benrimo),[34] *Yellow Jacket* premiered in New York in November 1912. After its modest 1913 London run, the play continued to be produced in other European cities. By the end of the 1920s, it had been seen not only in the United States and Europe, but also in South America, the Caribbean, and even Japan and China.[35] As the *New York Times* put it in 1916, *Yellow Jacket* was the first American play that "went round the world," attaining international acclaim in the early twentieth century.[36] The most well-known work of Hazelton and Benrimo, *Yellow Jacket* can be considered the first Western (Euro-American) play that explicitly and extensively drew upon Chinese staging practices to explore an anti-realistic, alternative approach to theatre making.

To examine how Hazelton and Benrimo conceived *Yellow Jacket* and claimed to make use of Chinese theatre practices, the foreword to the published script deserves to be quoted in full:

> The purpose of the creators of this play is to string on a thread of universal philosophy, love and laughter the jade beads of Chinese theatrical convention. Their effort has been to reflect the spirit rather than the substance. To do this, the property man had to be overwrought; the Chorus had to be introduced. Signs usually indicate the scenes on the Oriental stage; the Chorus voices them for us.
>
> While the story of THE YELLOW JACKET is not taken from any direct source, it is hoped that it may convey an imaginative suggestion of all sources and reflect the childhood of drama.
>
> It might be said in a Chinese way that scenery is as big as your imagination.
>
> Primitive people the world over begin to build their drama like the make-believe of children, and the closer they remain to the make-believe of children the more significant and convincing is the growth of their drama.[37]

In their metaphor, *Yellow Jacket* is a necklace-like intercultural product on which the "jade beads," the eye-catching outer forms of Chinese theatre, are "strung" on an inner "thread" which consists of universal themes and dramatic narrative. In other words, Hazelton and Benrimo resorted to the by-now familiar approach of using Chinaface as an eye-catching visual novelty on a dramatic narrative of their creation, but they did so by drawing upon the formal aspects of Chinese theatre. Their formalist approach, however, did not intend to reproduce exactly the "substance" of Chinese practices but rather to reflect their "spirit." Therefore adjustments were made, such as their creative interpretation of the property man's tasks on stage (discussed below) and the use of the Chorus character, a narrator, to fulfill stage functions in ways that were different from the Chinese conventions. While hinting at the play's abstract use of scenery, which imitates the Chinese practice, the foreword makes clear that the story does not derive from specific Chinese sources but depicts a universal, primitive drama that resembles childhood make-believe.

In their inventive adaptation of Chinese theatre practices, Hazelton and Benrimo were ahead of their contemporary Euro-American theatre practitioners and about two decades earlier than both Bertolt Brecht, who took inspiration from Chinese theatre to develop his theory and practice of epic theatre, and Thornton Wilder, who adopted a similar approach in his writing and staging of *Our Town*. Hazelton and Benrimo incorporated as much actual Chinese material as possible in their stage setup, costume, props, and character names, which they were able to do with assistance from the local Chinese community in New York. The creative process that led to *Yellow Jacket* therefore can therefore be deemed an intercultural collaboration with a notable contribution from the Chinese.

While the Chinese participation made the formal aspects of *Yellow Jacket* seem highly authentic when compared with plays like *Chinese Honeymoon*, its achievements remained largely superficial and *Yellow Jacket* can best be characterized as wearing a more authentic-looking and less imaginative Chinaface than the earlier productions. While Hazelton and Benrimo aimed to present a universal, primitive drama, they inadvertently contributed to the interculturated perception of Chinese theatre as ancient and childlike. They also created a poetic but stilted language for the dialogue and an effeminate Chinese male character to represent "the Oriental esthete." Taken as a whole, *Yellow Jacket* foreshadows later Western theatrical works that would take inspiration from the formal aspects of Chinese theatre, especially in staging; the play also furthers earlier orientalist depictions of China and its people and betrays its lack of a deeper textual understanding and appreciation of Chinese theatre.

Set in an unspecified time and date, in an unidentified province near the Yangtze River, *Yellow Jacket* tells the fable of Chee Moo and her son Wu Hoo Git. Chee Moo loses the favor of her husband, governor of the Flowery Kingdom, who schemes with his second wife's father to murder her. She flees with her infant son but soon dies of exhaustion. The son is rescued and raised by her maid and the maid's husband. Twenty years later, Wu Hoo Git has grown into a strapping youth who is eager to find his ancestors and regain his rightful position, which has been usurped by his effeminate half-brother, Wu Fah Din (Daffodil). With the assistance of a philosopher and blessings from his deceased mother and his beloved, a girl named Moy Fah Loy, Wu Hoo Git overcomes a series of challenges, which are schemes contrived by Wu Fah Din, such as the lure of worldly pleasure, the obstacle of a high mountain, and the snare of a spider. Eventually Wu Hoo Git wins back the throne and dons the yellow jacket of the play's title, the symbol of utmost power and honor.[38]

With its fairy-tale like setting and story, the fable of *Yellow Jacket* depicts episodes of rivalry, trickery, rescue, maternal care and sacrifice, life challenges, power struggle, and ultimately revenge. It reads like Ji's *Zhao Shi Gu Er* told in the style of Dibdin's *Chinese Sorcerer* (see Chapter Two and Chapter Three, respectively). Hazelton and Benrimo stated that, drawing on the theme of a pilgrim's progress, in the story they "carried a boy from the cradle to the grave in a fashion plausible to the Occidental mind, and yet developed the tale in an Oriental atmosphere."[39] That is, they portrayed a story that would be familiar to the Western audience in structure and content but gave it an outer Chinese ambience, which was created by imitating and creatively interpreting the formal styles of Chinese dramatic narrative, speech delivery, and staging convention, as well as by Hazelton and Benrimo's characterization of their Chinese characters.

The play begins with the Chorus—a single performer acting as the playwright, narrator, and prompter—telling the audience who he is, how Chinese theatre originated, and what the play is about. Throughout the play, he explains and comments on the stage actions. Similarly, the characters, who are mostly given generic names such as Kind Mother, Spirit, Spider, and Purveyor of Hearts, describe themselves to the audience when they first enter the stage. On stage, chairs and tables are used symbolically to construct various scenes such as mountains, a love boat, and tombs. The Property Man, a silent role who takes care of changing the scenes and props, is visible on stage, as are the musicians.

The Chorus's opening of the play and the characters' direct addresses to the audience clearly resemble the introductory act and self-introduction speeches of Chinese drama. However, as the name "Chorus" suggests, Hazelton and Benrimo were also inspired by Greek theatre and interculturalized Chinese and Greek conventions in one character. The generic names they used for the characters recall the stock role type system in Chinese theatre, but the generic types they created were mostly their own invention. Similarly, Hazelton and Benrimo used chairs, tables, and other props in a symbolic, Chinese manner, but some of their specific usages were not seen in Chinese staging practices. Last but not least, they adopted the Chinese method of employing the property man (Jianchang, 檢場) to move props without disguising his presence in the midst of dramatic action. Their adaptation, however, exploited his presence for laughs.

Figure 4.3 offers a visual document of Hazelton and Benrimo's design and use of "Chinese theatrical convention." Starting clockwise from top left,

Wu Fah Din (Daffodil) smells a posy held by the Property Man; Wu Hoo Git climbs a mountain; Wu Hoo Git (front) and Ling Won (Spirit, back) ride a chariot; and Wu Hoo Git is caught in a spider's web. In the examples of mountain climbing and chariot riding, the chairs, table, and banners were used similarly to the Chinese practices. The Spider and his web, however, closely resemble the character and prop from the Japanese *noh* play *Tsuchigumo* (Ground Spider), suggesting that this is an example of Hazelton and Benrimo's interculturalization of Chinese and non-Chinese theatre practices. It is noticeable that the Property Man is present for and central to the construction and depiction of the dramatic actions: he supplies the posy for Wu Fah Din, holds the chair for Wu Hoo Git, and provides the paper threads for the Spider. He smokes a cigarette and exhibits an aloof, even contemptuous attitude toward the stage actions, demonstrating Hazelton and Benrimo's creative adaptation of this stagehand from Chinese theatre as a character in his own right.

The spider scene in Figure 4.3 also documents the use of a conventional Chinese stage. The stage is empty, with entrance and exit doors visible on the two sides of the back stage. In the middle of the back stage, a balcony opens above a circular alcove in which the musicians sit. Long scrolls, together bearing a congratulatory couplet, are hung on either side of the balcony. Signs with the Chinese words for entrance and exit are placed above the doors. The Chinese texts on the scrolls and signs are intelligible, suggesting that they were supplied by someone capable of composing classical Chinese poetry and knowledgeable about Chinese theatre practices.[40] *Yellow Jacket*'s functional Chinese stage with real, meaningful Chinese writing stood in sharp contrast to *Chinese Honeymoon*'s fantasized, intercultured Chinese stage with Chinese-looking gibberish writing (see Figure 4.1). Hazelton and Benrimo's ability to reproduce such an authentic-looking stage manifests their research efforts, life experiences, and assistance they received from the Chinese.

The origin of *Yellow Jacket*, as Benrimo admitted sixteen years after the premiere of the play in 1912, was an illustrated article written by Henry Burden McDowell about Chinese theatre that he had clipped and treasured.[41] McDowell's article, published in the 1884–1885 issue of *Century* magazine, provides an interesting but questionable interpretation of the origin of Chinese theatre, followed by detailed and admiring accounts of its stage performances and dramatic literature based on performances of *yueju*, the Cantonese regional genre, staged in a theatre on Jackson Street in San Francisco's Chinatown. Among the illustrations is a drawing of this theatre's stage, which would provide the model for the Chinese stage of *Yellow Jacket*.[42] The play's genesis, therefore, was informed by the practice of Chinese theatre in diaspora in the United States.

Besides crediting McDowell's article, Benrimo also stated that he was brought up by Chinese servants in San Francisco, his interest in China was stimulated by a trip to Asia, and he had once acted in *The First Born*, a play dealing with San Francisco's Chinatown. After some futile attempts in seeking

Figure 4.3 "In the Chinese Manner: 'The Yellow Jacket,' at the Duke of York's."
The Sketch (Supplement), vol. 82 April 9, 1913, p. 4. Photograph.
General Research Division, The New York Public Library, Astor, Lenox
and Tilden Foundations.

interest in collaboration, he eventually found Hazelton, who took interest in his play idea.[43] According to Hazelton's and Benrimo's manuscript collections and various clippings, programs, and reports on *Yellow Jacket*,[44] Hazelton and Benrimo began to collaborate in the summer of 1910, and the first draft was completed in the spring of 1911.[45] In their collaboration Hazelton was the actual writer of the script, and Benrimo served as an expert on China, as he was comparatively more familiar with the country and culture. Hazelton appears to have been responsible for the plot structure and dialogues. Throughout the rewriting process he stayed faithful to a note he had written to himself, "1st wife has a son=crux of play," but kept revising the title of the play, the names of the characters, and the content of the story.[46] Benrimo, on the other hand, seems to have provided most of the Chinese aphorisms and facts about Chinese theatre, culture, and society that were integrated into the script. Benrimo and Hazelton also visited libraries and made use of English translations of Chinese philosophy and literature. Hazelton's manuscripts and correspondence indicate that Benrimo appears to have suggested and explained suitable Chinese idioms for the play and corrected Hazelton's misconceptions.[47] To use their own metaphor from the play's foreword, Hazelton constructed the thread of the story, while Benrimo identified, appraised, and recommended the Chinese jade beads that were strung on it.

Based on the documents in their manuscript collections, Benrimo and Hazelton appeared to have consulted some local Cantonese-speaking Chinese in New York, at least for the names of the characters. In the Benrimo Papers, for example, there is a piece of paper showing the characters' names, written in English, with the corresponding Chinese as pronounced in Cantonese dialect. Among Hazelton's drafts of the script is a business card from a Chinese printing company attached to several pieces of paper on which some of the characters' names were translated into Chinese.[48] As a result of this consultation, the names of most characters acquired not only Cantonese pronunciations but also literal meanings such as Chee Moo (Kind Mother, 慈母), Wu Hoo Git (Young Hero of the Wu Family, 伍豪傑) and Moy Fah Loy (Plum Blossom, 梅花蕾). Although there is no proof of this, it is possible that the Chinese printing company might also have helped with the Chinese scrolls and signs, which were made in a proper and elegant Chinese style.

However, perhaps out of a desire to demonstrate the extent of their knowledge and research, the language of *Yellow Jacket* is embellished so extensively with rhetoric and poetic expressions that the speeches and dialogues of characters often sound stilted and exaggerated. For example, when the mandarin Wu Sin Yin and his second wife's father Tai Fah Min meet and plot the murder of Chee Moo, they address each other as follows:

Wu: Tai Fah Min, my exalted second father-in-law, I receive you into my palace and presence with exuberance of fancy. My beloved second father-in-law may assume that Wu Sin Yin, the Great, has bowed to him with filial obeisance.

Tai: And my celestial son-in-law may felicitate himself with the glorious fancy that his second father-in-law also has bowed. The palace of the great Wu Sin Yin breathes incense of happiness. The gods smiled and it rose like a flower from the earth for the habitation of our master. The teak-wood was carved by moon-rays dancing on its surface, the rugs were woven by humming-bird beaks as they played hide-and-seek with their love-mates among the silken threads on the loom. The gods—(13)[49]

The son-in-law and father-in-law greet each other with elaborate formality in observance of filial piety and deference to their official positions. They embellish their speeches with modifiers such as "exalted," "celestial," and "glorious" to convey respect and adoration. The result is that the script, while poetic, is excessively verbose. It may be that Hazelton and Benrimo were influenced by the Chinese honorific addresses, aphorisms, and idioms they encountered to script the above dialogue, but its actual wording, styling, and poetic imagery were products of their own literary invention. The poetic language they created is a textual manifestation of their formalist approach to exploring Chinese theatre practices, as the language has a seemingly Chinese outward appearance, but its inner substance is highly contrived.

It is likely that Hazelton and Benrimo scripted the horticultural analogies in the cited dialogue in order to reflect Wu's position as the governor of the Flowery Kingdom, that is, the dramatized locale for China. Perhaps for this reason, most of the female characters in the play, such as Due Jung Fah (fuchsia), Suey Sin Fah (lily), Mow Dan Fah (peony), and Yong Soo Kow (hydrangea), are named after flowers. The most curious example is Wu Fah Din, the rival and half-brother of Wu Hoo Git, who describes himself as a man who possesses "a daffodil nature" (62).[50] He views Wu Hoo Git as "simply vulgarly manly," while he has "feminine qualities of great luxuriance." Wu Fah Din, then, is Wu Hoot Git's half-brother more in the sense of his half man, half woman qualities than blood relationship. His "feminine qualities of great luxuriance" are presumably related to his "daffodil," narcissist self-indulgence. Wu Fah Din boasts that his "[c]raft, guided by cruelty" will prevail over Wu Hoo Git's "brawn" and "vulgar manliness" (62–63). Thus, their rivalry is a battle between Wu Hoo Git's daring manliness and Wu Fah Din's cunning effeminacy. When all of his schemes ultimately fail, Wu Fah Din does not put up a fight. He simply steps down from the throne and begs to be retired to a garden filled with smiling flowers (185–186). The unsympathetic depictions of Wu Fah Din and his confrontation with Wu Hoo Git suggest that Hazelton and Benrimo associate effeminacy with luxury, self-indulgence, evil, and fragility, which, in their universal moral tale, is no match for righteous manliness.

Wu Fah Din's first scheme is to have his aide present his "porcelains," that is, women, to Wu Hoo Git in order to divert his attention from the throne. As his aide "deals deliciously in porcelains," Wu Fah Din contemplates, "[h]e will drop flowers of pleasure in Wu Hoo Git's path that my rival may inhale their odors of vice" (63). In this depiction, Chinese women are objectified not only as flowers, but also as porcelains, which, as discussed in the previous chapters, had been associated with China in the West since the late seventeenth century. Along with flowers, Hazelton and Benrimo interculturalized this popular Chinese commodity to highlight and dramatize the delicacy, fragility, and appeal of Chinese femininity in Wu Fah Din's perception. Benrimo acknowledged that a character like Wu Fah Din is nowhere to be found in Chinese theatre, but they constructed him as a "representative of the Oriental esthete."[51] In creating this character, Hazelton and Benrimo resorted to a gendered, orientalist stereotype to characterize and satirize an effeminate, self-indulgent Asian male.

In sum, the ultimate goal of Hazelton and Benrimo's efforts to write and stage *Yellow Jacket* was to demonstrate their belief that Chinese theatre "was something better than the realistic drama which demanded fresh butter on the stage if the plot called for fresh butter."[52] They invented a plot of primitive, childlike drama that called for the "fresh butter" of Chinese staging methods. Hazelton and Benrimon's intercultural experiment thus represents one of the early examples by modern Western theatre practitioners to reinvigorate their theatre practices by exploring and engaging Asian performing traditions. Despite their good intention and regard for Chinese theatre, Hazelton and Benrimo's primitive drama reinforces the association of China with backwardness and underdevelopment, and their formalist approach informs superficial imitation, as in the case of language discussed earlier, in its focus on imitating the formal aspects of Chinese theatre.

After he arrived in London to take charge of the production, Benrimo kept Hazelton informed about the preparations and also sought his assistance, for example, requesting him to send over props made by Chinese artisans in New York.[53] Although the London program stated that "the costumes and properties are supplied by Kwong Sun Chong of Canton and San Francisco,"[54] they seem very likely to have come instead from New York, modeled after those used in the New York production. William Furst, whose life is not much known, composed the incidental music to accompany the stage actions. Benrimo told reporters in London that they "sent to Canton and had records made in the Chinese theatre by means of the Victor gramophone. From these Mr. William Furst eliminated the clanging noises and the beating of drums, keeping the colour and the atmosphere, and it was no easy task."[55] This colorful account appears to be a tall tale invented by Benrimo to promote the production. Examination of the published scores reveals that the melody and structure of Furst's composition resembles Chinese folk songs and not music for the theatre.[56] In addition, the London production also issued a small booklet, "The Chinese Drama" written by Lionel Giles, an expert in Chinese studies working in the Oriental Department of the British Museum.[57] In the booklet Giles described the origin, the history, the genres, and the performance of Chinese drama, enhancing the production's truthful appeal as authentic Chinese theatre performance.

After its London premiere, *Yellow Jacket* drew mixed reviews. The production was, first of all, difficult to categorize within conventional English theatrical genres. It was called "an odd mixture of the comic and the tragic, the ridiculous and the sublime," "[a] curious medley of melodrama, farce, pantomime, and Miracle Play," "a curio," and "quaint and picturesque entertainment."[58] "Quaint" and "novel" were the most common depictions of the production. Beliefs and opinions varied about the story. Some, apparently taking it as a genuine adaptation of Chinese theatre, reported that it was two thousand years old and originally took nine nights to perform, while others doubted whether it was genuinely Chinese, and some thought it resembled the morality play *Everyman*. Most critics agreed that the play was too long and would have benefited greatly from curtailment.[59] Although some reviewers appreciated the flowery imagery that pervaded the script, most were turned off by the exaggerated formality and found the play lacking in true poetry and good writing.[60]

What drew the most diverse responses, however, were the play's claims about staging and acting in the "Chinese manner." Its single-scene setting was likened to Elizabethan drama, and the make-believe, symbolic acting was interpreted as naïve and primitive, not unlike a children's game.[61] "The Chinese element [in *Yellow Jacket*]," said the *Sunday Times*, "is its double appeal to our imaginative powers—double, because on the one hand many of our stage illusions are destroyed and because, on the other, we are expected to fill in by our own vision gaps of scenery and all the creations of decorative art."[62] That the absence of scenery did not prevent the audience from enjoying the play showed "how needless is realism, how prodigiously an audience is capable of make-believe."[63] However, some critics found that make-believe was "a pretty but tiring game" and that the unconvincing acting of the performers reduced them to "mechanical dolls." Worse than the slapstick of Punch and Judy, one reviewer said, *Yellow Jacket* might be successful as a puppet show.[64]

The reviewers extensively discussed the always bored, "intensely invisible" Property Man played by Holman Clark. As discussed earlier, the character was memorable for the comic effect created by his ubiquitous presence and his indifference to the stage actions. However, taking the character more seriously, S. O. of the *English Review* was intrigued by how Property Man enriched the significance of the play. According to this review, he both highlighted and shattered the illusion of the theatre by revealing the stage business, and he also became the audience's representative on stage, as his dull routine recalled the dreariness of day-to-day life. Property Man therefore became "essential and constructive"; he was "more tragic than the tragedy, comic because of his reality."[65] The review suggests that some saw meaning and significance in the comic depiction of the character.

Overall, though, it was the "Chinese manner," the form rather than the substance, that sustained the interest of the London public. The form, the game of make-believe in staging and acting, impressed the audience with its novelty. By contrast, the content was described as too thin or too poorly structured to sustain the audience's interest. "As an entire evening's entertainment for a London audience," one critic concluded, "it has something of the same order of success as would have an attempt to dine on chocolate dogs and gingerbread men."[66] *Yellow Jacket*, in other words, was considered a delectable confection, but not substantial enough to satisfy the appetite of some London theatergoers. *Yellow Jacket*, for all its attempts at innovation, marks another example of a play that attracted and appealed to the London audience with Chinaface novelty.

MR. WU

Shortly after *Yellow Jacket* was staged at Duke of York's, *Mr. Wu*, subtitled "an Anglo-Chinese Play in Three Acts and Two Tableaux," premiered on November 27, 1913, at the Strand theatre and ran for a whole year with 404 performances.[67] Similar to *Chinese Honeymoon*, *Mr. Wu* was developed upon established British theatre traditions, but in the melodrama genre. It offers a cautionary tale warning of the possible disastrous consequences of imperial expansion and intercultural contact. While also depicting an interracial, Anglo-Chinese encounter that involves romantic pursuits, *Mr. Wu* stands in sharp contrast to *Chinese Honeymoon* for the gravity of its subject matter, the terrifying threats posed by its Chinese villain, and its realistic setting in the British colony of Hong Kong. If *Chinese Honeymoon* covertly conveys the superiority and anxiety Britain felt toward China by comically depicting its exoticized attractions and idiosyncratic mannerisms, *Mr. Wu* exhibits fear, even paranoia, that China might acquire Western knowledge and use it to assert the worst possible revenge on the colonial power. In this regard, the depiction of the Chinese character Mr. Wu as an outsize, ferocious villain exhibits a distinct kind of orientalist discourse on China that counters the prevalent feminized characterization.[68] While the play's moral lesson is subject to debate, the play's successful long run benefited from the distinguished performance of Matheson Lang who was praised for his convincing portrayal of the Chinese villain. His performance, nevertheless, heightens the importance of the text in order to go beyond a Chinaface portrayal of the Chinese.

Written by Harry Vernon (1880?–1942), a playwright and screenwriter, and Henry Owen (1872–1930), a journalist and playwright,[69] *Mr. Wu* dramatizes the revenge of its eponymous character, a powerful and wealthy Chinese merchant in contemporary Kowloon, on the English businessman Mr. Gregory. Enraged and humiliated by a secret love affair between his daughter, Nang Ping, and Mr. Gregory's son, Basil, Mr. Wu ends his daughter's life and resolves to ruin the Gregory family. He kidnaps Basil, creates disturbances that bring down Mr. Gregory's business, and forces the distracted Mr. and Mrs. Gregory to seek his help. Upon meeting the Gregorys,

Mr. Wu outwits Mr. Gregory and talks Mrs. Gregory into visiting him to learn the whereabouts of Basil. Her visit becomes a nightmare as Mr. Wu gradually leads her to understand that he perceives only one option to settle the score with her son—to rape her. Horrified, Mrs. Gregory finds herself trapped with no way to escape. At a critical moment, her faithful maid casts a vial of poison into the room from a high window. The poison, intended for Mrs. Gregory so that she might kill herself rather than be raped, instead kills Mr. Wu when he drinks Mrs. Gregory's poisoned tea (Figure 4.4).[70]

The dramatic structure of *Mr. Wu* conforms to the conventions of melodrama in which the villain, Mr. Wu, is the driving force of the play.[71] He initiates the action, manipulates his victims, and almost succeeds in accomplishing his plan until the last sudden turn of fortune. The physical dangers to which the characters are subjected create drama and suspense, while the final meting out of justice seemingly assures that virtue is rewarded and vice punished (see further discussions on this point below).

A powerful and menacing villain, Mr. Wu was educated at Oxford and is therefore versed in Western society and culture. However, the traditional Chinese value of filial obedience and the taboo of interracial courtship are so deeply rooted in Mr. Wu that his daughter's affair with a foreigner is taken as a grave offence to his family and his honor. Although he himself may be considered as having an interculturalized persona due to his ability to function in both English and Chinese, at heart Mr. Wu, a Jekyll-and-Hyde-like character, keeps these two cultural systems separate within himself. It is precisely his inability to interculturalize and integrate the two identities of his character that gives rise to the tragedy. The dramatization of Mr. Wu's inner conflict also plays on the interculturated depiction of filial piety that has been shown in the earlier examples in this book to be a persistent and prominent feature in characterizing Chinese culture and the Chinese characters.

Placed in its historical context, the story of *Mr. Wu* dramatizes the possible contentious Anglo-Chinese relations in Hong Kong in the late nineteenth and early twentieth centuries.[72] Vernon and Owen appear knowledgeable about the function of Hong Kong as a trading hub for British merchants. They might have encountered news describing Anglo-Chinese conflicts in the colony, and their portrayal of Mr. Wu as a college graduate from Oxford might have been influenced by the presence of Chinese students in Britain.[73] However, as interactions between the Chinese and English communities in Hong Kong were quite limited, the likelihood of an interracial courtship seems improbable.[74] The realistic setting notwithstanding, Vernon and Owen's depiction of Mr. Wu and his cruel revenge may be better read as the writers' imagination of a possible conflict between the colonizer and colonized than a dramatization of a realistic occurrence. *Mr. Wu*, in other words, is a cautionary tale of the possible dangers in an inevitably intercultural environment, the colony, created by British imperial

Figure 4.4 "Mr. Wu drinks the poisoned tea which Mrs. Gregory intended for
herself." *The Play Pictorial*, vol. 23, no. 140, 1914. Billy Rose Theatre
Division, The New York Public Library for the Performing Arts, Astor,
Lenox and Tilden Foundations.

expansion. Mr. Wu, a highly dramatized melodrama villain rather than a truthful depiction of a Chinese man, personifies the Anglo-Chinese conflict and becomes the play's source of danger due to his conflicted intercultural identity, as discussed earlier. In Vernon and Owen's dramatization, Mr. Wu's omnipotent threat to the English characters lies in his ability to play with his Chinaface appearance and mannerisms while demonstrating that he is as much British as they are in his mastery of Western culture and values.

To resolve his inner dilemma, Mr. Wu kills his daughter, thus eliminating any prospect of intercultural contact between her and Basil. He further seeks revenge: as Basil tarnished his honor, he plans to violate the honor of the British. His doing so, as Mr. Wu tells Basil and Mrs. Gregory, is simply following the Western practice of an eye for an eye and a tooth for a tooth; in fact, it will be conducted it in a more "civilized" method—raping Mrs. Gregory and ruining her honor, rather than killing Basil. Using an approach that, he says, shows "the advantage of an European education" (III; 6, 16),[75] Mr. Wu intends to cunningly and perversely use his knowledge of Western values (that is, female virtue) to take his revenge upon the Gregorys.

When he first meets Mr. Gregory, Mr. Wu is depicted as "dressed in the height of Western fashion, but not overdressed." He is articulate and sharp in his responses. When Mr. Gregory insolently addresses him as "Wu," Mr. Wu wittily challenges him: "Wu is so short a name that you could say Mr. Wu whilst I was saying Gregory." He not only corrects Mr. Gregory's slip of the tongue in English but also demonstrates his knowledge of Latin and French. When his verbal threats and coercion prove ineffective, Mr. Gregory pulls a revolver on Mr. Wu, who, after momentarily giving in to his "Oriental ferocity," calmly talks Mr. Gregory into putting down the weapon. Mr. Wu then pulls his own revolver on Mr. Gregory and holds him hostage (II; 11–20). During the confrontation, Mr. Wu so outsmarts Mr. Gregory verbally and in mental and physical strength that he seems both monstrous and invincible. The characterization of Mr. Wu as an anglicized Chinese villain who turns his Western learning against the British exemplifies what Heidi Holder calls the "most paranoid of melodramatic fantasies," in which native subjects threatened the well-being of the British empire by acquiring Western knowledge and, consequently, power, in the early years of imperial decline in the early twentieth century.[76]

Mr. Wu's character impresses the English not only by his Western education and intelligence but also by his understanding of Western taste. When Mrs. Gregory visits his home, which the stage direction describes as that "[e]verything suggests wealth and taste": the ebony furniture, elegant cabinets in which china is displayed, and a room decorated with "Chinese antiques of every description," including bowls, weapons, statuettes, and figures. The house, Mrs. Gregory admits with a slight, awkward laugh, is not only civilized, but "refined to the last degree" (III; 8). The display of numerous Chinese goods and antiques that were treasured in Britain is not only another symbol of Mr. Wu's refined taste and keen understanding of

British material interests, but also a persistent, interculturated Chinaface convention. His death by drinking poisoned tea may be read as Vernon and Owen's admonishment that the British may, while consuming this Chinese material obsession, be consumed by it.

Mrs. Gregory is depicted as a caring mother whose eagerness to find her lost son leads her into Mr. Wu's trap. She seems resolute when she suggests that Mr. Gregory "meet cunning with its like" if Mr. Wu is as evil as rumored (II; 11). When confronted by Mr. Wu's threat of rape, however, Mrs. Gregory appears naïve and vulnerable in her belief that suicide is her only choice. The depiction of Mrs. Gregory as easy prey only heightens the likelihood for her to be victimized. The power relationship of a defenseless British woman at the mercy of an overpowering, seemingly omnipotent Chinese man challenges the prevailing orientalist discourse in which China is depicted as a weaker, feminized other. It may be argued that the play exhibits a related and opposite kind of orientalist discourse in which Chinese, if not exotically feminized, are villainized as monsters.

Basil and Mr. Gregory, while not villains, are not as naïve or innocent as Mrs. Gregory. Basil is depicted as a womanizer who Mr. Wu's daughter, Nang Ping, dreams of marrying, and he encourages her vain hopes, asserting that he will return to her after a journey to Britain when in fact he is leaving to marry an Englishwoman. Mr. Gregory is "a rather pompous, would-be-stern, bustling, unsympathetic man" who is "full of Western prejudices" (I; 10). He is unsophisticated in his dealings with the Chinese characters and offers only bluster and threats during his confrontation with Mr. Wu. As Basil and Mr. Gregory are not plain, righteous characters who contrast neatly with the evil Mr. Wu, the moral lesson at the end of *Mr. Wu* seems ambiguous. If Mr. Wu is punished for his devious plans, his thirst for revenge is nevertheless provoked by Basil's misconduct, whose culpability escapes judgment.

In the original version of the play, there is no last-minute reprieve in the form of a vial of poison, and Mrs. Gregory, with no opportunity to commit suicide, presumably succumbs to Mr. Wu's sexual assault. As noted on the manuscript, the ending was greatly modified for the London production in order to obtain the license of the Lord Chamberlain. In the revised version, Mr. Wu's rape scheme ("hideous bargain") is still proposed to Mrs. Gregory, but not carried out, so that "the drama remains painful, but ceases to be revolting; while there is now nothing necessarily hurtful to Chinese susceptibilities in either action or dialogue."[77] The censor's justification appears to rest on the taboo and graphic ("revolting") nature of rape and the possibility of offending the Chinese. Nonetheless, the revised ending little changes the depiction of Mr. Wu as a psychotic Chinese villain, as he is still depicted as killing his own daughter and scheming to ruin the Gregorys. Instead, it may be argued that the revised ending actually heightens the artificiality, and therefore the melodrama, of the Gregorys' escape, as they are saved purely by Mr. Wu's inadvertent drinking of the poisoned tea. The villain eventually dies, but the moral lesson is not entirely clear-cut.

Although commercially successful, *Mr. Wu* triggered comments that were no less diverse and extreme than those about *Yellow Jacket*. For some reviewers, the revenge, feud, and interracial conflict depicted in the play recalled Shakespeare's *Measure for Measure*, *The Merchant of Venice*, and *Othello*.[78] However, most critics found that Mr. Wu's death from drinking the poisoned tea resulted in an abrupt and unsatisfactory ending. As the review in *Sketch* put it, "... when it comes to the pinch, the authors funk their theme, and are rather like little boys who ring and run away."[79] The ending was interpreted as demonstrating the authors' inability to unknot the complicated plot they had conceived.[80]

Defending the play, the review in *Illustrated London News* stated that while at first glance the play might "seem mere melodrama with an Oriental veneer," it also showed that there were places, such as the East, where "the spirit of law-abidingness has not entered into the blood of the people, ... suppressed instincts may rise any moment against the suppressing power."[81] In this reading, the play depicts the revolt of outlaw or unrestrained human instincts against order and sense. It suggests that while well educated, smartly dressed, articulate, and exhibiting refined tastes, Mr. Wu actually has not absorbed the "suppressing power" of civilization and could turn barbaric at any moment. The same review also commented that the play handled "a problem of colour and sex in two aspects," namely, while the Western world is inclined to "view lightly" a white man's dalliance with a nonwhite woman, it "sees red" in the case of a nonwhite man's pursuit of a white woman.[82] The play exposes this double standard by contrasting Basil's exemption from punishment in his irresponsible flirtation with Nang Ping with Mr. Wu's punishment by death in response to his attempted rape of Mrs. Gregory. However, John Palmer of the *Saturday Review* compared the experience of viewing the play to the sensation of an English naturalist beholding for the first time "a monstrous insect or growth of the tropical forest,"[83] by which he presumably meant shock and disgust at the existence of something so impossible in an alien environment, i.e., the play and its setting in Hong Kong. Palmer considered that the playwrights inadequately handled the subject of interracial romance and depicted the English characters as no match for Mr. Wu. To him, there was "no good fight between intelligent protagonists" in the play.[84]

Amid diverse critical opinion, what sustained the production for a whole year was the powerful portrayal of Mr. Wu by Matheson Lang. "This Mr. Wu is an uncanny blend of Oriental ferocity and Western culture," the review in the *Times* commented. "Mr. Matheson Lang is wonderfully Chinese in appearance and demeanour as Mr. Wu, and with such an irreproachable English as well as Chinese suavity that you feel sure Mr. Wu, in his Oxford time, was a Fellow of All Souls."[85] "Mr. Lang," said the review in *Illustrated London News*, "besides doing wonders in the way of make-up and indications of accent and manner, seems to get right inside the skin of the Chinaman. There is a realistic thoroughness about his work, just as there is 'local colour' in the play."[86] This high praise suggests that Lang's portrayal went well beyond superficial Chinaface novelty. Beneath the yellowface make-up and Chinese mannerisms, Lang portrayed the character with "realistic thoroughness" and got "right inside the skin" of the character, managing to become a convincingly Chinese Mr. Wu. It may thus be argued that in performance, Lang succeeded in interculturalizing himself and the character.

Although he played mostly Shakespearean roles during his career, Lang earned such fame for his portrayal of Mr. Wu that he named his memoir *Mr. Wu Looks Back*, and when *Mr. Wu* was made into a film, Lang played his signature role.[87] As described in his memoir, Lang first thought of playing a Chinese character while he was touring in China. The Chinese he met in Shanghai were "men of high culture and great artistic intelligence," "with charming manners and an extraordinary sense of dominant personality," and Lang was excited by the idea of playing "a real Chinese of the type of these men" who would differ from the "ridiculous, comical little figure of musical comedy" or the "rather exaggerated monster of villainy in melodrama."[88] After he returned to London, Lang enthused over the script of *Mr. Wu* and set to work on the title role. Like Hazelton and Benrimo, he received help from the Chinese, in this case, the First Secretary of the Chinese Legation in London who, unknowingly, became his role model.[89]

According to Lang's account, his encounter with Chinese of high social class and culture inspired him to depict a Chinese character that would be different from the conventional Chinaface characters who typically appeared in both musical comedies and melodramas. Lang believed that the character Mr. Wu differed from other melodrama villains in his high social status and cultural refinement. Furthermore, Lang's personal contacts with the Chinese, especially the Chinese secretary in London, enabled him to observe and imitate the mannerisms of Chinese in high social positions. According to Lang, the Chinese secretary came frequently to the theatre to discuss the play, and Lang took advantage of these visits to observe and imitate him for the character Mr. Wu. However, it may be argued that in Lang's case, the Chinese assistance could only add a superficial appeal of authenticity to what as still, at root, a Chinaface role, as the character had already been cast in the script as a fictional embodiment of the Anglo-Chinese conflict. Although Lang enjoyed the script and saw the role as unique, the critics viewed Mr. Wu as a typical melodramatic villain, possibly even more exaggeratedly ferocious than usual for the genre; Lang's performance of Mr. Wu in the final tea drinking scene would make viewers gasp, said the *Times* review, which is "of course just the effect desired."[90] Despite Lang's outstanding performance, *Mr. Wu* highlights the critical and fundamental role played by the text in further interculturating Chinaface conventions.

Chinese Honeymoon, *Yellow Jacket*, and *Mr. Wu* could easily be treated as typical orientalist products of colonialism and imperialism that caricatured, mystified, and demonized the Chinese. Among the three plays, only *Yellow Jacket* has received some attention from later critics, most of whom severely criticize its portrayals of China and the Chinese. It is derided for its romantic fantasies and exaggerated exoticism, its depiction of China as culturally and aesthetically inferior to the West, its propagation of anti-feminist ideas, and its disapproval of femininity. Above all, it is deemed unfit for the modern stage.[91]

In its representation of China and the Chinese, as discussed earlier, *Yellow Jacket* does contain biased and exoticized interpretations. However, it would be unfair to say, as modern critics suggest, that Benrimo and Hazelton intended to portray China as inferior to the West culturally and artistically. "I saw in the Chinese theatrical conventions," wrote Hazelton, "the simplicity of Shakespeare productions and the forceful way of the Greeks." He liked the machine of Chinese theatre and asked Benrimo to give him the throttle of the engine.[92] Hazelton's comparison to Shakespeare and Greek theatre recalls Davis's analogy (discussed in Chapter Three) that similarly praises but antiquates Chinese theatre. As his machine metaphor suggests, Hazelton's comparison concerns the technical, staging aspects of these theatres. For all of the play's novel staging innovations, the contemporary reviews highlight the importance of substantial dramatic content, which, they suggest, would do more to provide the audience with meaning than the technical novelty of staging.

Matheson Lang visited China just after the 1911 revolution that ended the Qing Dynasty. While he was there, the requirement that men tie their hair into a queue (a long braid), which had been enforced by the deposed monarchy, was abolished. Lang quickly brought this new development back to the London production of *Mr. Wu* and claimed that the play was the first presented in London to show Chinese characters without queues.[93] This account demonstrates Lang's efforts to portray the Chinese as authentically as possible by updating the Chinaface appearance with new information. As cited earlier, he was enthusiastically praised by reviewers for his consistency as a character and effectiveness as a melodrama villain. His carefully studied Chinese mannerisms, including the updated Chinese hairstyle, enhanced his look, but could not make up for the conventionalized depiction of the character. The contemporary reviews suggest that while the critics were aware that the character was not a truthful representation of the Chinese, and that they were captivated by the thrill and horror created by the villain, they also regarded Lang's performance as realistic, implying an association of the role with actual Chinese.

Among the three plays examined in this chapter the least controversial in audience reception was *Chinese Honeymoon*. As discussed earlier, its dramatic content exceeded its audience's expectations by maintaining a discernible plot amid all the whimsical escapades. Unlike *Yellow Jacket* and *Mr. Wu*, *Chinese Honeymoon* did not claim to authentically depict Chinese theatre or the Chinese, and its audience well understood that it followed the conventions of musical comedy. *Yellow Jacket*, by contrast, was a novelty that set very different expectations for its audience, which may help explain its doubtful or negative reviews. Advertised as "A Chinese Play given in the Chinese Manner," and with its stage and props modeled after actual Chinese practice, the audience was led to anticipate a truthful depiction, both in story and staging, of the country and its people. This may also explain the critical comments recent critics have expressed toward the play—it was not what it said it was.

During its London run, *Yellow Jacket* drew the attendance of the Chinese ambassador in London, among other Chinese. He was said to have assisted in the rehearsal of the play.[94] After the production finished its run in London, Benrimo wrote Hazelton to report that he was invited to a lunch with Chinese high officials and thanked for showing "some of the poetry of China to the European world."[95] These accounts suggest that during the play's London run, its content and staging may have been further modified or interculturalized with assistance from the Chinese ambassador, and that the Chinese appreciated Benrimo's attempt to introduce Chinese theatre to the London (British) audience. Moreover, Benrimo's promotional work for *Yellow Jacket* had showed his enthusiasm for and positive view of the Chinese art form. Despite the problematic dramatic content of the play, the Chinese may have genuinely appreciated Benrimo's efforts to promote Chinese theatre when the country's image in the West had suffered from negative portrayals since the time of the first Opium War.

Commenting on *Yellow Jacket*, the review in *Daily Mail* questioned whether it was authentically Chinese. However, as various aspects of the production were enjoyable, the review surmised that it carried one away, "if not to China, at least to Chinatown."[96] The review fortuitously, if unknowingly, identifies the origin of *Yellow Jacket* in the inspiration it took from McDowell's illustrated article on the Chinese theatre performance in San Francisco's Chinatown and the assistance Hazelton and Benrimo received from Chinese in New York. The review may also be read as a reflection on London's own Chinatown, with which the London audience would have been familiar and therefore referenced as they watched the play. Given the assistance they gave to *Yellow Jacket* and *Mr. Wu*, it is apparent that diasporic Chinese played a crucial role in the conception and performance of both plays, yet the intercultural collaboration appeared to operate mostly on the visual, Chinaface level. These historical precedents indicate that the establishment of diasporic Chinese communities gave Westerners a shortcut means of engaging in intercultural collaboration with Chinese outside Asia. The precedents also hint at the possibility of more fruitful results if future intercultural collaborations could go beyond formalistic adaptations of Chinese theatre and Chinaface imitations in the portrayal of Chinese characters.

NOTES

1. The fall of the Qing dynasty, a difficult history to assess, has generated a huge body of scholarship. See, for example, Che Xu and Shouyi Dong, vol. 9 of *Qing Dai Quan Shi* [Complete History of the Qing Dynasty], ed. Rongsheng Wang (Shenyang Shi: Liaoning Ren Min Chu Ban She, 1991); Wenhai Li, Dunkui Lin, and Keguang Lin, eds., *Yi He Tuan Yun Dong Shi Shi Yao Lu* [Chronicle of the Movement of the Righteous and Harmonious Militia] (Jinan: Qi Lu Shu She, 1986); Qing Hua Da Xue Li Shi Xi, ed., *Wu Xu Bian Fa Wen Xian Zi Liao Xi Ri* [Chronicle of the Wu Xu Reform Movement] (Shanghai: Shanghai Shu Dian Chu Ban She, 1998); John King Fairbank, chap. 11 in *China: A New History* (Cambridge, MA: Belknap Press of Harvard University Press, 1992); Bruce A. Elleman, chaps. 7 to 9 in *Modern Chinese Warfare, 1795–1989* (London: Routledge, 2001); Jean Chesneaux, Marianne Bastid, and Marie-Claire Bergère, chaps. 9 and 10 in *China from the Opium Wars to the 1911 Revolution*, trans. Ann Destenay (New York: Pantheon Books, 1976); Chien-nung Li, chaps. 3 to 9 in *The Political History of China, 1840–1928*, trans. Ssu-yu Teng and Jeremy Ingalls (Princeton, NJ: D. Van Nostrand, 1956).
2. John Francis Davis, "Preface," in *China, During the War and Since the Peace* (London: Longman, Brown, Green, and Longmans, 1852), 1:vi.
3. Ibid., 1:vi–vii.
4. Ross G. Forman, *China and the Victorian Imagination: Empires Entwined* (Cambridge: Cambridge University Press, 2013), 4–5.
5. J. P. Wearing, *The London Stage, 1900–1909: A Calendar of Plays and Players* (Metuchen, NJ: Scarecrow Press, 1981), 1:123–124; Kurt Gänzl, *The Encyclopedia of the Musical Theatre*, 2nd ed. (New York: Schirmer Books, 2001), 1:364–366 (hereafter cited as *Encyclopedia*); Gänzl, *The British Musical Theatre* (New York: Oxford University Press, 1986), 1:720. Wearing records that *A Chinese Honeymoon* had a consecutive run of 1,071 performances (123), while Gänzl states that it had a run of 1,075 (*British Musical Theatre*, 1:725). For biographical accounts of Dance and Talbot, see, for example, the entry of Dance in Gänzl, *Encyclopedia* (1:459–461); the entry of Dance in Gale Research Company, *Who Was Who in the Theatre, 1912–1976: A Biographical Dictionary of Actors, Actresses, Directors, Playwrights, and Producers of the English-Speaking Theatre* (Detroit: Gale Research Company, 1978), 2:593; the entry of Talbot in John Tyrrell and Stanley Sadie, eds., *The New Grove Dictionary of Music and Musicians*, 2nd ed. (London: Macmillan, 2001). Dance's birth date is uncertain. *Who Was Who* gives 1865 as his birth year, while Gänzl states that Dance was born in 1857 (*Encyclopedia*, 1:459).
6. John M. MacKenzie, *Propaganda and Empire: The Manipulation of British Public Opinion, 1880–1960* (Manchester: Manchester University Press, 1984), 53–54. "Escapist musicals" is a term coined by Ronald Pearsall and cited by MacKenzie. See Ronald Pearsall, *Edwardian Popular Music* (Rutherford, NJ: Fairleigh Dickinson University Press, 1975), 11.
7. George Dance and Howard Talbot, "A Chinese Honeymoon," The Lord Chamberlain's Plays, Add. 53693 J (1899), Department of Manuscripts, the British Library.
8. For the libretto of *The Mikado*, see, for example, W. S. Gilbert, *The Best Known Works of W. S. Gilbert* (New York: Illustrated Editions, 1932), 101–161.

9. For the lyrics of *The Geisha*, see Sidney Jones, *The Geisha; A Story of a Tea House* (London: Hopwood and Crew, 1896). Synopses of its story are provided in Gänzl, *Encyclopedia*, 1:731–733; *British Musical Theatre*, 1:585–590.

10. For the libretto of *Fleur de thé*, see Charles Lecocq, *Fleur-de-thé; Opera Bouffe in Three Acts* (New York: Gray and Green, 1869). The similarity in plot structure between *A Chinese Honeymoon* and *Fleur de thé* is noted in Gänzl, *Encyclopedia*, 1:664–665.

11. For brief discussions of *San Toy, Florodora* and *See See*, see Gänzl, *Encyclopedia*, 1:665–668, 3:1790–1792, 1828.

12. Jeffrey Richards, *Imperialism and Music: Britain, 1876–1953* (Manchester: Manchester University Press, 2001), 262.

13. John M. MacKenzie, *Orientalism: History, Theory and the Arts* (Manchester: Manchester University Press, 1995), 180–181, 189–197.

14. MacKenzie, *Propaganda and Empire*, 53.

15. MacKenzie, *Orientalism*, 181; *Propaganda and Empire*, 53–54.

16. George Dance and Howard Talbot, *A Chinese Honeymoon. Musical Comedy*, Nineteenth Century English Drama: Plays Submitted to the Lord Chamberlain ([1902]; reprint, New Canaan, CT: Readex, 1985–), 5. This program, reproduced in microfiche, is undated. However, it includes a song titled "Tit-bits from the Plays" (29–30), which comments on contemporary productions. The most recent play it describes is *Ulysses*, produced between February and May 1902.

17. Dance and Talbot, "A Chinese Honeymoon." Hereafter all the page numbers cited are from this manuscript.

18. The expansion of Britain's imperial power in China at Wei-Hai-Wei (威海衛) was a real historical event with which the authors were apparently familiar.

19. Penny Summerfield, "Patriotism and Empire: Music-Hall Entertainment, 1870–1914," in *Imperialism and Popular Culture*, ed. John M. MacKenzie (Manchester: Manchester University Press, 1986), 37–38.

20. Paul Greenhalgh, *Ephemeral Vistas: The Expositions Universelles, Great Exhibitions and World's Fairs, 1851–1939* (Manchester: Manchester University Press, 1988), 74–75, 148–149; MacKenzie, *Orientalism*, 124–128; Richards, 262–266.

21. Jones, 3, 6.

22. The same allusion was also made in *San Toy* (1899), another musical set in China.

23. Heidi J. Holder, "Melodrama, Realism and Empire on the British Stage," in *Acts of Supremacy: The British Empire and the Stage, 1790–1930*, by J. S. Bratton et al. (Manchester: Manchester University Press, 1991), 141–142.

24. In the imperialist dramas of Holder's study, the native, non-European characters were replaced by European characters in the depiction of dramatic conflict. See ibid., 142.

25. Ibid., 143.

26. "Strand Theatre," *Times*, October 7, 1901, p. 5.

27. "'A Chinese Honeymoon,' at the Strand," *Illustrated London News*, October 12, 1901, p. 520.

28. Ibid.

29. "Strand Theatre," *Times*, October 7, 1901, p. 5.

30. "'A Chinese Honeymoon,' at the Strand," *Sketch*, October 9, 1901, p. 462.

31. "The Strand," *Stage*, October 10, 1901, p. 14.

32. "A Chinese Honeymoon," *Era*, October 12, 1901, p. 15.

33. J. P. Wearing, *The London Stage, 1910–1919, A Calendar of Plays and Players* (Metuchen, NJ: Scarecrow Press, 1982), 1:328.

34. For bibliographical accounts of Hazelton and Benrimo, see, for example, the entry of Hazelton in Allen Johnson and Dumas Malone, eds., *Frauces-Hibbard*, vol. 4 of *Dictionary of American Biography* (New York: Charles Scribner's Sons, [1964]), 2: 475–476; the entry of Benrimo in John Parker, ed., *Who's Who in the Theatre*, 9th ed. (New York: Pitman, 1939), 298–299; "J. Harry Benrimo, Actor, Playwright," *New York Times*, March 27, 1942, p. 23.

35. George C. Hazelton and J. Harry Benrimo, "The Record of 'The Yellow Jacket,'" in *The Yellow Jacket: A Chinese Play Done in a Chinese Manner in Three Acts* (New York: Samuel French, 1939), 116–117.

36. "The Play that Went Round the World," *New York Times*, November 26, 1916, p. X7.

37. George C. Hazelton and J. Harry Benrimo, "Foreword," in *The Yellow Jacket: A Chinese Play Done in a Chinese Manner in Three Acts* (Indianapolis: Bobbs-Merrill, 1913).

38. Hazelton and Benrimo, *Yellow Jacket* (1913).

39. J. Harry Benrimo, "Legend and Truth: The Facts about 'The Yellow Jacket,' Again in Revival Here," *New York Times*, November 4, 1928, p. 118 (hereafter cited as Benrimo, "Legend and Truth").

40. The New York and London productions employed an almost identical stage setup. While the complete picture of the stage is partially cropped in the spider scene, a different photo of the New York production ("Stage Setting From 'The Yellow Jacket,'" *Upholster*, January 15, 1913, p. 73) and another of the London production ("The Intensely Invisible Property Man Holds a Bamboo, with Dangling Noose," *Sketch* supplement, April 9, 1913. p. 3) help complete the picture. The two long scrolls bear a Chinese couplet that comments on the stage performance, "Don't take the wearing of Chinese costumes as bizarre / Foreigners will surely admire this wonder and novelty" (裝成中國衣冠 莫言鬼怪，想必異邦人物 共贊神奇). According to the traditional Chinese reading style, which is from top to bottom and right to left, the first scroll of the couplet should be hung on the right hand side of the balcony from the audience's perspective, and the second scroll on the left. In the London production the scrolls were hung in the reverse order. In both the New York and London productions, the entrance (出將) and exit (入相) signs were mismatched with the doors. The entrance sign should have been placed above the door on stage right, and the exit sign on stage left.

41. Benrimo, "Legend and Truth"; Henry Burden McDowell, "The Chinese Theatre," *Century* 29, no. 1 (1884): 27–44.

42. For the illustration, see McDowell, 42. The illustration is missing the congratulatory couplet seen in the photos of *Yellow Jacket*'s stage. For their play, Hazelton and Benrimo also adapted McDowell's account of the origin of Chinese theatre and used another of McDowell's illustrations depicting a painted-face character as inspiration for the costume and make-up design of the character Tai Fah Min.

43. Benrimo, "Legend and Truth."

44. The Billy Rose Theatre Collections of the New York Public Library for the Performing Arts holds the "George Cochrane Hazelton Papers, 1848–1941" (hereafter cited as Hazelton Papers), which contains various editions of manuscripts,

correspondence, programs, and clippings of reviews of *Yellow Jacket*. Additional programs and clippings of *Yellow Jacket* are also kept in this library. In addition, the Manuscripts and Archives Division of the Stephen A. Schwarzman Building, New York Public Library, holds the "Joseph Henry Benrimo Papers, 1906–1941" (hereafter cited as Benrimo Papers), which contains relevant correspondence and manuscripts of *Yellow Jacket*. Together these resources provide rich information about how *Yellow Jacket* took shape, how it was staged, and how audiences responded to its depiction of China and employment of Chinese theatre conventions.

45. Benrimo, "Legend and Truth"; Hazelton Papers, Box 6 (28,985), fol. 7.
46. Hazelton Papers, Box 28 (29,006) and Box 29 (29,007).
47. David H. Wallace, "Writing a Chinese Play: George C. Hazelton and Harry Benrimo Tell How It Is Done," *New York Dramatic Mirror*, November 13, 1912, p. 9; Benrimo, "Legend and Truth"; letter from Benrimo to Hazelton dated March 8, 1912, Hazelton Papers, Box 7 (28,986), fol. 1; Hazelton Papers, Box 29 (29,007), fols. 8 and 9.
48. Benrimo Papers; Hazelton Papers, Box 29 (29,007), fol. 9.
49. Hazelton and Benrimo, *Yellow Jacket* (1913). Hereafter all the references to the play script are cited from this edition.
50. The name Wu Fah Din does not correspond with the flower daffodil in Chinese saying, *shuixian*, which could also mean lily. As the female character representing lily has been named, in the Cantonese pronunciation, Suey Sin Fah (i.e., *shuixian* flower, Fah or *hua* meaning flower), Hazelton and Benrimo appeared to adopt a transliteration approach by translating the syllables ffodil in daffodil into Fah Din and place them after the family name Wu of the character, in the order of Chinese names.
51. Benrimo, "Legend and Truth."
52. Ibid.
53. The letters from Benrimo written in London to Hazelton in New York are kept in Hazelton Papers, Box 7 (28,986), fol. 3.
54. Duke of York's theatre, playbill of *Yellow Jacket*, March 27, 1913.
55. "London's Play in the Chinese Way: Mr. Henry Benrimo Explains 'The Yellow Jacket,'" *"London Budget,"* April 6, 1913, quoted from Hazelton Papers, Box 48 (29,026), 75.
56. William Furst, *Piano Score of The Yellow Jacket*, ed. Paul Taubman (New York: Samuel French, 1941). I am indebted to Ms. Sheng-Chieh (Holy) Chang, a graduate of the Department of Music and Performing Arts Professions at New York University, who helped me examine Benrimo's claim by playing through the scores and reconstructing some of the incidental music pieces.
57. Lionel Giles worked for the British Museum and translated various Chinese literatures. His father, Herbert Allen Giles, was a Chinese scholar who popularized the Wade-Giles romanization system and wrote extensively on China. See, for example, Janette Ryan, "Giles, Herbert Allen (1845–1935)," in *Oxford Dictionary of National Biography* (Oxford University Press, 2004–), doi:10.1093/ref:odnb/33401.
58. "The Yellow Jacket," *Era*, March 29, 1913, p. 14; "The Duke of York's," *Stage*, April 3, 1913, p. 20; "Duke of York's Theatre: 'The Yellow Jacket,'" *Times*, March 28, 1913, p. 10; "The Playhouses," *Illustrated London News*, April 5, 1913, p. 444.
59. "The Yellow Jacket," *Era*, March 29, 1913, p. 14; "Duke of York's Theatre: 'The Yellow Jacket,'" *Times*, March 28, 1913, p. 10; S. D., "Property Man Hero:

Chinese Drama at the Duke of York's. 'The Yellow Jacket,'" *Daily Express*, March 28, 1913; St. John Ervine, "'The Yellow Jacket': Amusing Chinese Play Given in Chinese Manner," *Daily Citizen*, March 28, 1913. The last two are quoted from Hazelton Papers, Box 48 (29,026), 52–53, 60.

60. "Duke of York's Theatre, 'The Yellow Jacket,'" *Morning Post*, March 28, 1913; S.R.L., "'Yellow Jacket': Chinese Play at Duke of York's. Delightful Production," *Daily Chronicle*, March 28, 1913; E. F. S., "'The Yellow Jacket' at Duke of York's," *Westminster Gazette*, March 28, 1913; "Another Chinese Play: 'The Yellow Jacket,' at the Duke of York's," *Pall Mall Gazette*, March 28, 1913. All of these reviews are quoted from Hazelton Papers, Box 48 (29,026), 45–47, 55–58.

61. "Duke of York's Theatre: 'The Yellow Jacket,'" *Times*, March 28, 1913, p. 10; "The Yellow Jacket: Simple Chinese Play Delights a London Audience. The Glorification of Pretence," *Sketch*, n.d., quoted from Hazelton Papers, Box 48 (29,026), 50.

62. "(4) Duke of York's: 'The Yellow Jacket,'" *Sunday Times*, March 30, 1913, quoted from Hazelton Papers, Box 48 (29,026), 65.

63. E. F. S. (Monocle), "The Stage from the Stalls: 'The Yellow Jacket' in an English Dress," *Sketch*, April 9, 1913, 10.

64. "The Theatre: In the Chinese Manner," *Globe*, March 28, 1913; "'The Yellow Jacket': A Chinese Play Given in the Chinese Manner," *Daily News and Leader*, March 28, 1913; "In the Chinese Manner: An Oriental Play—Without an Oriental Audience," *Daily Graphic*, March 28, 1913. All of these reviews are quoted from Hazelton Papers, Box 48 (29,026), 51, 54–55.

65. S. O., "Play of the Month: The Yellow Jacket," *English Review*, 14 (April–July 1913): 320.

66. "The Yellow Jacket: Simple Chinese Play Delights a London Audience. The Glorification of Pretence," *Sketch*, n.d., quoted from Hazelton Papers, Box 48 (29,026), 50.

67. J. P. Wearing, *London Stage, 1910–1919*, 1:402–403.

68. Among the examples discussed in this book, Lycungus in Settle's *Conquest* (see Chapter One) may be regarded as a historical precedent comparable to the character Mr. Wu.

69. For bibliographical accounts of Vernon and Owen, see, for example, the description of Vernon in the Harry M. Vernon papers kept at the Margaret Herrick Library, the Academy of Motion Picture Arts and Sciences, http://collections.oscars.org/link/papers/103; the entry of Vernon in Parker, *Who's Who in the Theatre*, 1484, and the entry of Owen in Gale Research Company, *Who Was Who*, 3:1860. Parker gives Vernon's birth date as 1878, which is different from that (1880) in the description of the Harry M. Vernon Collection.

70. Harry Vernon and Harold Owen, "Mr. Wu," The Lord Chamberlain's Plays, 1913/36 (1913), Department of Manuscripts, the British Library.

71. Michael R. Booth, "The Character of Melodrama," in *English Melodrama* (London: Herbert Jenkins, 1965), 18.

72. For a general history of Hong Kong, see, for example, G. B. Endacott, *A History of Hong Kong* (London: Oxford University Press, 1973).

73. Chinese students began to arrive in Britain in the late nineteenth century for advanced education. Though their number was very small, their presence was likely visible to the British. See, for example, Gregor Benton and Edmund Terence Gomez, *The Chinese in Britain, 1800–Present: Economy, Transnationalism,*

Identity (Basingstoke: Palgrave Macmillan, 2008), 47–50; Kwee Choo Ng, *The Chinese in London* (London: Oxford University Press, 1968), 12–14.

74. See, for example, Endacott, 70, 243–244.
75. Vernon and Owen, "Mr. Wu." Hereafter all the act and page numbers are cited from this manuscript.
76. Holder, "Melodrama, Realism and Empire on the British Stage," 146–147.
77. Ernest A. Bendall, notes of recommendation for license, in Vernon and Owen, "Mr. Wu." In this manuscript accepted for license the rape scene is cut.
78. "An Anglo-Chinese Play: 'Mr. Wu' at the Strand," *Times*, November 28, 1913, p. 12; "London Theatres: The Strand," *Stage*, December 4, 1913, p. 26; John Palmer, "The Worst Play in London," *Saturday Review*, May 9, 1914, p. 598.
79. "Things New: At the Theatres," *Sketch*, December 3, 1913, p. 260.
80. "'Mr. Wu,'" *Era*, December 3, 1913, p. 14.
81. "The Playhouses: 'Mr. Wu' at the Strand," *Illustrated London News*, December 6, 1913, p. 976.
82. Ibid.
83. Palmer, "The Worst Play in London."
84. Ibid.
85. "An Anglo-Chinese Play: 'Mr. Wu' at the Strand," *Times*, November 28, 1913, p. 12.
86. "The Playhouses: 'Mr. Wu' at the Strand," *Illustrated London News*, December 6, 1913, p. 976.
87. Matheson Lang, *Mr. Wu Looks Back: Thoughts and Memories* (London: Stanley Paul and Company, 1940).
88. Lang, *Mr. Wu Looks Back*, 112.
89. Ibid., 113–116.
90. "An Anglo-Chinese Play: 'Mr. Wu' at the Strand," *Times*, November 28, 1913, p. 12.
91. See, for example, Dave Williams, "The State and the Self-Sacrificing Woman: *The Daughter of Heaven* and *The Yellow Jacket*," in *Misreading the Chinese Character* (New York: Peter Lang, 2000), 157–174; Wenwei Du, "Traditional Chinese Theatre on Broadway," in *Cultural Encounters: China, Japan, and the West*, eds. Søren Clausen, Roy Starrs, and Anne Wedell-Wedellsborg (Aarhus, Denmark: Aarhus University Press, 1995), 197, 206–207; James Harbeck, "The Quaintness—and Usefulness—of the Old Chinese Traditions: *The Yellow Jacket* and *Lady Precious Stream*," *Asian Theatre Journal* 13, no. 2 (Fall 1996): 238–247; Erika Fischer-Lichte, "What Are the Rules of the Game? Some Remarks on *The Yellow Jacket*," *Theatre Survey* 36 (May 1995): 21–36.
92. Hazelton, letter to Mr. Leupp, dated March 22, 1913, Hazelton Papers, Box 7 (28,986), fol. 3.
93. Lang, *Mr. Wu Looks Back*, 103–106; "An Anglo-Chinese Play: 'Mr. Wu' at the Strand," *Times*, November 28, 1913, p. 12.
94. See, for example, *Daily Herald*, March 24, 1913; J. T., "'The Yellow Jacket': Chinese Play in Chinese Fashion in London," *Evening News*, March 28, 1913; G. M., "Quaint Effects in 'The Yellow Jacket,'" *Daily Mail*, March 28, 1913. All these reports are quoted from Hazelton Papers, Box 48 (29,026), 44, 52–53.
95. Benrimo, letter to Hazelton, dated October 6, 1913, Hazelton Papers, Box 7 (28,986), fol. 4.
96. "The Letters of An Englishman: In the Chinese Manner," *Daily Mail*, April 2, 1913, quoted from Hazelton Papers, Box 48 (29,026), 76.

REFERENCES

Anonymous. "(4) Duke of York's: 'The Yellow Jacket.'" *Sunday Times*, March 30, 1913.

———. "An Anglo-Chinese Play: 'Mr. Wu' at the Strand." *Times*, November 28, 1913, p. 12.

———. "Another Chinese Play: 'The Yellow Jacket,' at the Duke of York's." *Pall Mall Gazette*, March 28, 1913.

———. "A Chinese Honeymoon." *Era*, October 12, 1901, p. 15.

———. "'A Chinese Honeymoon,' at the Strand." *Sketch*, October 9, 1901, p. 462.

——— "The Duke of York's." *Stage*, April 3, 1913, p. 20.

———. "Duke of York's Theatre, 'The Yellow Jacket.'" *Morning Post*, March 28, 1913.

———. "Duke of York's Theatre: 'The Yellow Jacket.'" *Times*, March 28, 1913, p. 10.

———. "In the Chinese Manner: An Oriental Play—Without an Oriental Audience." *Daily Graphic*, March 28, 1913.

———. "The Intensely Invisible Property Man Holds a Bamboo, with Dangling Noose ..." *Sketch* supplement, April 9, 1913. p. 3.

———. "J. Harry Benrimo, Actor, Playwright." *New York Times*, March 27, 1942, p. 23.

———. "The Letters of An Englishman: In the Chinese Manner." *Daily Mail*, April 2, 1913.

———. "London Theatres: The Strand." *Stage*, December 4, 1913, p. 26.

———. "London's Play in the Chinese Way: Mr. Henry Benrimo Explains 'The Yellow Jacket.'" *"London Budget,"* April 6, 1913.

———. "'Mr. Wu.'" *Era*, December 3, 1913, p. 14.

———. "The Play That Went Round the World." *New York Times*, November 26, 1916, p. X7.

———. "The Playhouses." *Illustrated London News*, April 5, 1913, p. 444.

———. "The Playhouses: 'Mr. Wu' at the Strand." *Illustrated London News*, December 6, 1913, p. 976.

———. "Stage Setting From 'The Yellow Jacket.'" *Upholster*, January 15, 1913, p. 73.

———. "The Strand." *Stage*, October 10, 1901, p. 14.

———. "Strand Theatre." *Times*, October 7, 1901, p. 5.

———. "Things New: At the Theatres." *Sketch*, December 3, 1913, p. 260.

———. "The Yellow Jacket." *Era*, March 29, 1913, p. 14.

———. "'The Yellow Jacket': A Chinese Play Given in the Chinese Manner." *Daily News and Leader*, March 28, 1913.

———. "The Yellow Jacket: Simple Chinese Play Delights a London Audience. The Glorification of Pretence." *Sketch*, n.d.

Academy of Motion Picture Arts and Sciences. Harry M. Vernon Collection. Margaret Herrick Library. http://collections.oscars.org/link/papers/103.

Benrimo, J. Harry. "Joseph Henry Benrimo Papers, 1906–1941." Manuscripts and Archives Division. Stephen A. Schwarzman Building. New York Public Library.

———. "Legend and Truth: The Facts About 'The Yellow Jacket,' Again in Revival Here." *New York Times*, November 4, 1928, p. 118.

Benton, Gregor, and Edmund Terence Gomez. *The Chinese in Britain, 1800–Present: Economy, Transnationalism, Identity*. Basingstoke: Palgrave Macmillan, 2008.

Booth, Michael R. *English Melodrama*. London: Herbert Jenkins, 1965.

Chesneaux, Jean, Marianne Bastid, and Marie Claire Bergère. *China From the Opium Wars to the 1911 Revolution.* Translated by Ann Destenay. New York: Pantheon Books, 1976.

Daily Herald. March 24, 1913.

Dance, George, and Howard Talbot. "A Chinese Honeymoon." The Lord Chamberlain's Plays, Add. 53693 J (1899). Department of Manuscripts. The British Library.

———. *A Chinese Honeymoon. Musical Comedy.* [1902]. Reprint, Nineteenth Century English Drama: Plays Submitted to the Lord Chamberlain. New Canaan, CT: Readex, 1985–.

Davis, John Francis. *China, During the War and Since the Peace.* 2 vols. London: Longman, Brown, Green, and Longmans, 1852.

Du, Wenwei. "Traditional Chinese Theatre on Broadway." In *Cultural Encounters: China, Japan, and the West: Essays Commemorating 25 Years of East Asian Studies at the University of Aarhus,* edited by Søren Clausen, Roy Starrs, and Anne Wedell-Wedellsborg, 192–214. Aarhus, Denmark: Aarhus University Press, 1995.

Duke of York's Theatre. Playbill of *Yellow Jacket,* March 27, 1913.

———. "'A Chinese Honeymoon,' at the Strand." *Sketch,* October 9, 1901, p. 462.

E. F. S. "'The Yellow Jacket' at Duke of York's." *Westminster Gazette,* March 28, 1913.

E. F. S. (Monocle). "The Stage From the Stalls: 'The Yellow Jacket' in an English Dress." *Sketch,* April 9, 1913, p. 10.

Elleman, Bruce A. *Modern Chinese Warfare, 1795–1989.* London: Routledge, 2001.

Endacott, G. B. *A History of Hong Kong.* London: Oxford University Press, 1973.

Ervine, St. John. "'The Yellow Jacket': Amusing Chinese Play Given in Chinese Manner." *Daily Citizen,* March 28, 1913.

Fairbank, John King. *China: A New History.* Cambridge, MA: Belknap Press of Harvard University Press, 1992.

Fischer-Lichte, Erika. "What Are the Rules of the Game? Some Remarks on *The Yellow Jacket.*" *Theatre Survey* 36 (1995): 21–36.

Forman, Ross G. *China and the Victorian Imagination: Empires Entwined.* Cambridge: Cambridge University Press, 2013.

Furst, William. *Piano Score of the Yellow Jacket.* Edited by Paul Taubman. New York: Samuel French, 1941.

Gale Research Company. *Who Was Who in the Theatre, 1912–1976: A Biographical Dictionary of Actors, Actresses, Directors, Playwrights, and Producers of the English-Speaking Theatre.* 4 vols. Detroit: Gale Research Company, 1978.

Gänzl, Kurt. *The British Musical Theatre.* 2 vols. New York: Oxford University Press, 1986.

———. *The Encyclopedia of the Musical Theatre.* 2nd ed. 3 vols. New York: Schirmer Books, 2001.

Gilbert, W. S. *The Best Known Works of W. S. Gilbert.* New York: Illustrated Editions, 1932.

G. M. "Quaint Effects in 'The Yellow Jacket.'" *Daily Mail,* March 28, 1913.

Greenhalgh, Paul. *Ephemeral Vistas: The Expositions Universelles, Great Exhibitions and World's Fairs, 1851–1939.* Manchester: Manchester University Press, 1988.

Harbeck, James. "The Quaintness and Usefulness of the Old Chinese Traditions: *The Yellow Jacket* and *Lady Precious Stream.*" *Asian Theatre Journal* 13, no. 2 (1996): 238–247.

Hazelton, George C. "George Cochrane Hazelton Papers, 1848–1941." Billy Rose Theatre Collection. The New York Public Library for the Performing Arts.

Hazelton, George C., and J. Harry Benrimo. *The Yellow Jacket: A Chinese Play Done in a Chinese Manner in Three Acts*. Indianapolis: Bobbs-Merrill, 1913.

———. *The Yellow Jacket: A Chinese Play Done in a Chinese Manner in Three Acts*. New York: Samuel French, 1939.

Holder, Heidi J. "Melodrama, Realism and Empire on the British Stage." In *Acts of Supremacy: The British Empire and the Stage, 1790–1930*, by J. S Bratton, Richard Allen Cave, Breandan Gregory, Heidi J. Holder, and Michael Pickering, 129–149. Manchester: Manchester University Press, 1991.

Johnson, Allen, and Dumas Malone, eds. *Frauces-Hibbard*. Vol. 4 of *Dictionary of American Biography*. New York: Charles Scribner's Sons, [1964].

Jones, Sidney. *The Geisha; A Story of A Tea House. A Japanese Musical Play*. London: Hopwood and Crew, 1896.

J. T. "'The Yellow Jacket': Chinese Play in Chinese Fashion in London." *Evening News*, March 28, 1913.

Lang, Matheson. *Mr. Wu Looks Back: Thoughts and Memories*. London: Stanley Paul and Company, 1940.

Lecocq, Charles. *Fleur-de-thé; Opera Bouffe in Three Acts*. New York: Gray and Green, 1869.

Li, Chien-nung. *The Political History of China, 1840–1928*. Translated by Ssu-yu Teng and Jeremy Ingalls. Princeton, NJ: D. Van Nostrand, 1956.

Li, Wenhai, Dunkui Lin, and Keguang Lin, eds. *Yi He Tuan Yun Dong Shi Shi Yao Lu* [Chronicle of the Movement of the Righteous and Harmonious Militia]. Jinan: Qi Lu Shu She, 1986.

McDowell, Henry Burden. "The Chinese Theatre." *Century* 29, no. 1 (1884): 27–44.

MacKenzie, John M. *Orientalism: History, Theory and the Arts*. Manchester: Manchester University Press, 1995.

———. *Propaganda and Empire: The Manipulation of British Public Opinion, 1880–1960*. Manchester: Manchester University Press, 1984.

Ng, Kwee Choo. *The Chinese in London*. London: Oxford University Press, 1968.

Palmer, John. "The Worst Play in London." *Saturday Review*, May 9, 1914, p. 598.

Parker, John, ed. *Who's Who in the Theatre: A Biographical Record of the Contemporary Stage*. 9th ed. New York and Chicago: Pitman, 1939.

Pearsall, Ronald. *Edwardian Popular Music*. Rutherford, NJ: Fairleigh Dickinson University Press, 1975.

Qing Hua Da Xue Li Shi Xi, ed. *Wu Xu Bian Fa Wen Xian Zi Liao Xi Ri* [Chronicle of the Wu Xu Reform Movement]. Shanghai: Shanghai Shu Dian Chu Ban She, 1998.

Richards, Jeffrey. *Imperialism and Music: Britain, 1876–1953*. Manchester: Manchester University Press, 2001.

Ryan, Janette. "Giles, Herbert Allen (1845–1935)." In *Oxford Dictionary of National Biography*. Oxford University Press, 2004–. doi:10.1093/ref:odnb/33401.

S. D. "Property Man Hero: Chinese Drama at the Duke of York's. 'The Yellow Jacket.'" *Daily Express*, March 28, 1913.

S. O. "Play of the Month: The Yellow Jacket." *English Review* 14 (1913): 320.

S. R. L. "'Yellow Jacket': Chinese Play at Duke of York's. Delightful Production." *Daily Chronicle*, March 28, 1913.

Summerfield, Penny. "Patriotism and Empire: Music-Hall Entertainment, 1870–1914." In *Imperialism and Popular Culture*, edited by John M. Mackenzie, 17–48. Manchester: Manchester University Press, 1986.

Tyrrell, John, and Stanley Sadie, eds. *The New Grove Dictionary of Music and Musicians*. 2nd ed. 29 vols. London: Macmillan, 2001.

Vernon, Harry, and Harold Owen. "Mr. Wu." The Lord Chamberlain's Plays, 1913/36 (1913). Department of Manuscripts. The British Library.

Wallace, David H. "Writing a Chinese Play: George C. Hazelton and Harry Benrimo Tell How It Is Done." *New York Dramatic Mirror*, November 13, 1912, p. 9.

Wearing, J. P. *The London Stage, 1900–1909: A Calendar of Plays and Players*. 2 vols. Metuchen, NJ: Scarecrow Press, 1981.

———. *The London Stage, 1910–1919: A Calendar of Plays and Players*. 2 vols. Metuchen, NJ: Scarecrow Press, 1982.

Williams, Dave. *Misreading the Chinese Character: Images of the Chinese in Euroamerican Drama to 1925*. New York: Peter Lang, 2000.

———. "Things New: At the Theatres." *Sketch*, December 3, 1913, p. 260.

Xu, Che, and Shouyi Dong. Vol. 9, *Qing Dai Quan Shi* [Complete History of the Qing Dynasty]. Edited by Rongsheng Wang. 10 vols. Shenyang Shi: Liaoning Ren Min Chu Ban She, 1991.

Epilogue
Aladdin Pantomimes, Chinesely British

During the 2012–13 and 2013–14 Christmas seasons, I attended eight different British pantomime productions of *Aladdin* presented at theatre venues in London and towns near London.[1] All the *Aladdin* pantomimes I saw are set in China and depict Aladdin as a carefree Chinese boy living with his mother Widow Twankey, who operates a laundry, and his younger brother Wishee-Washee; they are denizens of the city of Peking. At these performances, I join excited children and their adult companions, who throng the packed theatre houses. Rarely have I experienced such electrifying energy in a theatre audience; young and old alike develop an intimate and reciprocal bond with the performers on stage. The audience members knowingly and loudly boo and hiss the villain, the African magician Abanazar, as soon as he enters the stage, scream to direct Aladdin to the magic lamp and exhort him to rub it to escape from the cave in which he is trapped, loudly shout "No!" when asked if the Chinese princess Jasmine should exchange the magic lamp for the new ones offered by the disguised Abanazar, and participate in sing-alongs and dance-alongs at their seats during the performance and the post-performance singing contest, the latter of which is designed especially for the younger ones, who are awarded with goodie bags for their efforts at the end of the contest. Toys and souvenir programs are sold at concession counters decorated as "Peking Stores"; the holiday atmosphere is exuberant and festive.

Now a family entertainment for the Christmas season, British pantomime (or panto as it is usually called in Britain) and Pantoland (the world of panto) traces its roots back to Italian *commedia dell' arte* and has continued to evolve and reinvent itself since its beginnings in the late seventeenth and early eighteenth centuries.[2] The *Aladdin* productions I have attended vividly demonstrate panto's current popularity and vitality more than three hundred years after its invention. In its most recent reincarnation, panto is increasingly musicalized and reliant on celebrity drawing power, while maintaining many signature conventions that were interculturated into the panto tradition at different historical moments. The *Aladdin* pantos, from historical precedents to the most recent productions, are lively and thriving exemplars of British theatre practice that cultivate the phenomenon of interculturalization and embody the ongoing process of interculturation in their Chinaface approach to representing China.

The Chinese setting of the current *Aladdin* pantos, which feature both Chinese and African/Muslim characters, can be traced to the very origin of the Aladdin tale and bears the unmistakably interculturalized, fictitious qualities of a highly imaginative Oriental tall tale. The laundress Widow Twankey exemplifies the process of interculturation that retains in one role both tea jokes in her name from the early nineteenth-century popular entertainments and the reference in her profession to a common occupation held by Chinese immigrants in the early twentieth century. The stage visual elements that reflect contemporary society, such as scenery depicting international chain-store logos, costumes shaped like Chinese restaurant takeaway boxes, and panda suits worn by children performers, demonstrate that the interculturation process, while retaining popular images from the historical past, continues to take in new information and reshape stage Chinaface representations. The numerous topical and local references made within the tale's story frame manifest the close ties the *Aladdin* pantos build with the specific communities in which they are performed. Despite the nominal setting, the *Aladdin* pantos are not really about China at all but rather utilize the clearly artificial Chinaface look to joke, share, and commiserate as an intimate community in a comic, holiday spirit. Numerous references show that the panto producers are fully aware of the existence of British Chinese community, and some aspects of the pantos suggest participation and contributions from the Chinese. However, it is apparent from the conspicuous absence of Chinese both on stage and in the audience that the Chinese are largely not included in panto's Saturnalian merrymaking and the heartwarming community it builds. I speculate that their greater participation and presence could contribute to and reshape this remarkable Chinesely specimen of the long British panto tradition.

Possibly the earliest English publication of the Aladdin story, the 1721–22 English version included in *Arabian Nights Entertainments* opens with:

> Sir, in the Capital of one of the largest and richest Provinces of the Kingdom of *China* ... there liv'd a Taylor, whose Name was *Mustapha*, who had no other Distinction but that which his Profession afforded him, and was so poor, that he could hardly subsist himself and Family, which consisted of a Wife and Son, by his daily Labour.
>
> His Son, whom he called *Aladdin*, had been brought up after a very careless and idle Manner, and by that Means had contracted many vicious Habits.[3]

This opening passage depicts Mustapha's meager means of providing for his family and Aladdin's idleness, which sets up the very beginning of Aladdin's magical journey from rags to riches and exhibits several characteristics in terms of locale and character that have been influential in shaping the conception and dramatization of the tale in British pantos. Most notable is the combination, or interculturalization, of its Chinese locale with characters in Muslim names, which creates an impossible Oriental setting that clearly demonstrates the tale's fictitiousness.[4] Despite these Muslim names, which could have informed the story's locale, China has become the standard story backdrop in *Aladdin* pantos. Furthermore, the tale's unspecific "Capital of one of the largest and richest Provinces" in China has given British pantos leeway to variously construe its location, and their creative interpretations have shifted with changes in Anglo-Chinese relations and perceptions of China. Although he is lured into and becomes trapped in a mysterious cave and travels to Africa in order to win back his princess and palace, Aladdin mostly spends time in his Chinese city, giving panto practitioners the opportunity to create views of the city featuring various Chinese sites and Chinese people. In all, the tale's setting in a clearly stated Chinese but not precisely specified locale opens up creative opportunities for British pantos to create locational Chinaface attractions. Similarly, the lack of proper names for the unnamed characters in the tale has given panto writers latitude to invent designations for them, notably the tailor Mustapha's wife, who would become known as Widow Twankey.

The very first traceable *Aladdin* panto prefigures the social satire and the deliberate references to the artificial framework of the performance that would become prominent features of later pantos. Presented at the Covent Garden theatre in 1788, *Aladin; or, The Wonderful Lamp*, by John O'Keeffe (1747–1833), presents the magic lamp as hidden in "Arabia's spicy vales," in "a valley dark and deep." [5] Amid the scenes depicting the quest for the lamp in the fragrant and mysterious orientalist setting are songs that directly address the audience with contemporary and topical references. In the drinking song, "Our Trade to Work in Clay Began," the potter sings of a "noble christening bowl" so large that "The Covent Garden swell at Jupps [possibly a drinking and/or eating place], / In this [the cup] may take his Go—." In the next stanza the potter complains to the audience, "And why abroad our money fling, / To please our fickle fair? / No more from China, China bring, / Here's English China-ware."[6]

The lyrics are lighthearted, sarcastic, and seemingly jingoistic. The "noble christening bowl," a form of local English chinaware, is recommended to the fashionable London dandy to support heavy drinking. That is, this protest against the chinaware obsession satirically asks the English to purchase their local equivalent, presumably of a lower quality than that of the Chinese import, in order to support a social ill. China, then, was referenced not simply out of jingoism but, in a tongue-in-cheek manner, to ridicule English material and social foibles. This approach to creating social satire aimed at the English through references to China foreshadows those used in later productions such as *Chinese Honeymoon* (see Chapter Four). While seemingly disrupting the progression of the drama, the satire and its performance—a drinking song totally unrelated to the Aladdin story—creates a bonding experience in which the performer and the audience laugh together at their own foibles. When the drama resumes, the audience is well aware that the actors are the singers with whom they have just shared a song, heightening the artificial nature of the whole performance. As later pantos expanded upon this performance style and incorporated even more audience participation, what Millie Taylor calls "the framing of performance,"[7] the artificiality in performing the story and its depiction of China and the Chinese, would be repeatedly acknowledged for a knowing audience.

The creative opportunities provided by the original Aladdin tale to invent Chinese sites and character names, and the use of textual references to China to create social satire and commentary, were exemplified in a few popular nineteenth-century *Aladdin* theatrical productions, which, according to the study of V. C. Clinton-Baddeley, constitute the progenitors of modern-day *Aladdin* pantos.[8] The traceable influences, which Clinton-Baddeley calls pedigrees, from the earlier to later productions, demonstrate the process of interculturation, through which certain usages in text, scenery, and costume have been retained and continuously drawn upon to represent and reference China. Central to this process, however, has been its openness to new inputs to influence and reshape this representation, which, I argue, is the vital force that has enabled the *Aladdin* pantos to remain relevant to their audience. The visual Chinaface look and the Chinese textual references, in other words, are not simply time-trapped and fixed but have evolved with changing British perceptions of China and the Chinese.

In the 1813 "Melo-Dramatic Romance" of *Aladdin* arranged by Charles Farley (1771–1859), one of the scene sets is titled "Mountains and Waterfalls, over them ... Chinese bridges,"[9] a choice which shows Farley's awareness of Britain's appreciation of Chinese architecture (a phenomenon discussed in previous chapters). Particularly notable in this production is that Aladdin's mother is named Widow Ching Mustapha and the African magician is called Abanazar. Farley's invention of the widow's name, which interculturalizes a Chinese-sounding word with the Muslim name of her late husband, is an early instance in which the widow, unnamed in the original tale, is given a Chinese identity. Furthermore, Farley's invention of the name Abanazar for the African magician has proven highly enduring and is still used for the character in the *Aladdin* pantos of today.[10] To put it in the terms used in this book, after its very invention two hundred years ago, the name Abanazar has been interculturated and become the staple designation of the character. The name appears to owe its continued appeal to its comic potential. In the productions I have seen, the other characters pause and look confused after being told the name, asking if the magician means, for example, 'ave a banana, Abbey National, or even Abercrombie and Fitch, which are contemporary references recognizable to the current British audience.[11]

In the 1861 burlesque extravaganza, *Aladdin, or the Wonderful Scamp!*, written by Henry James Byron (1835–1884), the story takes place in

Pekin (Peking), which is now the common setting for the *Aladdin* pantos, and Aladdin's mother is named Widow Twankay Mustapha. Similar to Farley's invention of Ching Mustapha, Byron's invented name for the widow interculturalizes an English spelling of a Chinese word with her late husband's Muslim name. In this case, Twankay, a reference to the Chinese tea port Tunxi (屯溪) (which is also known as a kind of Chinese green tea), continues the use of Chinese commodities to name Chinese characters, as seen earlier in *Chinese Sorcerer* (Chapter Three). In the opening aria of the burlesque, the Vizier character drinks tea and sings gleefully, "I'm on for tea! / For the savour sweet that doth belong / To the curly leaf of the rough Souchong." His son is named Pekoe, which is the English spelling of another kind of Chinese tea.[12] Byron's joking references to the Chinese beverage, featuring several varieties the British consumed, poke fun at their intemperate taste for it.

While Byron named the widow Twankay, in the *Aladdin* pantos I have attended the widow's name has been invariably spelled Twankey, which is an alternative English spelling for the same Chinese tea. According to Clinton-Baddeley, the two spellings coexisted for about two decades in performance, and Twankey eventually replaced Twankay as the common spelling of the widow's name in the late nineteenth century.[13] The name Twankey exemplifies the longevity of tea jokes and has been interculturated as the staple name for the character. On the other hand, in tracing the creative association of Widow Twankey with laundry washing, Clinton-Baddeley locates a production in 1844 in which the widow was depicted as "a washerwoman with mangled feelings," and he observes that the association firmed up in the 1890s, along with the appearance of the new character Wishee-Washee as Aladdin's brother.[14] By the late nineteenth century, the current panto depiction of the Aladdin family had been formed and further interculturated.

A final historical *Aladdin* panto from the nineteenth century that appears to have had significant influence on contemporary practice is the 1874 Christmas pantomime of *Aladdin* at Drury Lane by Edward L. Blanchard (1820–1889). Set in Canton, China, the first scene opens with "Illustrations of Chinese life," with shop signs that include "Chow Chow Canton Dining Rooms—bird's-nest soup always ready—original house for puppy pies" and "Chin-Chin, barber—pigtails dressed in the latest fashion." Soon Abanazar arrives. To "assume a suitable disguise," he puts on a "skull cap with ornamental appendages, [and] shows himself in Chinese suit."[15] Blanchard's choice of the port city as the story's locale indicates his identification of China with Anglo-Chinese trade. The opening scene depicting Chinese local life has been reworked in current *Aladdin* pantos as an opening musical number that introduces the cast and the location, which is now Peking. The shop signs demonstrate Blanchard's comic but somewhat racist depictions of the Chinese diet and the signature queue hairstyle required by the Qing government. The description of Abanazar's disguise as Chinese suggests an on-stage, comic improvisation in which the character puts on the signature Chinese hairstyle by means of a skull cap with "ornamental appendages." In the *Aladdin* pantos I have seen, the opening number has usually been performed against a backdrop depicting a marketplace in Peking, with various shops and their signs displayed. Performers' costumes have incorporated the queue hairstyle in a few of the productions.

As I have argued earlier, the process of interculturation is open and takes in new influences as it progresses. The modern-day *Aladdin* pantos not only retains familiar characters and other interculturated historical elements, but also incorporate contemporary references, which they use to reinterpret old conventions and satirize contemporary society. In the Old Vic production, for example, Widow Twankey described herself as the "Wigan-born widow of Saddam al-Twankey" and the victim of the dictator's "hidden weapon."[16] This modern-day example of interculturalizing. Muslim and Chinese names references a British town, makes the widow a British subject, and combines a political joke about the Iraq invasion with sexual innuendo. At the time the production was staged, this topical reference would have played well with the audience.

In the scenery depicting Chinese shops in these productions, the banners or signs are written in English or Chinese-looking gibberish. Gone are the references to bird's-nest soup, puppy pies, and pig tails; instead, the shops now include noodle houses, takeaway places, and Widow Twankey's laundry, which indicate more recent perceptions of Chinese business and perhaps increased sensitivity to the offensiveness of the older shop signs. Interestingly, in the Hackney Empire production of *Aladdin* from January 2010, which I watched in an archival recording, the painted front curtain that serves as the backdrop for a few scenes contained signs for Starbucks, T.K.Maxx, and ToysAmWe, references to contemporary brand-name shops, with the name of the last comically distorted. The production thereby updated the stores in the tale to the twenty-first century, demonstrating the creative license British theatre practitioners have used to depict China as a backdrop for commentary on contemporary society.[17]

Similarly, costume designs bear motifs taken from both historical and contemporary Chinese references. In the Sevenoaks production, colors and decorative patterns on the extravagant dress Widow Twankey wore in the final "walkdown" (costume display) of the characters were modeled on the signature patterns of Chinese blue-and-white porcelain. Twankey in the Wimbledon production, by contrast, appeared in a walkdown dress that folded and opened like a Chinese fan. More literal and comic designs of Twankey's costumes in several productions included dresses shaped like a Chinese lantern, a Chinese porcelain vase, and a Chinese restaurant takeaway box, which provoked much laughter from the audience. Last but not least, the Hackney Empire production dressed its child-actors in panda suits, a creative idea that took advantage of the growing visibility and popularity of the animal that is most associated with China in the contemporary imagination.

The depictions of contemporary *Aladdin* pantos I offer above may paint these productions as disjointed, or even jarring, hodgepodges that amassed a wide range of names, scenery, and costumes from separate historical origins with varying degrees of relation to China. I was myself struck by this open-ended inclusiveness in the productions' creative approaches, which I believe exemplifies the mechanism of interculturation. Within the overall framework of the fictitious tale and its Chinese locale, these *Aladdin* pantos continue to remain open to new input and influences that affect scenery, costume, character, and plot. Interculturation is manifested as an ongoing process which acquires various and separate contemporary elements while retaining and continuing historical and familiar examples. As discussed earlier, British pantos make explicit their highly artificial nature, which they use to build intimate bonds with their audiences through direct interaction and social commentary, and given that China is only a fictitious backdrop to this function, it may be considered unreasonable to criticize pantos' depictions of China and the Chinese. Nevertheless, among the popular historical and contemporary images that have entered the interculturation process are notable references to the British Chinese community, which raises questions about the implications of these references and the Chinese community's participation, or lack thereof, in pantos.

One of the highly entertaining scenes in the modern-day *Aladdin* pantos I have seen involves Widow Twankey's laundry, which in these productions includes both an antique mangle (a machine that presses laundry between rollers) and automatic washer-dryers.[18] In the Guildford production, for example, the Chinese policeman PC Pongo, after chasing Aladdin to the shop, was caught in the mangle and flattened into a cut-out figure. In the Ilford production Wishee-Washee was accidentally put into the dryer and came out as a shrunken, tiny figure played by a child performer. These highly improbable, comic transformations brought out much laughter in the audience and vividly exemplify how some of the panto comic business identified by Clinton-Baddeley and Taylor is made possible by the laundry shop, helping explain this sustained creative choice in *Aladdin* panto performance.[19]

While the comic possibilities alone might have sustained the association of Widow Twankey with laundry, which can be traced as far back as the mid-nineteenth century, another likely explanation for its persistence may relate to the historical development of the professions of the British Chinese. Due to a combination of factors (discrimination, low capital requirements, minimal contact with customers), the laundry trade was indeed the main business of the British Chinese in the early twentieth century. It was later surpassed in importance by the catering trade.[20] Underneath the fun and entertainment, the association of Widow Twankey with laundry may also be considered a manifestation of prejudice. Similarly, among the comic costumes Widow Twankey wears is one shaped like a Chinese takeaway box, which, like the laundry trade, refers to a business the British Chinese entered for economic and social reasons. Perhaps the most jarring example is the O2

Arena production's make-up and costuming of the Chinese emperor, who appeared in yellowface make-up, Fu Manchu moustache, and a long queue, a racist stereotype from the historical past that recalled the image of the evil Chinese doctor created by the British author Sax Rohmer (pseudonym of Arthur Henry Sarsfield Ward, 1883–1959).

The Chinese emperor in the O2 Arena production is not the only example of yellowface that I have witnessed in these productions. Reading through the biographies (with photos) of the performers, I have only been able to identify a handful of performers of Asian heritage, and all the Chinese characters that I have seen have been played by non-Chinese (or Asian) performers. To represent themselves as Chinese, the chorus members in these productions resort to distinct Chinese costumes and, noticeably for female characters, black wigs. The main characters also conveyed their Chinese identity mostly through their dress, with some male characters wearing varying levels of yellowface make-up. As an audience member at the *Aladdin* pantos, I am very aware of being an outsider in the crowds: I traveled from out of town specifically to catch the shows as a lone attendee, and I was one of the few Asian faces in the audience. This lack of diversity in the audience may be a reflection of the demographic makeup of the areas where the theatre venues are located. Nevertheless, in the town of Ilford, which has a large South Asian population, the *Aladdin* panto I attended did attract quite a few South Asian families, but the majority of the audience was still white. As British panto is a longstanding theatre tradition closely associated with the Christmas holiday, it might take some time for newer British audiences, who may be unaware of or unfamiliar with it, to get to know and take part in the tradition. At present, I observe that instead of joining the panto community either on stage or in the audience, the British Chinese are being interculturated as part of the explicitly artificial Chinaface look of the *Aladdin* pantos.

Flawless, a group of black street dancers and stars from the TV program *Britain's Got Talent* in 2009, joined the Wimbledon production as the Peking Police Force and would, quoting the production's souvenir program, take the audience's breath away with their "technical abilities and sophisticated yet fresh style."[21] The casting choice of Flawless as the Peking Police Force not only brought street dance to pantomime; it also heightened on stage a sharp contrast, in terms of skin color, between the members of Flawless and the rest of the cast, who were mostly white. The performance I attended, in my observation, drew a small number of black audience members, which I associated with the casting of Flawless in the show.

In his review of the Wimbledon production, Dominic Maxwell commented on the star attraction of Flawless: "On the flimsiest of the pretexts," he stated, they performed (as Peking's police force) several "pulsating routines, throwing shapes and defying gravity with thrilling panache." Maxwell thought the production had come into its own as a variety show: "Loud, lavish, rude, spectacular: it has something for everyone."[22] In his review of the Old

Vic production, on the other hand, Christopher Hart wondered in passing if it ought to be deemed as politically incorrect as minstrel shows in that it was, among other things, "peopled with wicked Arabs and Chinese laundry workers." "But never mind," Hart concluded, for "it's panto: a riotous feast of filth and folly, more Saturnalia than Christmas."[23]

While Maxwell saw through the pretext of Flawless as Chinese police and Hart was aware of the racism inherent in depicting the Chinese as laundry workers—that is, both were aware of the artificiality of the Chinese characters in the productions—they found justification in the creative license granted to panto to be unrestrainedly Saturnalian, loud (riotous), rude, and silly, which demonstrates their regard for pantos as runaway holiday entertainments. However, whether the Wimbledon production, and by extension panto, is for everyone, as Maxwell claimed, may be debated. The limited presence of Chinese or Asians, either on stage or in the audience, suggested that the Saturnalian fun might be exclusive, poking fun at specific ethnic groups that were not present, or only marginally so.

Among the productions I have watched, the Hackney Empire production stands out as the only one that employed a cast with black performers in many leading roles. Veronica Lee reported that it reflected the northeast London borough of Hackney's multi-ethnic make-up and that "McKenna [the writer-director] proves that one can make affectionate jokes about diversity that are neither offensive nor po-faced."[24] While thoroughly enjoying the production in terms of script, acting, and staging, Charles Spencer offered this retrospection on panto: "But at its best, pantomime is the most joyous and democratic form of theatre, the last miraculously surviving relic of traditional variety, in which everyone in the audience is both welcome and generously catered for."[25] While Lee identified the close connection the production built with the immediate community it served, both Lee and Spencer highlighted the critical factor of the open, warm, and welcome attitude toward their audience. In line with the openness of the intercultura-tion process to new elements, this attitude made panto "the most joyous and democratic form of theatre."

The artificiality of the Hackney Empire production was obvious from its very setting, as the story took place in "Ha Ka Ney," described as a well-known eastern suburb of old Peking (a similar connection was made between the story setting and the local community in several other productions). The multi-ethnic cast and their costuming and make-up styles also made it explicit that they were non-Chinese playing Chinese characters. For example, the Chinese Empress, described as "an African queen with fly squatter ting" named "Ngingimbooboo Hu Rich now," decided to order "600 more traffic wardens for Ha Ka Ney" so that she could raise funds quickly. Her identity and name interculturalize African and Chinese references, and her joke hinted at local controversies, prompting the audience to laugh. The obvious social satire immediately created a bonding moment between performers and audience, establishing the theatre house as a close, intimate community. Mi fut Pong, the Peking Police Officer and the empress's secret lover, in exaggeratedly bad whiteface make-up, commented on the facial features of Clive Rowe, who played Widow Twankey: "Your face is your chaperone, you've got more chins than a Chinese phone book."[26] In this homonymic reference to a Chinese surname, the joke was on Rowe, who has a plump, smiling face. Through these "affectionate jokes," as Lee called them, the production used gentle sarcasm that made its audience feel welcome and "in on the jokes."

Even in this production the presence of Chinese or Asian performers was marginal. However, at one point during the opening number, "The Chinese Way," in which the cast celebrated Chinese New Year with joy and exuberance, a Chinese lion dance entered through the audience and shared the stage, if only momentarily. This instance shows that the production was aware of the dance's actual function and used it to enhance the stage version of celebration. Judging by the authentic design of the lion, it is very possible that the production received assistance from the local Chinese community. Perhaps it is not entirely coincidental that the production used this particular dance, which Chinese communities worldwide use to beckon good fortune, to welcome the Chinese into the panto world. It may, indeed, be an auspicious suggestion that the years to come may bring more fruitful collaboration with the local Chinese community and that future *Aladdin* pantos may welcome the Chinese themselves to participate in the interculturation process, and not only to enhance their artificial Chinaface look.

NOTES

1. In January 2013, I attended pantomimes of *Aladdin* presented in London (O2 Arena), St Albans (Alban Arena), Sevenoaks (Stag Theatre/Stag Community Arts Centre), Guildford (Yvonne Arnaud Theatre), and Richmond (Richmond Theatre). In January 2014, I attended those presented in Wimbledon (New Wimbledon Theatre), Basingstoke (Anvil), and Ilford (Kenneth More Theatre). In addition, I watched two taped pantomime performances of *Aladdin* (Old Vic, London, January 20, 2005; Hackney Empire, London, January 9, 2010) at the Theatre and Performance Collection, Victoria and Albert Museum.

2. For the origins of British pantomime, see, for example, David Mayer, "Pantomime, British," in *The Oxford Companion to Theatre and Performance*, ed. Dennis Kennedy (Oxford: Oxford University Press, 2011), 451–452; Gerald Frow, "Origins" in *"Oh, Yes It Is!" A History of Pantomime* (London: British Broadcasting Corporation, 1985), 15–33; Dawn Lewcock, "Once Upon a Time: The Story of the Pantomime Audience," in *Audience Participation: Essays on Inclusion in Performance*, ed. Susan Kattwinkel (Westport, CT: Praeger, 2003), 133–147; and Millie Taylor, *British Pantomime Performance* (Bristol: Intellect, 2007), 12–14.

3. See *Arabian Nights Entertainments. Consisting of One Thousand and One Stories* (London: W. Taylor; W. Chetwood; and S. Chapman, 1722), 9:89–90. While vol. 9 of the publication is dated 1722, vol. 10 is dated 1721. The Aladdin

story begins in vol. 9 and continues into vol. 10. The first initial of the bookseller Chapman is printed S. in vol. 9, and J. in vol. 10.

4. Mayer comments that from the mid-eighteenth century onwards, the English have lumped the various African, Near Eastern, and Asian worlds into "one confused aggregate" in the wholly imaginary world of stage and novel such that there is no consistent or clear distinction between the separate and distinct cultures. Pantomimes fuse everything together under the headings of "Moghul" or "Oriental" and quite successfully manage to blur distinctions. Mayer, e-mail correspondence with the author, April 28, 2014.

5. See, [John O'Keeffe], *The Recitatives, Airs, Chorusses, &c. in Aladin; or, the Wonderful Lamp* (London: T. Cadell, 1788), 8.

6. Ibid., 11, 12. The title of the song is given in *The Pantomime of Aladin, or the Wonderful Lamp; as Perform'd with Universal Applause at the Theatre Royal, Covent Garden* (London: G. Goulding, n.d.).

7. Taylor, 14.

8. V. C. Clinton-Baddeley, "Aladdin," in *Some Pantomime Pedigrees* (London: Society for Theatre Research, 1963), 31–37.

9. See, for example, *Songs, Chorusses, &c. &c. in the Grand Melo-Dramatic Romance Called Aladdin; or, The Wonderful Lamp* ..., Nineteenth Century English Drama: Plays Submitted to the Lord Chamberlain (n.d.; reprint, New Canaan, CT: Readex, 1985–), 15.

10. In the Old Vic production Abanazar is spelled Abbanazar, while in the Hackney Empire production it is spelled Abanazer.

11. Mayer notes that even before 9/11 and the drawing of British forces into Iraq and Afghanistan, there were concerns about vilifying the United Kingdom's considerable Muslim population or depicting Muslims unfavorably. Pantomime management has to monitor what Abanazer, who Mayer calls the "unmistaken villain" in the Aladdin tale, says and does and how he is costumed in order to disassociate him from Islam. The jokes I cited here may represent examples in which the character is teased in a nonreligious manner. Mayer, e-mail correspondence with the author, April 28, 2014.

12. See Henry J. Byron, *Aladdin; or, the Wonderful Scamp!* (London: Samuel French, n.d.), 2, 5.

13. Clinton-Baddeley, 32, 36–37.

14. Ibid., 34, 36.

15. See Edward L. Blanchard, *Aladdin; or, Harlequin and the Wonderful Lamp. Grand Comic Christmas Pantomime* (London: Tuck & Co., 1874), 15, 16.

16. See Benedict Nightingale, "First Night: Infectiously Funny But One Dose Is Just Enough," *Times*, December 20, 2005, p. 28.

17. As of 2014, Starbucks and Toys "R"Us, though not T.K.Maxx, have stores in China. In 2007, two years before the Hackney Empire production, a Starbucks outlet located in Beijing's Forbidden City was forced to close due to protests against its presence that "trampl[ed] on Chinese culture." See, for example, "Forbidden City Starbucks Closes," *BBC News*, July 14, 2007, http://news.bbc.co.uk/2/hi/asia-pacific/6898629.stm. This incident might have inspired the depiction of Starbucks in the production's scenery.

18. While mangles were first invented in the late eighteenth century, they were eventually replaced by the inventions of, among others, automatic spin-drying washing machines and tumble dryers in the early twentieth century. See, for

example, Christina Hardyment, *From Mangle to Microwave: The Mechanization of Household Work* (Cambridge: Polity Press, 1988), 55–69; David J. Cole, Eve Browning, and Fred E. H. Schroeder, *Encyclopedia of Modern Everyday Inventions* (Westport, CT: Greenwood Press, 2003), 269–275. A mangle side-by-side with automatic washer-dryers is a very unlikely, and therefore comic, situation; it also demonstrates the interculturation of two laundry jokes from different historical moments.
19. Clinton-Baddeley, 34–35; Taylor, 40.
20. See, for example, Gregor Benton and Edmund Terence Gomez, *The Chinese in Britain, 1800–Present: Economy, Transnationalism, Identity* (Basingstoke: Palgrave Macmillan, 2008), 89–102, 109–131; David Parker, "Chinese People in Britain: Histories, Futures and Identities," in *The Chinese in Europe*, ed. Gregor Benton and Frank N. Pieke (Basingstoke, Macmillan Press, 1998), 67–95.
21. See First Family Entertainment, "Flawless: Peking Police Force," in *The Magical Book of Panto 2013/14*, New Wimbledon Theatre souvenir programme.
22. Dominic Maxwell, "Aladdin at New Wimbledon Theatre, SW19," *Times*, January 6, 2014, p. 11.
23. See Christopher Hart, "Dame for Laughs," *Sunday Times*, January 8, 2006, p. 32.
24. Veronica Lee, "Fun at the Ha Ka Ney Empire: From Aladdin to Peter Pan—the Best Panto This Season," *Sunday Telegraph*, December 6, 2009, p. 21.
25. Charles Spencer, "Is This the Best Panto of the Year?" *Daily Telegraph*, December 7, 2009, p. 31.
26. Susie McKenna, "Aladdin: Typescript." Theatre and Performance Archives. Victoria and Albert Museum, U.K., 13, 19, 21.

REFERENCES

Anonymous. *Songs, Chorusses, &c. &c. in the Grand Melo-Dramatic Romance Called Aladdin; or, The Wonderful Lamp, As Performed at the Theatre Royal, Covent Garden. The Scenery, Machinery, Dresses, and Decorations Are Entirely New; ... The Whole Arranged and Produced Under the Direction of Mr. Farley.* n.d. Reprint, Nineteenth Century English Drama: Plays Submitted to the Lord Chamberlain. New Canaan, CT: Readex, 1985–.
Arabian Nights Entertainments. Consisting of One Thousand and One Stories. vols. 9 and 10. London: W. Taylor; W. Chetwood; and S. [J.] Chapman, 1721–22.
Benton, Gregor, and Edmund Terence Gomez. *The Chinese in Britain, 1800–Present: Economy, Transnationalism, Identity.* Basingstoke: Palgrave Macmillan, 2008.
Blanchard, Edward L. *Aladdin; or, Harlequin and the Wonderful Lamp. Grand Comic Christmas Pantomime.* London: Tuck & Co., 1874.
Byron, Henry J. *Aladdin; or, the Wonderful Scamp!* London: Samuel French, n.d.
Clinton-Baddeley, V. C. "Aladdin." In *Some Pantomime Pedigrees*, 31–37. London: Society for Theatre Research, 1963.
Cole, David J., Eve Browning, and Fred E. H. Schroeder. *Encyclopedia of Modern Everyday Inventions.* Westport, CT: Greenwood Press, 2003.
First Family Entertainment. "Flawless: Peking Police Force." In *The Magical Book of Panto 2013/14.* New Wimbledon Theatre souvenir programme.
"Forbidden City Starbucks Closes." *BBC News.* July 14, 2007. http://news.bbc.co.uk/2/hi/asia-pacific/6898629.stm.

Frow, Gerald. "Origins." In *"Oh, Yes It Is!" A History of Pantomime*, 15–33. London: British Broadcasting Corporation, 1985.

Hardyment, Christina. *From Mangle to Microwave: The Mechanization of Household Work*. Cambridge: Polity Press, 1988.

Hart, Christopher. "Dame for Laughs." *Sunday Times*, January 8, 2006, p. 32.

Lee, Veronica. "Fun at the Ha Ka Ney Empire: From Aladdin to Peter Pan—the Best Panto This Season." *Sunday Telegraph*, December 6, 2009, p. 21.

Lewcock, Dawn. "Once Upon a Time: The Story of the Pantomime Audience." In *Audience Participation: Essays on Inclusion in Performance*, edited by Susan Kattwinkel, 133–147. Westport, CT: Praeger, 2003.

Maxwell, Dominic. "Aladdin at New Wimbledon Theatre, SW19." *Times*, January 6, 2014, p. 11.

Mayer, David. "Pantomime, British." In *The Oxford Companion to Theatre and Performance*, edited by Dennis Kennedy, 451–452. Oxford: Oxford University Press, 2011.

McKenna, Susie. "Aladdin: Typescript." Theatre and Performance Archives. Victoria and Albert Museum, U.K.

Nightingale, Benedict. "First Night: Infectiously Funny But One Dose Is Just Enough." *Times*, December 20, 2005, p. 28.

[O"Keeffe, John]. *The Recitatives, Airs, Chorusses, &c. in Aladin; or, the Wonderful Lamp*. London: T. Cadell, 1788.

The Pantomime of Aladin, or the Wonderful Lamp; as Perform'd with Universal Applause at the Theatre Royal, Covent Garden. London: G. Goulding, n.d.

Parker, David. "Chinese People in Britain: Histories, Futures and Identities." In *The Chinese in Europe*, edited by Gregor Benton and Frank N. Pieke, 67–95. Basingstoke: Macmillan Press, 1998.

Spencer, Charles. "Is This the Best Panto of the Year?" *Daily Telegraph*, December 7, 2009, p. 31.

Taylor, Millie. *British Pantomime Performance*. Bristol: Intellect, 2007.

Index